MAKE IT LEGAL

LEE WILSON

ALLWORTH PRESS, NEW YORK

Published by Allworth Press, an imprint of Allworth Communications, Inc., 10 East 23rd Street, New York, NY 10010.

Distributor to the trade in the United States and Canada: North Light Books, an imprint of F&W Publications, Inc., 1507 Dana Avenue, Cincinnati, Ohio 45207. To order additional copies of this book, call toll-free 800-289-0963.

Book Design by Douglas Design Associates, New York, NY.

Library of Congress Catalog Card Number: 90-80448

ISBN: 0-927629-08-9

Anecdotes which illustrate various points of law appear throughout this book. Although they recount realistic situations and occasionally use the names of actual copyright or trademark owners, celebrities, companies, and organizations, they are wholly fictitious and do not refer to any actual events. No parallels should be drawn from these anecdotes to any actual persons, companies, or organizations or to any clients or acquaintances of the author.

The information contained in this book is intended only to educate readers generally in selected areas of the law relating to the creation of graphic design and advertising and is not meant to substitute for legal advice applicable to specific situations, for which it may be inadequate. Further, because laws change, the information given in this book may become outdated and inaccurate. The author and the publisher therefore disclaim any responsibility for any consequence of the use by anyone of the information contained in this book and urge the reader to seek legal advice from an attorney competent in the area of the law pertinent to any particular legal concern or problem of the reader.

Table of Contents

Preface

In a former life, and for more than five years, I was the creative director for a national marketing corporation. I met with clients, designed campaigns and programs, wrote ad copy, newsletters, manuals, and trade press articles, worked elbow-to-elbow with graphic designers, art directors, and photographers, attended photo sessions, proofed bluelines, produced radio spots and advertising jingles in dark little recording studios and pretty good television spots in studios and on location, hired and fired free-lancers and talent, answered to the chairman when a deadline was missed, and learned to eat pencils instead of lunch. I had prepared for my brilliant career in advertising by majoring in English Lit in college and working, during one brief, shining moment in the annals of journalism, as a reporter for a daily newspaper.

When I left my glamorous job in advertising for the drudgery of law school, I supported myself, badly, as a free-lance writer. Today I am an intellectual property lawyer who represents design studios, advertising agencies and advertising production companies, photographers, artists, and writers. Because I used to do what you do, I have a good idea of the daily concerns of advertising creative people and of the problems you face. Because I am now a lawyer, I know that you have problems that you don't even know you have.

Until I began studying law, I knew far too little about the areas of law that concern advertising and graphic design. I never stepped on anyone's rights during my tenure in advertising, but it was more through instinct than through knowledge. That was very dangerous, for me and my job, for the company for which I worked. Even well-meaning, honorable people can get into trouble without the right information. That's what this book's about — giving you the information you need to stay on the right side of the law and to protect what you create and the interests of your clients.

A word about the audience for this book. This book is primarily addressed to graphic designers and advertising agency creative staffs, and most of the examples used illustrate graphic design or advertising agency situations. However, because design and advertising job categories don't always represent neat divisions of labor, but instead often have floating, overlapping boundaries (many small graphic design studios produce ads for some clients, for instance, and most agency account executives routinely participate in advertising creative decisions), this book is potentially useful to everyone who works in graphic design or advertising.

This book will also be useful to free-lance designers, illustrators, copywriters, and commercial photographers, especially since they often do not have the information and other support available to people in similar jobs who work for studios or agencies. It will even be useful to people who work in in-house agencies of corporations which also have in-house legal departments to review ads and advise creative personnel regarding legalities, since time is always a problem in such settings and no one can ever know too much about his or her job.

My thanks to the last real man in America who cooks dinner, my very good friend Dane Bryant, who offered me unfailing aid and comfort during the often tedious process of writing this book, to my old and dear friend Todd Waterman, who gave me the same moral support during law school and who helped me edit parts of the manuscript for this book, and to my good friend and former co-worker, Eric Stein, the most vicious grammarian in captivity, who read every single word I wrote and complained, justifiably, about usage, punctuation, and sentence structure.

Lee Wilson
Nashville, Tennessee
January, 1990

Introduction

Ignorance Is Not Bliss

If you earn your living by creating advertising, you need a good working knowledge of copyright law, trademark law, libel law, the law governing privacy and the right of publicity, and false advertising law. That's true whether you work for an ad agency, own your own design studio, or free-lance out of your spare bedroom. In fact, as a graphic designer, art director, creative director, producer, advertising copywriter, illustrator, or commercial photographer, you really need to know *more* about these narrow but important areas of United States law than most lawyers know, because every day your professional activities involve copyright considerations, trademark decisions, libel, privacy, and publicity issues, and questions involving false advertising law, whether you know it or not.

If you photograph a sunset for the cover of a client's annual report, who owns the copyright in that photograph, you or the client? What if an ad agency hired you to create the photograph for its client — does the agency own the copyright, or does its client, or do you?

If an agency hires you to come up with a new logo for a restaurant chain and you do and they like it, but it looks a whole lot like the Coca-Cola logo, is The Coca-Cola Company going to cause trouble, and who's in hot water, you or your client?

Is it libel to say in a political campaign ad that your client's opponent has the worst voting record on environmental issues of any member of the legislature? What about saying that he takes bribes, if you have good reason to believe that he does but can't prove it?

Can you use a letter from a consumer to your client, complimenting your client's laundry detergent, in an ad? If you do, can you use the consumer's name and address?

If you find a photo of Meryl Streep wearing your client's wristwatch, can you feature the photo in an ad? Do you need Ms. Streep's permission if the photo was taken in a public place?

If you substitute nice, big chunks of beef for the puny ones that came out of your client's can of vegetable beef soup before you take a photo of a bowl of it for a magazine ad, will the Federal Trade Commission notice? What will it do to you, or your client, if it does notice?

Duck and Cover If you don't know the answers to these questions you are, at best, simply ignorant of the law in several matters that may be crucial to your professional advancement and, at worst, a sitting duck for lawsuits, unemployment, and financial disaster.

When did things get to be so complicated?

Advertising, and the laws governing it, got to be complicated when our technology made it possible to reach millions of people in one minute on network television. In the last twenty years, the rules have become much more complex and the stakes exponentially higher for anyone who creates any communication that is disseminated by any of our sophisticated, far-reaching communications media. That means that even if you merely stick your toe in the vast river of information that flows daily into almost every household in the country, you must know how not to drown.

If you expect either to protect and profit from what you create or to avoid infringing the rights of others, you cannot ignore questions of copyright, trademark, libel, privacy, publicity, and false advertising law. If you do, you risk losing valuable rights or the trust of clients or your job and, even worse, being sued. All it takes to put a small agency or studio out of business or you out of a job is one medium-sized lawsuit. Even if you win the lawsuit, you've lost money spent in legal fees and the respect of your client or employer.

The good news is that you don't have to be scared of learning what you need to know. Anybody who is smart enough to design an ad or create a television spot can easily learn enough to stay on the right side of the law and out of lawsuits, as well as profit from knowing more. Raises, new clients, and fat paychecks come to those who know; those who don't know face lives too sad to contemplate. Read on. Knowledge is power.

More Than Most Lawyers Know About Copyrights, Patents, and Trademarks

A rose is a rose is a rose, but a copyright is not a patent or a trademark, even though all three terms name varieties of "intellectual property" (valuable intangible products of the imagination), which, in this country, have their origins in our Constitution.

The framers of the U.S. Constitution lived in an era during which science and philosophy bore exotic fruit — inventions and ideas that changed forever the way men and women lived their lives and viewed their condition. Because of this important explosion of thought and technology, the men who wrote our Constitution provided for the encouragement and reward of the thinkers and creators in the new American nation.

In Article I, Section 8, Clause 8 of the Constitution, they empowered Congress "to promote the Progress of Science and useful Arts, by reserving, for limited Times to Authors and Inventors, the exclusive Rights to their respective Writings and Discoveries." The theory was that Americans would write great books and invent useful inventions if they were rewarded for their efforts by being made the only ones entitled to profit from their creations. This provision of the Constitution is the source for both the U.S. copyright law and the U.S. patent law.

United States trademark law has its origins in an entirely different section of the Constitution, the "commerce clause," in which Congress is given the power to regulate interstate commerce. As commerce in the nation grew, Congress realized that legislation was needed to protect consumers from confusion as to the sources of the goods they bought and to allow manufacturers to profit from their own good commercial reputations without interference from unscrupulous imitators, so it passed a trademark statute. The current federal trademark law was passed in 1946; all the states also have trademark statutes.

Wake Me When It's Over

Now this boring stuff really isn't boring, if you think about it. If you live in the United States, you are a part of the world's largest free enterprise society and should be concerned about having and preserving the ability to profit from your own commercial activities unimpeded by anyone who wants a free ride on your commercial coattails. That's trademark law. And whether you create photographs, print ads, broadcast ads, jingles, or illustrations, if you earn your keep by what you create, you need to know what rights the law gives creators. That's copyright law.

Further, anyone who creates copyrights or trademarks must know how to avoid infringing the trademark and copyright rights of others.

Patent law really *is* boring, unless you are an engineer or chemist or plant biologist, and after we talk about it enough to understand what patents are and how they differ from copyrights and trademarks, we will forget about it.

All You Ever Need to Know About Patents

A patent is a seventeen-year monopoly granted by the U.S. Patent Office to the creator of a new invention, such as a new industrial or technical process, chemical composition, or plant variety. Shorter patents called design patents are granted for ornamental designs used for manufactured items. An inventor must meet very strict standards before the Patent Office will grant a patent for his or her invention; then, the inventor can stop everyone else from manufacturing her or his invention without permission or even importing an infringing invention into the United States, even if the infringer of the patent independently came up with the same invention.

No product name is protectable by patent law; a product name is a trademark and trademark protection is, as we shall see, earned in the marketplace rather than being awarded like a patent. And no song, story, painting, or play can be patented; copyright gives writers and artists the right to keep others from copying their works, but not a complete monopoly on the creation or importation of similar works. If you create advertising and help your clients select new trademarks for a living, there is almost no chance that your work will require that you know any more about patents than you can learn in this paragraph. The same is not true of copyrights and trademarks.

Copyright Law 101

A copyright is like the "deed" to a literary or artistic work. The owner of a copyright has the exclusive right to copy or reproduce the work, to prepare alternate or "derivative" versions of the work, to distribute and sell copies of the work, and to perform or display the work publicly. The only way someone else can legally exercise one of these rights is by permission of the copyright owner or by becoming the owner of one or more of these rights. Any unauthorized exercise of any of these rights is copyright infringement.

On January 1, 1978, a new United States copyright law became effective. For any copyrightable "work," that is, for any photograph or poem or musical composition or other original product of the imagination created on or after that date, the law is very different from what it was for works created earlier. The first thing to know about the new copyright law is that, for any "work of authorship" created after December 31,

1977, copyright exists at the moment the work is "fixed in any tangible form." Although a copyright is, itself, a set of intangible legal rights which are entirely separate from any physical object which embodies the work, under the new law the existence of copyright is triggered by the reduction of the work to a tangible form that allows the work to be perceived by the senses.

This means that when your pen leaves the paper, when your camera clicks, you own the copyright in what you have created. This is true even if you never publish your work, even if you do not put a copyright notice on it, and even if you never register the copyright in your new work. Your copyright rights automatically exist the moment you "fix" your work.

You own the copyright in what you create *unless* you copied someone else's copyrighted work. That is copyright infringement and the law does not grant you rights in something you wrongfully took from someone else.

You own the copyright in what you create *unless* you work full-time for someone else and create your photograph or advertising copy for them as a part of your regular duties. Then your creation is considered to be a "work-for-hire" and your employer owns the copyright in it from the beginning.

You own the copyright in what you create *unless* you have created something which is not protectable under copyright law. There only a few categories of works which are not copyrightable; they include blank forms, slogans, titles, raw information, ideas, methods, and systems.

If you remember nothing else about copyright law, remember this most basic concept: copyright protects not ideas, but only *particular expressions of ideas*.

You can grasp this concept, which confuses even lawyers and sometimes judges, by remembering a simple example. If a dozen photographers took simultaneous photographs of the same still-life arrangement of fruit and flowers, each photograph would be a separate expression of the same idea — the idea of an image of a still-life arrangement of fruit and flowers. There would be variations in the photographs because of the photographers' individual approaches to the angle and composition of the photographs and because of their varying choices of cameras, film, and filters, but even if by some chance two of them independently took identical photographs of that one still-life arrangement, *both* of the identical photographs would be copyrightable.

Trademarks for the Beginner

A trademark represents the commercial reputation of a product or service as embodied in a design (a logotype) or a word or name. Trademark law is a variety of the law of "unfair competition." This means that trademark law prohibits certain trade practices which are considered unfair, such as the imitation of another's trademark in order to profit from consumers' mistaken belief that the imitation trademark and the product it names are the real thing. That is trademark infringement.

Trademark law also exists to protect consumers. It ensures, for instance, that when you buy a pair of running shoes marked with the Nike name, they are of the high quality you have come to expect in Nike products because they are, indeed, manufactured by Nike.

The two things graphic designers and advertising creative people need to know about trademarks are how to choose them and how to use them.

Choosing a new product name is not a simple undertaking, or should not be. Certain kinds of names are not registrable as trademarks with the U.S. Patent and Trademark Office; the knowledgeable person who christens a new product will take these restrictions into account, since federal registration is, or should be, the goal of every trademark owner. The other major consideration in choosing a trademark is picking one that no one else is using. This process is called "trademark clearance." You ignore it at your peril, since adopting and using someone's established trademark, even innocently, is trademark infringement, and trademark infringement can result in lawsuits that are expensive to settle and hopelessly expensive to defend.

We Earned It

In the United States, trademark ownership accrues by use of the trademark in commerce. Unless a trademark is used in the marketplace, there *is* no trademark, because there is no commercial reputation which can be exemplified by the word or symbol. Roughly speaking, trademark owners earn the right to prevent others from using the same symbol or word to represent or name a product or service similar to theirs in direct proportion to the extent of their use of that name or symbol, geographically and otherwise.

The owner of the four Bonet's Boutique ladies' clothing stores in northeast Idaho can probably keep other retailers from calling new clothing stores of any kind by the Bonet's Boutique name or any name which is confusingly similar to Bonet's Boutique only within the same general area — that is, within the geographic area where the commercial reputation of Bonet's Boutique has spread.

The longstanding fame of Bloomingdale's, however, allows Bloomingdale's to stop the use of that or any confusingly similar name for a department or specialty clothing store anywhere in the United States, even in areas geographically remote from the famous New York store (or any of its outposts), because although the famous store is physically located in New York City, its reputation has spread across the United States, and United States trademark law prohibits competitors anywhere in the country from competing with it unfairly by appropriating its name.

Once a trademark is "cleared for takeoff" and is in use, *how* the mark is used is very important. If a trademark is used as a noun rather than as an adjective ("Winkles" rather than "Winkles toy trucks"), it can lose its status as a trademark. That's what happened to "aspirin," "cellophane," and "escalator," all of which once named particular brands of the products for which they are now the generic names.

If the ® symbol is not used properly in conjunction with a federally-registered trademark, the trademark owner's right to collect money damages in a lawsuit against a trademark infringer may be diminished.

In the abstract, these may seem like niggling considerations; in actuality, proper trademark usage can be crucial to the overall health of the company that owns the mark, since the company trademark may represent the most valuable asset of the company, its goodwill. The Xerox Company thinks so, at least. Otherwise it would not run thousands of dollars worth of ads every year pointing out that photocopiers are not "xerox machines" and that their machines are "Xerox brand photocopiers."

Xerox doesn't want to end up like the once-famous Escalator Company, the name of which, ironically, lost its uniqueness because of that very fame, thanks to the popularity and success of the moving stairways marketed under the same name. When the name "Escalator" became a generic term applicable to all moving stairways, the Escalator moving stairway faded into the woodwork, so to speak, becoming so famous it became anonymous.

Trouble Comes in Threes — Libel, Privacy, and Publicity

Like copyright, trademark, and patent law, libel, privacy, and publicity law are related but very different areas of the law. Advertising creative people can avoid most of the tedious disputes and enormous problems that may result from even an unintentional trespass upon someone's right of privacy or publicity or a defamation (libel) of someone, by learning enough about these three areas of the law to recognize the red flags that signal a possible lawsuit.

Unlike learning about copyright and trademark law, getting up to speed about libel, privacy, and publicity law will not reward you directly. Your only reward for not stepping on someone's legal toes by libelling them or invading their privacy or infringing their publicity right is that you will stay out of lawsuits; this may seem like small benefit to some, but if you have ever been close to such a lawsuit, you know that virtue, in these areas of the law, is its own reward.

Liable for Libel

To "defame" someone is to damage his or her reputation by spreading false statements about him or her. Slander is *speaking* defamatory statements. Libel, which is probably the only sort of defamation of any real concern to advertising people, occurs when defamatory information is spread by written or printed materials (photographs, newspaper or magazine ads, etc.) or, in most jurisdictions, broadcast over the airwaves (any sort of broadcast advertising).

Private Lives

The right of privacy is the right of every U.S. citizen to be left alone, to live a life uninterrupted by intrusions into private matters or living areas, and to be free from unwilling exposure to public scrutiny or participation in the commercial process. There are four kinds of invasion of privacy.

"False light" invasion of privacy, which is a sort of cousin to defamation, is the placing of someone in a "false light" before the public, usually by publishing a photograph or story that portrays that person in a misleading way that is very offensive to him or her.

"Intrusion" invasion of privacy involves some invasion of a person's private space or solitude. The invasion of privacy does not have to result from a *physical* invasion of private space; eavesdropping on private conversations and taking photos of someone through a window with a long-range lens are examples of this sort of invasion of privacy.

"Public disclosure of private facts" invasion of privacy involves the publication of true but private information about an individual, such as details about the person's sex life or health or finances.

"Misappropriation" invasion of privacy is the unauthorized use of a person's name or likeness for commercial purposes, such as in an ad, and represents the most common sort of privacy lawsuit involving advertising creative people.

The infringement of someone's "right of publicity" consists of the exploitation of someone's name or image in some commercial context without his or her permission. Unlike invasion of privacy, which is related to the right of private people to be left alone, the right of publicity is more in the nature of a property right of a famous person to exclusively exploit his or her own fame. The right of publicity is really the "flip side" of the right of privacy, since a violation of someone's right of publicity is a violation of his or her right to be the only one to make use of the "publicity value" of his or her name and a private individual's name usually has no such publicity value.

That is not to say that the name and photograph of a private individual would never be used without permission by a manufacturer in an endorsement for that company's products, but the usual lawsuit for infringement of someone's right of publicity involves a famous person who is suing because someone has used his or her name or picture to imply such an endorsement or to attract consumers' attention. In other words, people concerned with preserving their right of publicity are usually well-known.

True or False

"False advertising" refers to two separate kinds of trouble that are of special concern to advertising creative people since the genesis of both kinds of false advertising claims is the content, visual and verbal, of advertising.

The Lanham Act, the federal trademark statute, contains one section, Section 43(a) that has given rise over the years to a body of case law that has little to do with trademarks. Section 43(a) allows people who feel they have been harmed by misrepresentations made in someone else's advertising to sue for false advertising. Usually the people who feel they have been harmed and who sue are the competitors of the company which places the allegedly false ad, and usually they sue for significant false claims made about the advertised products. Recently, however, Section 43(a) was changed to also allow suits to be brought because of false claims made about the products of the *competitors* of the advertiser.

Transgression Trouble

The other kind of false advertising claim is not a private suit like a Section 43(a) claim but is, rather, an action taken by the Federal Trade Commission because the FTC believes that an ad transgresses its regulations governing advertising and is "materially misleading" to consumers. The FTC may decide that an ad is materially misleading either because of specific claims made in the ad or because of omissions of information which could, if included, influence a consumer's purchasing decision.

In other words, if you are not very careful to tell the *whole* truth in advertising materials you create, including in photos and copy and fine print, you and your client may end up, because of the content of one ad, fending off both your client's angry competitors and the federal government. As with the other areas of the law covered in Section IV of this book, false advertising claims present a danger even to honest people, who can't depend simply on their good intentions to shield them from the ire of competitors or the righteous indignation of the federal government.

Don't Worry, Be Happy

If you have read this far, you may be worried that you haven't understood and absorbed everything you have read. Don't worry. We have the rest of this book to consider copyright, trademark, libel, privacy, publicity, and false advertising law, at a more leisurely pace and in more detail. We will look at how each works and, especially, how each impacts your work. We will learn how to recognize problems and how to avoid or solve them, often without the advice of a lawyer. By the time you get to the end of this book, you will have a good working knowledge of these areas of the law as they relate to your job and, better still, some confidence that you can deal with questions that you are likely to encounter. You'll find it well worth the effort.

Copyright, trademark, and libel law, their brothers the rights of privacy and publicity, and the orphan false advertising law are not the most important things in the world. However, your knowledge of them does affect one of the most important things in *your* world: your competence at your work. If you are competent at what you do, your work will be better and your worklife will be happier. Listen up, so you can whistle while you work.

The Basics of Copyright Law

Chapter *1*

Copyright Basics

Reward Offered   Copyright law rewards creators by granting them the exclusive right to exploit and control their creations. Under the United States copyright statute, the creator of a copyrighted creative work has the exclusive right to copy or reproduce the work, to prepare alternate or "derivative" versions of the work, to distribute and sell copies of the work, and to perform or display the work publicly. With a few narrow exceptions, which we will discuss later, these rights may not be exercised by anyone other than the author of the work or a person to whom he or she has sold or licensed one or more of these "exclusive rights" or a portion of one of them.

Our copyright statute encourages the production of new works by allowing them to be withheld from free use by the public for a time. The public benefits doubly from the rights awarded artists, writers, and composers by the statute, since it enjoys immediate controlled access to the works they create and because those works eventually become public property, available for use by anyone.

As we have seen, American copyright law has its origins in a constitutional provision that allows Congress "to promote the Progress of Science and useful Arts, by reserving, for limited Times to Authors and Inventors, the exclusive Rights to their respective Writings and Discoveries." You may think from reading this that only authors of books are protected by copyright law. That is not the case.

Historically, American copyright law has interpreted broadly the "writings" granted constitutional protection. During the two centuries since the first

U.S. copyright law was passed in 1790, U.S. copyright statutes (there have been several) and court decisions have extended copyright protection to new subjects of copyright as previously non-existent classes of works emerged, needing protection.

This system of enumerating the classes of "writings" protected by copyright worked well enough until it became obvious that technology would create new methods of expression faster than the courts and lawmakers could amend copyright law to include the new technologies within the scope of copyright protection. The present U.S. copyright law abandons the effort to enumerate every class of work protected by copyright and states simply that "copyright protection subsists . . . in original works of authorship fixed in any tangible medium of expression, now known or later developed, from which they can be perceived, reproduced, or otherwise communicated, either directly or with the aid of a machine or device."

Your Government Loves You

So. George Washington, James Madison and all those other guys in wigs who wrote our Constitution, your Congress (they write our laws), the current administration (they are charged with enforcing our laws), the Supremes (Sandra Day O'Connor and the other eight justices of our country's highest court), and various lesser governmental bodies, like the United States Copyright Office in Washington, D.C., and government officials, like federal judges and federal marshals, all think that you have something to say and are sworn to protect and uphold your rights in what you create. Now that you are aware of the awesome responsibility for creativity placed upon your narrow shoulders by your federal government, we will consider just exactly what it is that copyright protects.

Almost all the categories of materials ordinarily created by ad agency creative staffs, graphic designers, free-lance artists and advertising writers, and commercial photographers are protectable "works" within the meaning of the U.S. copyright statute. Print ads, photographs, advertising copy, radio commercial scripts and finished spots, drawings, advertising jingles, television storyboards and finished commercials, cartoon strips, corporation annual reports, posters, brochures, logo designs — all are protectable under copyright law.

However, not everything that you come up with, even after days of brainstorming and lots of work on the finished product, is protectable by copyright and it is important to know the difference between a protectable work and one that is not. There are several varieties of materials that are not protected by copyright.

I've No Idea

If you remember nothing else about copyright, remember this; copyright does *not* protect ideas, only *particular expressions* of ideas. The goal of our copyright law is to increase the free exchange of ideas in our society and to allow society to benefit from new ideas. We are all encouraged to express our ideas, since copyright protects our expressions. However, no monopoly is granted on the ideas themselves, so the ideas embodied in the protectable expression become available for use by anyone. The same is true for systems, methods, information, and procedures, which are really all particular varieties of ideas; copyright does not protect them, either.

This means that your *idea* of printing grocery coupons right on the brown paper bags of your grocery store chain client can be copied by anyone else, even a competing grocery store, although the particular expression of your idea, your copy and artwork for the bags and the advertisements publicizing the promotion, may not.

And your *system* of giving grocery store customers double the face-value discount of any coupon if they use it to buy two product items at the same time, is not protectable by your copyright in the grocery-store coupon promotion materials and can be employed at any time by anyone, without your permission.

Further, if you print recipes on the grocery bags in addition to the grocery store coupons, you cannot, of course, stop anyone from using the *method* outlined in the Low-Fat Meatloaf recipe to create a low-fat meatloaf. Nor can you stop anyone, even a competitor of your client, from using the *information* outlined in that recipe to create his or her own recipe for low-fat meatloaf, including a recounting of your procedure for diminishing the fat content of the finished dish, so long as he or she simply reads your recipe to learn how to create a *new* expression of that information.

Not an Original   There are also a few categories of materials that are too close to being mere unembellished ideas for copyright protection to apply. In other words, these categories of "creations" lack sufficient originality to be granted copyright protection. Categories of works that are deemed by the copyright statute or the courts to be unprotectable by copyright are:

- names of products, services, or businesses;

- pseudonyms or professional or stage names;

- titles of movies, books, songs, etc. (names and titles may be protected under trademark law, however);

- slogans, short catchphrases, short advertising phrases, etc.;

- mere variations on familiar symbols or designs, such as typefaces or designs for numerals or punctuation symbols;

- raw information (although some *compilations* of raw information are subject to copyright protection);

- blank forms, such as account ledger page forms, diaries, address books, blank checks, restaurant checks, order forms, and the like;

- measuring and computing devices like slide rules or tape measures; and

- calendars, height and weight charts, sporting event schedules, and other assemblages of commonly available information which contain no original material.

All this has a practical application. It may be that your beautiful new typeface design is free for use by anyone, no matter how laboriously worked out by you. And your great new slogan for your client's product may soon be on everyone's lips, in contexts that have nothing to do with that product. (Think of "Go For The Gusto!" or "Where's The Beef?" or "The Pepsi Generation.")

Cultured Pearls But the good news is that if you are designing a poster calendar for your client the sporting goods company, you may copy all the information you need concerning the days of the week on which the dates fall and the dates of holidays from anyone else's calendar and any information about the year's sporting events from schedules published in newspapers or by colleges, sports magazines, or anyone else. And, when you write copy for a client, you can make free use of slogans and catchphrases from popular culture without obtaining permission from the copyright owner of the work from which the slogan was taken; otherwise, you'd have to call up Edgar Rice Burroughs' heirs to use "Me Tarzan, you Jane," or George Lucas to use "May the Force be with you," in an ad.

Just the Facts, Ma'am

Copyright law treats facts of all sorts like ideas; the only thing relating to facts that is protectable under copyright law is the particular expression of those facts. You may write a movie script based on the historic facts surrounding the sinking of the Titanic; those facts are free for use by anyone who cares to gather them at the library or from other sources. However, if you believe that it's time for another movie about the Titanic and that Hollywood will buy your script, you may want to think twice before you mention your project to your brother-in-law the screenwriter, since he is free to recognize your idea as a good one and write his own competing script based on the very facts you planned to use.

The same is true of plots. Shakespeare's *Romeo and Juliet* has spawned many works based on the plot of his play: the play Abie's *Irish Rose* and the movie *The Cohens and The Kellys*, now both forgotten except for the well-known copyright infringement suit concerning their similar plots, the famous musical *West Side Story*, the old television series *Bridget Loves Bernie,* and the 1969 Zefferelli film *Romeo and Juliet,* which was only the latest in a long line of movies made from Shakespeare's play.

And if you think for a moment about the love songs you know, you will realize that themes are not protectable by copyright, either; at last count there were 2,438,042 songs written about somebody's broken heart—all perfectly legitimate uses of that theme—and there will, no doubt, be more.

Shakespeare's Dead and I Don't Feel So Good Myself

The largest category of literary and artistic material which is not protected by copyright is "public domain" material. Most public domain material is material for which copyright protection has expired, such as the works of "dead poets," — literary gentlemen who have been dead a long time, like Shelley, Keats, Shakespeare, and all those other guys you had to read in college. The trick is to make sure that the author whose work you want to use has been dead long enough.

Herman Melville has been dead long enough to allow your free use of the *Moby Dick* characters and story in your ad campaign; the copyright in that famous novel expired awhile ago. The same is not true of, for example, Tennessee Williams; his plays are still protected by copyright and his estate owns the copyrights in those plays and collects royalties from performances of them. All this applies to painters and composers, too, as well as to lesser mortals like you and me whose creations are not quite great literature or art but are valuable to us nonetheless.

Figuring out whether a work is in the public domain is not simply a matter of determining whether the author has been dead awhile, however, since the creators of many still-valid copyrights expired a long time before their copyrights will. Unless you know for sure that the copyright in a work has expired (anything showing a copyright date more than seventy-five years ago is a safe bet), you must investigate the copyright status of the work before reprinting it or copying it or otherwise exercising any right reserved to the owners of valid copyrights.

The best way to begin to do this is to follow the recommendations in the Copyright Office publication called "How to Investigate the Copyright Status of a Work," which is reprinted in the Appendix section of this book. You can also hire a copyright search firm to perform a search of Copyright Office records for you; these companies are almost all based in and around Washington, D.C., for obvious reasons, and usually charge by the hour for their work.

We Have Met the Public and It Is Us

There is one other category of public domain works of which you should be aware; that is works created by officers or employees of the U.S. government as a part of their government jobs. These works are in the public domain because the government has chosen not to claim copyright in works created at the taxpayers' expense.

This means that you may quote the entire text of a government publication on varieties of mortgage loans in the brochure you prepare for customers of a client bank without any special permission from the government. However, if your end creation consists preponderantly of material produced by the government, your copyright notice should acknowledge the fact, as in "Copyright 1990 Ads Extraordinaire, Inc., except material on pages 10 through 15, taken from U.S. Government Publication 428, 'Understanding Mortgages.'"

The only precaution necessary before using material from government publications is to make sure that the material used was prepared by the U.S. government proper and not by some private or semi-private agency of the government or government contractor. You can probably do this simply by looking at the title page of the government brochure or by calling the department or organization which published it. Anything published by the U.S. Government Printing Office or offered through the Consumer Information Catalog is almost certainly public domain material.

A Narrow Escape

The Greatest Ad on Earth

Miriam and Jerry owned a small graphic design firm and ad agency in a medium-sized city in the great midwest. Jerry was the graphic designer for the firm, Miriam was creative director, and they both sometimes also acted as account executives. They were in a predicament. The presentation that they had made to their biggest client, the municipal auditorium in their city, of their ideas to promote the circus that was soon to appear at the auditorium was a success. They had been given the go-ahead to produce the billboards, newspaper ads, and other elements of their campaign. The bad news was that the auditorium manager had particularly liked the old photos Jerry had used for the presentation mockups, which he had simply copied directly from a book on circuses he had checked out of the library, and wanted those photos used for the actual ads and billboards. Unfortunately, Jerry and Miriam were not sure they could use those photos for the campaign.

Miriam had checked the credits section of the book and had found that all four of the photos she and Jerry wanted to use had been taken by the same photographer. The copyright date on the book was 1956; there was no copyright date shown for the photos, but the clothing and hairstyles in them indicated that they also dated from the fifties. Miriam had called the book publisher, but the publisher had no information on the photographer other than his name and none for the author of the book besides a thirty-year-old Florida address. Miriam could find no telephone listing for the author at that address and there was no time to write the author in an attempt to secure information about the photographer, because the campaign ads and billboards had to be produced and billboard and newspaper space reserved right away if the campaign was to run on schedule.

Jerry thought that since they couldn't find the photographer, the photos were at least thirty-five years old, and the photographer was possibly even dead, they didn't need anyone's permission to use the photos and should simply copy them from the book. Miriam was worried that they'd be sued for copyright infringement.

Call for Help

They called their lawyer for advice. Their lawyer told them that using the old photos in any form without permission from the copyright owner would expose them to the threat of a lawsuit for copyright infringement. If the photos were taken in the fifties, the copyrights in them were very probably still valid. Even if the photographer had since died, he might have sold the copyrights in the circus photos to someone else, such as a stock photo house or a publisher, or they could have been inherited by his estate. Since the owner of the copyright in any photograph has the exclusive right to reproduce it or permit its reproduction and to publish it in any form or allow anyone else to publish it, Jerry and Miriam's use of the photos without permission would be infringement.

Jerry and Miriam were told further that they could have the Copyright Office or a private copyright search firm conduct a search of Copyright Office records to determine the copyright status of the photos and the owner of those copyrights, but that this could take several weeks and could cost several hundred dollars and could result even then in inadequate information to locate the copyright owner to ask for permission to use the photographs. In any event, there was no guarantee that such permission would be granted even if the owner of the photograph copyrights were located, since any copyright owner can grant or withhold any requested permission to use a copyright, for any reason at all or for no reason.

Miriam and Jerry's lawyer also warned them of two dangers they had not perceived. First, she told them that the circus performers in the photos, most of whom were recognizable as particular individuals and almost all of whom were probably still living, could sue Jerry and Miriam for violating their rights of publicity and privacy; that is, for using in newspaper ads and on billboards their recognizable, though dated, photographs.

She also warned them to beware of the tendency, epidemic among young people working in advertising and other creative industries that value current ideas, to assume that nothing that predates them could possibly have any effect on or relevance in their lives. The lawyer cited the lawsuit involving the once-famous silent screen actress Pola Negri, who successfully sued a cosmetics company because the company's ad agency creative staff had used, without her permission, a fifty-year-old photo of her in an ad, never thinking that the young kohl-eyed siren in the old photograph could have become a dignified elderly lady still very much aware of her rights.

French Fries

Further, Miriam and Jerry were told that even though their little agency might look like small potatoes to a potential plaintiff in a suit, the municipal auditorium, which was owned by the city, would not. In fact, their lawyer said, the city, as owner of the auditorium, would be what is known as a "deep-pocket" defendant; that is, a defendant with enough money to make a suit worthwhile. Since Jerry and Miriam were acting as the auditorium's, and hence the city's, agency, their actions in failing to secure permission for use of the photos from the copyright owner or the people pictured in them would be attributable to the city and could expose the city to the same liability faced by the agency.

Then their lawyer, being a resourceful soul as well as a practical lawyer, suggested some alternate courses to Jerry and Miriam. "If you can't find the person who could give you permission to use these photos," she said, "find someone who can give you permission to use similar photos that are too old to show living performers, like a photo archive. Maybe a circus historical society or a big museum would have what you need.

"Or commission a set of nice circus drawings from one of your free-lancers and frame the finished drawings for the office of the auditorium manager after the ads and billboards are finished. The new drawings can depict old circus scenes, if you wish, but don't copy the old photos you wanted to use, because that is also copyright infringement. Or, easiest of all, simply find some old illustrations for which copyright protection has expired."

1902 Solution Frightened, Miriam went that evening to the local university library and spent several hours poking around in the stacks. She arranged with the periodicals librarian to borrow for a few days a bound volume of the 1902 issues of a famous American illustrated children's magazine. The next day she and Jerry chose several of the lovely old illustrations she had found in a serial story about a circus. They shot stats of the by-now-public-domain illustrations and used them, with subtle coloring added and with a nice old-fashioned "circus-y" typeface, for the ads and billboards. The auditorium manager liked the "hand-tinted" old circus scenes, the low cost of the illustrations, and, especially, the framed set of illustrations hanging in his office.

The campaign won an award, Miriam and Jerry kept the account and everybody stayed out of the dungeon in the basement of the Copyright Office reserved for copyright infringers.

Copyright Protection

Life Plus Fifty   Creative people often believe that copyright law is a dark mystery, accessible only to lawyers, and that the mechanisms of copyright protection are incredibly complex. Fortunately, they're wrong.

"Copyright protection" means the protection the law gives copyright owners from any unauthorized use of their works. Copyright protection lasts a very long time. Copyrights created today will not expire until well into the next century and there are still-valid copyrights which were created close to the beginning of this century. The period of time during which the law offers copyright protection to a particular work is called the "term of copyright." Determining the term of copyright for a work is not hard if you know a few things about when, by whom, and under what circumstances the work was created.

The current United States copyright law went into effect on January 1, 1978. The copyright in works created on or after that date endures from the moment the work is first "fixed" in any tangible form until fifty years after the death of the author of the work, or, if two or more people created the work, until fifty years after the death of the last surviving co-author.

If the work is created anonymously or by someone using a pseudonym, and the actual name of the author is not revealed in Copyright Office records, copyright protection will endure for seventy-five years from the year of first publication or one hundred years from the year of creation of the work, whichever period expires first. If the work is created as a work-for-hire, the copyright in the work will last until seventy-five years from the year the work was first published, or one hundred years from the year of creation of the work, whichever period is shorter.

For works created before January 1, 1978, that is, before the new copyright law was in effect, the duration of copyright is determined differently. Under the old copyright law, copyright owners were granted an initial twenty-eight year term of protection and, if the copyright owner made a renewal of copyright at the proper time, a second twenty-eight year renewal term. For works which were in their renewal terms on January 1, 1978, the new law extended copyright protection an extra nineteen years past the second twenty-eight year term, for a total of seventy-five years of copyright protection, rather than the fifty-six years formerly available.

It's Up to You

Registration of your copyright is not mandatory, but it is a very good idea for any work which is published or otherwise disseminated or made public. You probably don't need a lawyer to help you register your copyright properly, but you do need to educate yourself about registration in order to avoid mistakes.

The Copyright Office in Washington, D.C., is the federal agency which has the responsibility for administering the registration of copyrights and performing other government functions relating to copyrights, such as maintaining records of copyright registrations and creating and disseminating regulations interpreting sections of the copyright statute. The Copyright Office is a division of the Library of Congress; the copies of works being registered for copyright may end up in the collections of the Library, depending on the work and the needs and collections policies of the Library.

There is no such thing as any state copyright law; this means that there is no state agency anywhere in the U.S. that grants copyright registrations or otherwise has anything to do with copyrights. All U.S. copyright registrations are granted by the Copyright Office; whether it is a child's poem or a hit song or a bestselling novel, if it is registered for copyright in the United States, it is registered in the Copyright Office in Washington.

The Copyright Office prescribes a specific form for the registration of copyright in each particular variety of work. Form TX is used for the registration of "literary" works, that is, works, other than dramatic works, which consist primarily of TeXtual matter. Form VA is used to register copyrights in works of the Visual Arts. Form PA is used to register copyrights in works of the Performing Arts, including plays, songs, and movies. Form SR is used to register the copyrights in Sound Recordings.

There are other forms for other sorts of works; the name of each variety of copyright registration form and the sort of work to be registered with each are listed in the Resources section of this book, along with information about obtaining registration forms (which are free), from the Copyright Office. A TX form and a VA form and instructions for filling them out are reproduced in the Appendix section of this book. Information about the Copyright Office, its services, publications, and twenty-four-hour hotline (202-707-9100) for ordering registration forms and publications is given in the Resources section of this book.

Do-It-Yourself Job

Copyright registration is usually routinely granted by the Copyright Office, and, in most cases, you can register your copyright yourself. At this writing, registration costs only ten dollars per registration. (A group of works may be registered as a collection for one ten-dollar fee if they were all created by the same person and if they are bound together or otherwise assembled in an orderly form under a single title. Many people use this method of registration to diminish copyright registration fees while gaining the advantages of copyright registration.)

Besides the registration fee, you must send the Copyright Office, in the same envelope with the registration fee, a non-returnable "deposit" (one or more copies of the work as specified by the Copyright Office according to the type of the work and whether it has been published and, if so, when), and a properly completed copyright form of the correct variety.

The best way to figure out the requirements for any particular copyright registration is to order the free Copyright Office publications "Copyright Basics" and "Copyright Registration Procedures," as well as the pamphlet that explains registration procedures for the type of work you are registering (for example , "Copyright Registration for Works of the Visual Arts") when you order the appropriate registration form from the Copyright Office. If you read these simply-written pamphlets and follow the instruction sheet that comes attached to the registration form, you should be able to fill out the form correctly and submit the correct deposit copies to register your copyright properly.

If, after reading the pamphlets and the instruction sheet, you still have questions, you can call a Copyright Information Specialist at 202-479-0700 for help. Information on ordering application forms and the Copyright Office publications mentioned above, as well as others, is given in the Resources section of this book.

When Was It Born?

Copyright registration is not required. The copyright law automatically grants copyright protection to every work created on or after January 1, 1978, without requiring any action at all from the creator of the work before copyright protection takes effect. However, it is a very good idea to register the copyright in any work which you believe to be of more than passing significance, for several reasons.

Copyright registration is a prerequisite for filing a copyright infringement suit. If registration is made before or within five years of the publication of the work, registration establishes *prima facie* evidence in court of the validity of the copyright and of the facts stated in the copyright registration certificate, such as the name(s) of the owner(s) of the copyright and the date of creation of the copyrighted work.

Further, if registration is made within three months after publication of the work or prior to any infringement of it, a copyright owner who prevails in a copyright infringement suit can collect his or her attorneys' fees as a part of any judgment awarded and may be awarded statutory damages (a range of money damages the copyright law allows the court to award, in its discretion, instead of the actual damages to the plaintiff plus the actual profits of the infringer, both of which can be very difficult and time-consuming for the owner of the infringed copyright to prove in a trial).

Equally important is the protection that registration provides if you are accused of having infringed someone else's copyright. Registration of your copyright establishes a public record that your copyrighted work existed in a certain form at least as early as the date of registration. This is all the proof necessary to prove that you are not guilty of infringement if the copyright you are accused of infringing was created later than yours. Otherwise, if the two works are similar, proving your innocence can be difficult.

For Deposit Only Whether or not you register your copyright, the law requires you to "deposit" with the Copyright Office certain works published in the United States with notice of copyright. In general, the copyright owner or the owner of the exclusive right to publish the copyrighted work has a legal obligation to deposit, within three months of publication in the United

States, two copies of the work for the use of the Library of Congress. Failure to do so does not invalidate copyright protection for the work, but the law does prescribe fines and other penalties for failure to made this mandatory deposit.

The good news is that the deposit of copies you made with your copyright registration application completely satisfies the mandatory deposit requirements of the copyright law. More good news is that Copyright Office regulations exempt certain categories of works entirely from the mandatory deposit requirements and reduce the requirements for other categories. The best way to make sense of this requirement with regard to any work that you publish but do not, for whatever reason, register, is to request from the Copyright Office the free publication "Mandatory Deposit of Copies or Phonorecords for the Library of Congress." Information on ordering that pamphlet is given in the Resources section of this book.

No Trespassing

Copyright notice is like a "no trespassing" sign. It is "notice" to the world that you claim ownership of the copyright in the work to which it is affixed. Copyright notice consists of three elements which should appear together in close proximity. They are: the word "copyright" (that is C-O-P-Y-R-I-G-H-T, *not* "copy-write") or the © symbol (or, in the case of a sound recording, the ℗ symbol), followed by the year of first publication of the work and the name of the owner of the copyright or an abbreviation or alternate name by which that copyright owner is generally recognized.

For example, International Business Machines, Incorporated, can call itself "IBM" for purposes of copyright notice. However, when in doubt, use the form of your legal name you commonly use for other formal purposes, e.g., "Aaron L. Bowers" rather than "Sonny Bowers."

The year-date of first publication may be omitted from copyright notice when a pictorial, graphic, or sculptural work, with any accompanying text, is reproduced on greeting cards, postcards, stationary, jewelry, dolls, toys, or useful articles.

In the United States, proper copyright notice consists only of some combination of the three elements mentioned above. "Copyright 1990 Natalie Marie Wilson," "© 1990 N.M. Wilson," and " ℗ 1990 Natalie M. Wilson" (for a sound recording) are all correct.

Occasionally copyright owners will also add to the title page of a book or magazine a paragraph something like this:

> All rights reserved. No portion of this publication may be reproduced or transmitted in any form or by any means, electronic or mechanical, including by photocopying, recording or use of any information storage and retrieval system without express written permission from ABC Publishing Company.

Other than possibly scaring off some potential copyright infringers who may not know or appreciate the full significance of copyright notice, added language of this sort has no effect and is not a substitute for proper copyright notice. However, there is also nothing in the copyright law that says you cannot use some language of this sort near your copyright notice to make more explicit your claim of ownership of copyright in the work.

Don't Be a Fool   The important thing to remember is that there is no legal substitute for proper copyright notice. It costs nothing to use and you don't need permission from anyone to use it—so not using notice on any work that leaves your hands seems foolish.

Foolish though it may be to fail to use copyright notice, it must be said that, copyright notice is not *required* for any work published after March 1, 1989. That is the date the United States' entry into the Berne Convention became effective. The Berne Convention is a very old and widespread copyright treaty, but the United States became a signatory to it only late in 1988, for a variety of complicated reasons, one of which is that Berne Convention signatory countries may not require as a condition to copyright protection any "formalities," such as using copyright notice.

The short of this long story is that you cannot now lose copyright protection for any work published after March 1, 1989, by failing to use copyright notice. However, in order to encourage the use of copyright notice in the U.S., the law now provides a valuable procedural advantage (in infringement lawsuits) to copyright owners who do use it. Specifically, an infringer cannot successfully claim that he or she did not know that his or her acts constituted copyright infringement if the copyright owner has used proper copyright notice. That takes care of people dishonest enough to ignore copyright notice. Using copyright notice also precludes the possibility that honest people, seeing no copyright notice, will believe that your work is free for anyone to use. Even after Berne, copyright notice remains one of the most useful tools for protecting your copyright.

Public Notice

Copyright notice does not have to be obtrusive. Copyright Office regulations specify only that notice be placed, in a durable form affixed in a permanent manner, in a location on the work where it is reasonably easy to discover.

For works published in book form, acceptable locations for copyright notice include the title page, the page following the title page, either side of the front or back cover, and the first or last page of the main body of the book.

For motion pictures and other audiovisual works, notice should be embodied in the film or tape as a part of the image itself so that it will appear whenever the work is played or broadcast or otherwise performed and may be located with or near the title or credits or immediately following the beginning of the work or at or immediately preceding the end of the work.

If the audiovisual work lasts sixty seconds or less (as in a television commercial), copyright notice may appear in any of the locations specified above or on the leader of the film or tape immediately preceding the work if the notice is embodied there electronically or mechanically (that is, is not simply written by hand on the leader). For audiovisual works or motion pictures distributed to the public for private use, such as a movie videotapes, notice may also appear on the permanent container for the work.

For pictorial, graphic, or sculptural works embodied in two-dimensional copies, copyright notice should be affixed directly, durably, and permanently to the front or back of the copies or to the backing, mounting, or framing to which the copies are attached. For such works embodied in three-dimensional copies, notice should be affixed directly, durably, and permanently to any visible portion of the work or any base, mounting, framing, or other material to which the copies are attached. If, because of the nature of the work, it is impractical to affix notice to the copies directly or by means of a durable label, notice may appear on a tag or durable label which is designed to remain attached to the copy.

For copies of sound recordings, such as audiotapes, cassettes and records, copyright notice should appear on the surface of the copy of the sound recording and on the container of the copy, so as to give reasonable notice to an observer of the claim of copyright ownership.

Prescriptions　There are other sorts of works for which the Copyright Office prescribes copyright notice placement. Further and more detailed information concerning copyright notice and placement is available in the free Copyright Office pamphlet "Copyright Notice," and in the Copyright Office circulars, also free for the asking, "Methods of Affixation and Positions of the Copyright Notice on Various Types of Works" and "Copyright Notice." Information on obtaining all three of these short publications is included in the Resources section of this book.

It is important to note that although individual articles and illustrations in periodicals are protected by the copyright notice for the publication even if the publisher does not own the copyrights in the individual articles, the *advertisements* which appear in magazines and newspapers should carry their own copyright notices, just like ads in any other format. This notice may be run up one vertical margin of the ad in small type, or appear in the footnote position, or be placed in any location in the ad where it is legible and "reasonably discoverable."

I Don't Care.　Many clients want to own the copyright in the ads they
I Do.　pay to have produced. Some don't care. This does not have to be a touchy question. The best way to avoid disputes is to discuss in advance the ownership of copyright in any materials produced for clients. Any other approach can result in outraged clients who won't listen to any explanations, however reasonable, about the copyright law and what it says. Agreements between clients and design studios or ad agencies should specifically address the question of copyright ownership, and ads produced under such an agreement should bear copyright notice which jibes with the contract. This necessitates, in the case of an agreement with a client that the client will own copyright in

materials produced for it, agreements with free-lancers to acquire rights that the client expects to own. (More about free-lancers, specifically photographers, and copyright in the next chapter.)

A photographer or illustrator who does not assign the copyright in his or her photo or illustration to the design studio or ad agency that uses it in a client's ad may request that separate copyright notice that applies only to the photo or drawing be included in the ad. This is not often done, but there is really no reason why it should not be done, since it reflects that situation as it actually exists. It is also an easy way to keep good free-lancers happy. Any designer can easily work out the positioning of copyright notice for the photo or illustration so that it is obvious that it refers only to the photo or illustration and not the ad as a whole, which should still carry its own copyright notice.

Works which consist preponderantly of one or more public domain U.S. government works must carry a special form of copyright notice, which must either disclaim copyright protection for the section of the work which is quoted from U.S. government material or must identify the particular parts of the whole work which are original and in which copyright ownership is claimed.

From Sea to Shining Sea

All rights of United States copyright owners are granted to them by the U.S. copyright statute, which is a "federal" law, that is, a law passed by Congress which governs copyright matters throughout the U.S. The provisions of the federal copyright statute are interpreted by court decisions. These decisions become another segment of United States copyright law, for they are used by other courts in deciding later copyright cases.

It is important to realize that all this law skids to a halt at the geographic boundaries of the United States because, of course, United States law has no power other than within the fifty states and possessions of the U.S.

Almost every other country in the world has its own copyright law, the provisions of which may diverge considerably from those of our copyright law.For example, the term of copyright in Great Britain is different from that in the United States. There are various copyright treaties, and the U.S. is now a signatory to the principal ones. These treaties are basically agreements among several nations that each treaty signatory will accord the same respect to the rights of copyright owners who are citizens of the other signatory countries as it does to those of its own citizens.

Although your United States copyright rights are governed by U.S. law, which has no power in other countries (other than that given it by treaty in most countries of the world), you can apply for copyright registration in other countries as well as in the United States. If you are curious about international copyright protection, you can order the free pamphlet "International Copyright Relations of the United States" from the Copyright Office. See the Resources section of this book for details.

Copyright Infringement Chapter 3

Trespassers Will Be Prosecuted

Copyright infringement is any trespass upon one or more of the rights that the law reserves to copyright owners. These "exclusive rights" are the right to copy or reproduce the work, the right to prepare alternate or "derivative" versions of the work, the right to distribute and sell copies of the work, and the right to perform or display the work publicly. Any unauthorized exercise of any of these rights is infringement. Knowing the test that courts apply in deciding copyright infringement lawsuits can help you know when someone violates your rights as a copyright owner and how to avoid infringing the copyrights of others.

What It Is Is What It Isn't

Essential to an understanding of copyright infringement is knowing what copyright does *not* protect. As we discussed in Chapter One, the most basic concept of copyright law is that copyright protects, not ideas, but only particular *expressions* of ideas; neither does copyright protect systems, methods or procedures, titles, slogans, raw information, blank forms, measuring and computing devices, plots, or public domain material. Further, copyright does not prevent another person's independent, coincidental creation of a work which is similar or even identical to yours. So long as that person did not copy your work, his or her creation is as entitled to copyright protection as yours.

This Is Only a Test

Most copyright infringement lawsuits are brought because a copyright owner believes that his or her work has been infringed by being copied without permission. Sometimes these suits are valid — an infringer has intentionally copied the copyright owner's song or book or painting in an effort to steal the successful features of that work and profit from them. Many copyright infringement lawsuits, however, are brought because the plaintiff wrongly believes that someone who has created a somewhat similar work has infringed the plaintiff's copyright by copying.

The test for copyright infringement, in the absence of an admission by the defendant of copying (which is rare), is a two-part circumstantial evidence test — "access" and "substantial similarity." That is, in order to prove copyright infringement, you must prove that the accused infringer did not merely accidentally create a work substantially similar to yours entirely *independent* of any copying from your work; you must prove that the accused infringer had access to your previously created work so that copying was possible. Secondly, you must prove that the work you suspect of infringing your work is more than just passingly similar to yours; that it is, in fact, *substantially* similar to your creation.

More Than a Little

Exactly what amount of similarity constitutes "substantial similarity" is hard to say. Slight or trivial similarities do not result in infringement; however, it is not necessary for the accused work to be nearly identical to the plaintiff's work in order to constitute substantial similarity. In other words, the degree of similarity which will get you in trouble is *substantial* — more than "sort of" like the copyrighted work, but less than exactly like it.

If this sounds like a vague standard to you, you are right. Each copyright infringement case must be determined on the facts of that particular case and it is simply not possible to formulate a precise test for infringement applicable in all situations. The test for copyright infringement is like the system one Supreme Court justice once said he used for determining if a work was obscene. "I can't define it," he said, "but I know it if I see it."

Fringe Detriments

Vague standard notwithstanding, it is possible to give some examples of actions which will always result in infringement if the work copied is not a public domain work or otherwise unprotected by copyright.

Outright duplication of significant portions of a work obviously results in substantial similarity; this sort of substantial similarity has been characterized as taking the "fundamental substance" of another's work and is the sort of copying that is often called simply "plagiarism."

Another sort of substantial similarity is what has been called "comprehensive literal similarity," where as a whole the accused work tracks the pattern of expression of the work said to have been infringed and uses the same theme or format.

A third variety of substantial similarity is the taking of portions of a work which are important to the impact and character of the work from which they are taken but which do not amount to a large portion of the infringing work. This sort of infringing substantial similarity points up the fact that what is important is the quantity and importance of the material taken from the infringed work rather than simply the portion of the infringing work that the stolen material constitutes. In other words, an infringer cannot escape responsibility for his or her infringing actions by pointing out how much of the infringing work was *not* stolen.

It's Only Fair

There are situations in which you may use parts of another person's copyrighted work without infringing that person's rights. This sort of use is called "fair use."

Fair use is a kind of public policy exception to the usual standard for determining copyright infringement; that is, there is infringing copying but because of a countervailing public interest, it is permitted and is not called infringement. The fair use defense can render otherwise infringing substantial similarity non-infringing.

Courts consider a long list of factors in determining whether a use is "fair." The purpose and character of the use that is claimed as fair use is important. Educational, research, criticism, and news reporting uses are almost always fair; commercial uses, such as uses in advertising, are seldom fair uses.

The nature of the copyrighted work is considered. Fair use for informational works is broader than fair use for creative works.

The amount and substantiality of the copied portion of the copyrighted work is examined. This is the "substantial similarity" question again. It is quantitative and qualitative; that is, did you quote the twelve-page climax of a mystery novel, thereby disclosing the identity of the killer, or did you quote only a three-paragraph section which describes the detective?

The effect of the would-be fair use on the potential market for the copyrighted work can be determinative in a court's evaluation of whether the use constitutes infringement. This is a very important factor in any such evaluation. If the market for the copyrighted work is significantly diminished because of the purported fair use, then it is not a fair use. Fewer readers want to buy the book if its most sensational and newsworthy sections have been previously excerpted in a magazine.

A related factor that is considered is the effect of the purported fair use on any of the rights in the copyright of the work said to be infringed. If one person writes and sells a screenplay based on another person's copyrighted novel, the right to prepare and sell a screen adaptation of the novel has been lost to the author of that novel.

Parody of copyrighted works is a kind of free-speech exception to the prohibition against the use of others' copyrighted works and is a sort of fair use. However, parody is never a permissable fair use unless the parody uses only so much of the parodied work as is necessary to "call to mind" the parodied work and is dangerous to attempt without careful attention to the question of infringement.

In fact, advertising parody is much more difficult to bring off safely than less commercial sorts of parody, because advertising is presumed to be a commercial use of the underlying parodied copyrighted work and therefore ineligible for the fair use defense to a charge of copyright infringement. This does not mean that satire and parody can never safely be used in the creation of advertising, only that when the satirized or parodied work is protected by copyright (as opposed to a parody of, say, *Robinson Crusoe*), great care must be taken to use only so much of the copyrighted work as is absolutely necessary to the parody or satire, and strict attention should be paid to the factors courts use in determining fair use generally.

Another sort of fair use is the quotation of portions of copyrighted works. Quotation of short passages, such as the sort of quoting found in book reviews or news stories, is generally safe in any context where the First Amendment protection of free speech can be reasonably invoked, such as, for example, in the text of a press release or a corporation annual report or a newsletter article, even if the piece in which the quotation is used has a partially commercial purpose.

The use of even a short quotation from a famous living person in a strictly commercial context, such as a newspaper or magazine advertisement, could be dangerous, however, as a violation of that person's right of publicity and, possibly, as falsely implying his or her endorsement of the product or service advertised. The same goes for quotations from people who are not famous, except that use of a quotation from, say, a letter from such a person in an ad would be construed as an invasion of that person's privacy. Unless you have express permission to use quotations from anyone in any advertising context, it is wise to avoid doing so. (See Chapter Nine for more detailed information.)

Direct quotations should always be attributed, as should closely paraphrased statements. It is very important to understand, however, that you cannot escape responsibility for copyright infringement simply by attributing the lifted portion of any work to its author; if the "borrowed" segment amounts to a substantial portion of the copyrighted work, attribution does not eradicate your sin. As indicated earlier, you should also avoid any use of even two- or three-paragraph direct quotations or close paraphrases if they embody the "meat" of the work from which they were taken or if use of them would diminish the salability of that work.

You Be the Judge The imprecision of the courts in defining copyright infringement need not confuse you, because you already have very good equipment to judge for yourself if one work infringes another. Courts judge substantial similarity by the "ordinary observer" test. This means that if an ordinary observer would recognize from the overall appearance or character of the two works that one had been copied or derived from the other, substantial similarity, and therefore infringement, exists. You, as an ordinary observer, are in a very good position to determine with your own eyes or ears whether you have infringed someone's copyright or if someone else has infringed yours.

In determining whether your work infringes some-one else's copyright, let your conscience be your guide; if you think that you have taken more than inspiration from another, copyrighted work, you could very well have stepped over the meandering boundary between permissible use of another's work and "substantial similarity."

If someone sues you for copyright infringement and is able to prove to the court that an infringement took place, that copyright owner may obtain an injunction to halt further sales or distribution or dissemination of the infringing publication or advertisement and you could be forced to pay a substantial judgment, includ-ing any profits you made from the infringement and, possibly, the attorneys' fees and costs of the success-ful plaintiff. The lawyers' fees incurred in defending through trial a copyright infringement suit can be, in themselves, enormous, even if the judgment is not. And even if the case is settled before it goes to trial, you still may have to pay a cash settlement to the plain-tiff, as well as your lawyer's fees for handling the case to the point of settlement.

It's a Matter of Principle

If you are an employee of an advertising agency or design studio or corporation, you should also realize that your acts, within the scope of your duties, are attributable to your employer and to any client for whom you prepare ads, under the principles of the law of agency. This means that both your employer and your client can be sued for something *you* did. In fact, they are far more likely to be sued than you are, since they are "deep pocket" defendants .

If you are ever tempted to steal from a copyrighted work, stop and think how you'd like to explain to your boss how a copyright infringement lawsuit ended up on her or his desk and why lawyers have been calling for an explanation as to why your client is now their client since becoming a defendant. Then, go back to your drawing board or typewriter and come up with your own work.

If you feel that someone has infringed your copyright, call a lawyer who is knowledgeable about copyright law. A good copyright lawyer will be able to predict your chances of success in a copyright infringement suit and will help you assess the wisdom of suing. Being right and being able to win in court are often two different things. Collecting a big enough judgment to make a suit worthwhile is another matter still. Further, a skilled copyright lawyer may be able to stop the infringement and secure a cash settlement from the infringer *without* filing suit.

A Short Survey of the Delights of Civil Litigation

Big Ideas, Big Trouble

People who believe that their copyrights have been infringed often have no idea how complicated copyright infringement lawsuits are and exaggerated ideas about how much money they might recover if they bring suit against the suspected infringer. Unfortunately, the unwarranted contemplation of the large amounts of money one feels certain he or she will be awarded is often the most satisfying stage of a copyright infringement suit. As with most civil litigation, copyright infringement suits are more fun for plaintiffs to think about than participate in. For defendants, lawsuits are no fun at all.

Here Be Dragons

Every ancient mapmaker knew that his very own country was the center of the world, but most were confused as to what lay over the horizon. They prudently decided that what they didn't know could hurt them and often marked these vast *terra incognita* areas with the warning "Heere Bee Dragons" to warn explorers of the perils there. If you have never been involved in a civil lawsuit, this is a wise attitude to cultivate toward suing and being sued, because today in the United States the dragons are called Litigants and Lawyers.

This doesn't mean that there are no issues worth going to court over — litigation is, regrettably, sometimes the only way to settle some disputes or pursue that elusive goal, justice. However, and especially with regard to business disputes of any sort, litigation should be viewed as a last resort. In civilized countries, if your neighbor offends you, you do not engage him and his clan in a feud; rather, you file your complaint in a court of law and let a judge decide the dispute. Unfortunately, the U.S. judicial system is so complex that a lawsuit can leave you as bloodied as a fistfight; even if you win you are bruised by the experience.

Quick, Call a Lawyer

If you decide to sue someone, the first thing you must do is find a lawyer to represent you. In Great Britain, lawyers are classified as either "barristers," that is, lawyers who represent clients in court, or "solicitors," lawyers who counsel clients concerning every sort of legal matter, including lawsuits, but who do not represent clients in court. In the United States, there is no such formal division among lawyers, but most lawyers consider themselves either primarily counselors or litigators. If you have an established relationship with a lawyer you trust, it is probably a good idea to take your lawsuit first to that lawyer for evaluation and advice, just as you would first consult your family physician for evaluation of any ailment and possible later referral to a specialist.

Litigators are specialist attorneys; their specialty is representing clients in lawsuits. For that reason, litigators may not always be the best source for objective advice on whether to sue, since their judgment in evaluating possible solutions to your problem may be too influenced by the remedy they know best — litigation. In addition, a good evaluation of whether to bring suit in a suspected case of copyright infringement involves a careful analysis of the question of whether the suspect actions actually do constitute copyright infringement. For this evaluation, only a lawyer who is well-versed in copyright law can reliably advise you, since lawyers who are not thoroughly familiar with the issues involved in copyright infringement cases, however well-meaning they may be, often are poor judges of copyright infringement.

It's the Best I Can Do

Responsible lawyers will not bring frivolous suits on your behalf; a lawyer has an ethical duty to determine that any lawsuit he or she files for you is founded on a reasonable interpretation of the law and that your allegations against your defendant are based in fact and are not merely unfounded claims. However, no lawyer can guarantee the outcome of any suit; the best your lawyer can do is make a prediction of your chances of prevailing, based on her or his assessment of the applicable state or federal statute and the precedents set by court decisions in similar cases.

Remember, your lawsuit is brought in *your* name, not your lawyer's; your lawyer is only a skilled agent acting on your behalf. It is *your* testimony that will be required, and you who stand to gain from any judgment in your favor. And it is *you* who will be footing the bill for all the work your attorney must perform to represent you adequately.

**Support Your
Local Lawyer**

Lawyers' fees run from a low of around $75 per hour to as much as $300 per hour in some cities. What your lawsuit will cost, in attorneys' fees and costs such as court filing fees, costs of court reporters for depositions, expert witness fees, etc., depends mostly on how complicated the issues in your case are, how many people are involved, how well-financed they are, how vigorously they defend against your claims, and whether the suit must be brought in another city or can be brought where you live.

Even a relatively uncomplicated suit, however, can cost you several thousand dollars to bring to the point of trial. Complicated lawsuits involving multiple plaintiffs and/or defendants are a litigator's dream; he or she knows that, even despite his or her best efforts to bring the suit to a quick resolution, the legal work involved may produce fat fees for several years.

And though most clients who have been through an expensive lawsuit would hesitate to admit it, there's nothing unfair about a lawyer charging for his or her work. If anything is unfair about a lawsuit, it is the fact that circumstances compel you to be involved in one in the first place. All your lawyer can do is use every tactic at his or her disposal to get you out of it as quickly as possible.

Sometimes lawyers will agree to represent clients in lawsuits on a "contingency fee" basis. This means that the lawyer will represent the client without payment for her or his services during the course of the lawsuit for a large share, usually one-third, of any sum eventually awarded the client by the court.

Before accepting any case on this basis, a lawyer will look at the amount of legal work involved, the probable amount of damages which could be awarded, and the likelihood that the plaintiff will win the suit, because a lawyer who accepts a case on this basis earns nothing in return for sometimes literally years of work if the court rules against her or his client. And bringing a suit even on a contingency fee basis can still be expensive for the client, since the client, not the lawyer, pays all the expenses of the suit, which can be considerable.

But Perry Mason Always Wins

If more people had fewer assumptions about lawsuits and the judicial process, the public image of lawyers as a group would be better. Clients somehow believe in their hearts that their lawyers can control the outcome of lawsuits and very often become disenchanted with their own lawyers, not to mention the lawyers of their adversaries, if they lose their suits. *Judges* decide cases based on *laws* passed by *legislators* who were elected by *you*. Lawyers are like guides through what is today in the U.S. often a legal jungle; they are stuck with the laws and the judges they encounter and must do their best to guide you through the litigation process, but cannot change the basic rules by which the litigation must be conducted.

Nevertheless, clients think, on some level, that all a lawyer has to do is to reach into the bottom drawer of his or her desk, fill out a form marked "Lawsuit," file it at the courthouse and — voila! — the worthless human being who has just been labelled the "Defendant" will be hauled to a cell under the courthouse that very afternoon by two or more burly federal marshals.

Unfortunately, it doesn't happen that way. You may know that your defendant is dead wrong and a sneaky, dishonest person besides, and the defendant may know it, too, but before the *court* knows it, you have to *prove* it, while simultaneously fighting the best efforts of the defendant to avoid admitting that he did anything wrong. That's why your lawyer will plot your lawsuit like a chess game and view the trial as a battle.

How Long Do You Have?

Litigation is a long process, and in real life, most of it takes place before the trial. The first thing your lawyer will do after investigating the facts surrounding your grievance against your adversary and the law governing your claim is to draft what is called your "complaint." A complaint is a carefully-worded document that sets out the facts of your dispute, relates them to the law, tells how the defendant has transgressed your rights under the law, and asks for certain "relief," from and on account of the defendant's transgressions, such as an injunction (an order from the court directing the defendant to do something or to stop doing something) or an award of damages (money awarded to compensate you for your losses or punish the defendant).

Plaintiffs should know that lawyers always ask for more than they have any hope of actually receiving; those "Million Dollar Lawsuit" headlines you see may result, long after the newsprint has faded, in actual awards of only a few thousand dollars, which may be barely enough to cover the legal fees of the plaintiffs.

The lawsuit officially begins when your complaint is filed with the court. After the defendant is formally notified of the suit, he or she has a specified period of time within which to file an "answer" with the court which responds to each allegation made in the complaint, giving the defendant's side of the matter.

In many suits, before and sometimes also after the answer is filed, the defendant will file various motions objecting to one or another important procedural aspect of the lawsuit in an effort to have the case dismissed, or, at least, to delay its progress. Your lawyer must file a response challenging any such motion and must support your position with a written "brief," which is a brief statement of the law and facts relating to the issue raised in the defendant's motion and which is meant to educate the judge and persuade him or her that the defendant's motion should be granted.

These motions, all duly supported by well-researched and carefully written briefs, can continue for a frustratingly long time.

Eureka! Meanwhile, another interesting and, for the lawyers, often lucrative part of the lawsuit is going on; this is "discovery," the minuet between the parties to the suit by which each litigant "discovers" from the other as many facts as possible related to the lawsuit. Discovery tools include interrogatories (written questions), requests for production of documents (written requests for pertinent paperwork), and depositions (oral testimony taken out of court, but under oath and recorded by a court reporter). Discovery can also take forever.

Once the complaint and answer are filed, all the motions are made, answered, and ruled on by the court, and discovery is complete, the case can be set for trial. Both your lawyer and the defendant's lawyer will pore over all the facts they've gathered, assess the strengths of their arguments and map out their plans to present those facts and arguments in court before the judge, if the trial is to be a "bench trial," or the jury.

A very large percentage of lawsuits are settled just prior to trial, sometimes literally in the hallway outside the courtroom just before the proceedings are to begin. This is because no one, least of all lawyers, wants to go through a trial if a settlement is offered on any basis that is at all acceptable. Even more persuasive is the attitude of most judges, who actively encourage settlements to reduce their heavy workload, to save taxpayers' money, and to clear perpetually clogged court dockets.

A settlement agreement between the litigants also usually eliminates the possibility that the lawsuit isn't over even after the fat lady sings. Many losing litigants can find reasons to appeal the judgments entered against them by their trial courts. Sometimes they appeal up the ladder of courts more than once, on one ground or another, until all the people involved in the original lawsuit feel that they have unwittingly wandered into Charles Dickens' famous never-ending fictional lawsuit, *Jarndyce v. Jarndyce.*

Bad to Worse

The only thing worse than being a plaintiff in a lawsuit is being a defendant. A plaintiff at least has the choice of filing the suit or not and chooses, to some extent, when and where the suit is filed and what issues are involved. A defendant has none of these choices. In a suit brought on meritorious grounds, a plaintiff has some justifiable hope of winning the suit, collecting an award of damages and, possibly, an award of the attorneys' fees and costs he or she has incurred in pursuing the suit.

The best most defendants can hope for is to have the court rule in their favor; in which case they pay their own often enormous legal fees and go home. At worst, a defendant is held to have transgressed the rights of the plaintiff, is ordered to pay the plaintiff money damages, is enjoined from further conduct of the sort the plaintiff sought to have stopped, and has to pay the plaintiff's legal fees in addition to his or her own legal fees. Sometimes plaintiffs come out ahead in lawsuits; defendants almost never do, even if the judgment is in their favor.

Theory 10, Practice 0

Our judicial system is, in theory, one of the best ever invented. In practice, it often leaves a great deal to be desired. Some disputes cannot be settled out of court and must be litigated to avoid injustice, but too often litigation is commenced because someone is trying to prove a point or holds a grudge or gets greedy. Those lawsuits make even lawyers tired. It is important to be right, but what you really should aim for is to be right *out* of court. That means careful choices in your business relationships, careful attention to the rights of others, and a careful lawyer who counsels you on ways to avoid disputes before they ripen into that bitter fruit, a lawsuit.

Is It Infringement?

Wood Anyone Mind?

You want to use Grant Wood's famous painting "American Gothic" in a magazine ad for your travel agency client ("Bored At Home?"), so you shoot a copy of it from an Art Institute of Chicago guidebook, blow it up a little, add copy and run the ad. Is it infringement?

Yes. You are in double trouble with this ad. Grant Wood painted "American Gothic" in 1930. Although he died in 1942, the copyright in the painting, which will endure through the end of 2005, is owned by his estate. Not only did you not have the right to use Wood's painting without permission, you also did not have the right to copy the photograph of the painting. The Art Institute of Chicago owns the copyright in that photograph and your copying the photo without permission constitutes a second infringement of copyright.

Big Lies, No Trouble

Your client Harry Hardwood the furniture store owner likes the "Joe Isuzu" television ads and wants the spring ad campaign for his store to mirror them as closely as possible. You study all the Isuzu ads you can and produce your best imitation of them, although you use a character named Josephine Hardwood who tells big lies about furniture instead of Japanese cars. Is it infringement?

No. You have every right to adopt the idea behind the Isuzu ads, that is, the idea of an off-the-wall character named after a product who tells obviously outrageous lies about its qualities. What you cannot do is copy the expression of that idea, which, in the case of Joe Isuzu, would be the dramatic content of the Isuzu spots, or Joe Isuzu's dialogue or, arguably, the particular events or plot devices used by Isuzu in any spot. So long as you only take inspiration and an idea from Isuzu, your actions are legal. (This may not be true, however, in any context where your product competes with the product advertised in the ads which inspire you. That could be a sort of trademark infringement because consumers could confuse your spots with the original ads because they are so similar.)

I Was Framed You reprint the entire text of Martin Luther King, Jr.'s famous "I Have A Dream" speech on "parchment" paper in a form suitable for framing for your *alma mater*, a small and struggling but well-regarded black college, which sells the printed speeches for ten dollars each to raise money for a new library. Is this infringement?

Almost certainly. Any use of the full text for Dr. King's 1960's speech without the permission of his estate constitutes infringement, especially if that use is made for commercial gain, as in this situation. It is possible that you could successfully argue that your otherwise infringing use of the speech is actually a "fair use" because it was made on behalf of and for the benefit of a non-profit educational institution, but it is more likely that Dr. King's estate would, at the very least, require your college to pay a royalty on each copy sold. The King estate could also stop the sale of the speech, compel the destruction of all unsold copies of it, and collect the profits from all sales made. Even national heroes have copyright rights.

Free Ride, Free Meal

You find a nice little poem about home cooking in an old book with an 1890 copyright date and reprint it, with proper credit to the author, on the front of the new menu for your client Granny's Family Restaurant. A Megan Bowers, great-granddaughter of Patricia Bowers, the author of the poem, eats at Granny's on her way back to Peoria. Megan sees the poem and tells Granny that, as the heir of Patricia Bowers, she is owed a royalty from Granny's use of the poem. Is she right?

No. The copyright in a poem written in 1890 or before expired no later than 1965. That means that "Home Cookin'" is now in the public domain and is free for use by anyone. You had no obligation to seek permission from any of the author's heirs before using the poem, and no one has any obligation to pay Megan Bowers any royalty. Try placating her with free Sunday dinner for two at Granny's.

They Said It, I Didn't

You use, on the cover of your corporation client's annual report, a photo of a small segment of a *Wall Street Journal* article which contains a twenty-five-word quotation naming the corporation as an innovator in its field. Is it infringement?

No. Your use of the *Wall Street Journal* quotation is a fair use of that publication's copyrighted story in two ways; it is a properly attributed short quote used in a First Amendment context, since the annual report is the corporation's way of informing its stockholders about the corporation, and you used only a small portion of the *Journal* story, not enough to constitute a taking of the "fundamental substance" of the news story or to make the annual report "substantially similar" to it. Reprinting the whole story without permission would be a different matter.

Dynamic Duo

Your auto dealer client calls himself "The Super-Dealer." You use a photo of him, dressed in blue long johns with a red cape and a wide gold belt, in an ad that depicts him standing shoulder-to-shoulder with those other super-heroes, Batman and Superman, who appear as their original cartoon-figure, comic-book selves. Is it infringement?

Yes, two kinds. You infringed the copyright rights of the publishers from whose comic books you copied the cartoon figures you used and you infringed their trademark rights by using the well-known super-heroes to attract attention to your ad. You are in more trouble for your trademark transgression than for your copyright infringement. Duck into a phone booth and disguise yourself as a smarter person.

In a Jam

Your client Old-Tyme Jams and Jellies wants to branch out into the instant beverage market. The president of the company brings you a beautiful drawing of his three young granddaughters, done by a local portrait artist and presented to him on his last birthday in a gilt frame. He wants to call his new instant lemonade "Three Sisters Lemonade Mix" and use the drawing on the packaging for the mix. You design beautiful labels and canisters around the drawing, which you color delicately in pastels. Is it infringement?

Yep. You were led astray by a doting grandfather, but down the primrose path nevertheless. Ownership of a physical object conveys no ownership of copyright in the work it embodies. Neither you nor your client had any right to reproduce or otherwise use the portrait drawing for any purpose other than hanging it on the wall to look at. And you had no right to prepare an alternate version of the drawing by coloring it, however delicately. You should have suggested that your client either obtain permission to use the drawing as he wished or sort through his family album for a nice turn-of-the-century photo of his long-dead great-aunts, Minerva, Miranda, and Matilda.

See No Evil

Your department store client has asked you to design entirely new shopping bags, wrapping paper, and boxes for customer purchases. The store is upscale and located in the nicest section of town, so you decide on a ritzy but traditional approach. You spend an afternoon in a wallpaper store, buy a half-roll of a beautiful hunter green and ruby red Jacobean stylized floral on a cream background, stat it and send it to the printers. Is it infringement?

Yes. Just because the Jacobeans all expired a few centuries ago, along with whatever copyright rights in their designs English law gave them at that time, you cannot assume that the wallpaper design you used is public domain. It is very probable that the wallpaper you used is a recent modern interpretation of a Jacobean design or of that style and was created by a real live designer hired by the wallpaper company. In fact, you really should have noticed that there was a copyright notice, " © The Beautiful Wallpaper Company," running down the edge of the paper you bought. Maybe you just didn't want to look.

A Cautionary Tale

One-Man Band

Albert was very pleased with himself. He had just picked up a new client for his struggling one-man advertising agency, The Albert Agency, and the concept for the ad campaign for the client, Vito's Italian Restaurant, had come to him as he drove back to his office from his meeting with Vito. As he drove, Albert had heard on his favorite oldies station the Billy Joel song "My Italian Restaurant," and had had the idea to use the song title for the theme of the Vito's ad campaign, using the personable Vito himself as spokesman and the Billy Joel song as the background for the radio and television spots, with Vito recording the voice-overs.

Albert presented his idea at his next meeting with Vito. The old gentleman was flattered and approved the campaign. Albert went out and bought a brand-new copy of the Billy Joel album that includes "My Italian Restaurant," had a photo taken of Vito in a tuxedo at the door of his restaurant, and produced the campaign in time to air the radio and television spots and run the print ads during the city's fall convention of independent insurance agents, who ate a lot of Italian food at Vito's, across the street from the convention center. Vito was very happy with The Albert Agency and Albert began to think that he could pay his office rent on time after all.

Letter Bomb   Then, Vito received by certified mail a scary piece of correspondence called a "cease and desist letter" from a New York law firm representing Billy Joel's record company and music publishing company. The letter informed Vito that his use of the Billy Joel recording of the song "My Italian Restaurant" in ads for his restaurant was an infringement of the copyright rights of both the record company, which owned the copyright in the recording of the song, and the music publishing company, which owned the copyright in the song itself.

Further, the letter said, Vito was to immediately "cease" use of the song and recording and "desist" from any additional use whatever of either and that if Vito would pay $10,000 within thirty days to compensate the record company and music publisher for Vito's unauthorized use of the recording and song, those companies would agree not to file a suit in federal court against Vito for copyright infringement. After reading this letter, Vito was considerably less happy than he looked in the big photo on billboards all over town that had gone up two weeks before. He called Albert in a rage.

Albert told Vito that he didn't believe their use of the Billy Joel recording and song was an infringement, since no more than sixty seconds of the recording were used in any spot, that he certainly had not meant to trespass on anyone's rights, felt certain that an innocent blunder was not actionable, and that, in any event, he didn't believe that Vito, who was considerably richer than Albert, could be held responsible for any mistake of Albert's or sued for something Albert did. Albert told Vito that he would consult a lawyer about how to respond to the letter, which Albert said he believed was unjustified and extortionary.

Deflated Ego

Then Albert called his old schoolmate Eddie, who was a lawyer with a Chicago intellectual property law firm. Eddie punctured Albert's unfounded righteous indignation about two minutes into the conversation.

Eddie told Albert that his use of the Billy Joel recording and song was, indeed, copyright infringement, since any broadcast of any copyrighted recording, if the broadcast is made without the permission of the copyright owner and if it cannot be considered a fair use of the recording, is a violation of the copyright owner's exclusive right to perform its copyrighted recording. Eddie said that sixty seconds of the recording was far too large a segment to be considered a fair use and that the same was true for thirty seconds or even ten seconds.

Eddie also told Albert that any use of any copyright for commercial purposes without the express permission of the copyright owner, including his use of the song "My Italian Restaurant," was very likely not to be a fair use of the copyright, merely by virtue of the commercial context of the use.

Worse still, Eddie told Albert that his ignorance of copyright law would not relieve him of his responsibility for the infringements, that copyright infringement is judged by evaluating the quantity, quality, and context of the use of the copyrighted work and not by gauging the wrongful intent of the accused infringer. Even more bleak was the news that, because Albert was acting as the "agent" for Vito, that is, on behalf of and in the place of Vito, Albert's actions could, indeed, be attributed to Vito and Vito could be held responsible for Albert's mistake, even though Vito had no knowledge of any wrongdoing on Albert's part and had certainly never countenanced any.

No Fairy Tale

This story has an unhappy ending. Vito's lawyers told him that he was responsible for Albert's actions, which they agreed were infringements of the rights of the record company and music publishing company, and advised him to settle the dispute before it became a lawsuit. Vito paid the $10,000 to avoid being sued, but immediately filed a lawsuit against The Albert Agency, which means that Albert was sued personally, since The Albert Agency was simply Albert doing business as The Albert Agency.

Vito won a judgment of $10,000 against Albert, plus the cost of producing all the broadcast ads that had to be pulled after Vito received the cease and desist letter, plus the cost of media time that Vito was unable to fill because he had no ads, plus Vito's attorneys' fees and other costs of bringing the suit against Albert and settling the infringement dispute. Vito never collected his judgment, however, because Albert was forced to declare bankruptcy.

At last report, Albert was selling used cars and Vito had turned his restaurant over to his nephew Guido and moved to St. Petersburg, Florida, which reminds him of his birthplace in Sicily.

Copyright in the Marketplace

Abracadabra The law says that a copyright is a bundle of exclusive rights that belong, in most instances, to the person who creates the copyrighted work. That's true, but what copyrights really are is magic. There's something wonderful in the fact that you can sit down with a pencil and paper and create something that pays the rent.

And nobody can tell what your copyright is worth; you may create a photograph today that you allow someone to use in an ad in return for payment of a few hundred dollars only to find that, years from now, that photograph is worth thousands, as a piece of art or because of its subject matter, or because of the growth of your own fame as a photographer. And this invisible thing called a copyright can be subdivided and sold to as many people as you choose for long or short periods and you can, in the end, still own it after profiting from these exploitations of it.

However, like any magician, you must know how to make the magic work for you. That involves a thorough understanding of the three ways copyright rights are owned and change ownership. These three "sorcerer's apprentices" are "License," "Assignment," and the much-feared "Work-For-Hire." If you will read the rest of this chapter, they will do your bidding, turn what you touch to gold, and protect you from the wolf at the door.

You're Hired

In ordinary circumstances, the creators of literary and artistic works own the copyrights in those works from the creation of the works. This is not true when an employee creates a work as a part of her or his job; in that case, the work is a "work-for-hire," which means that the employer is considered both the copyright owner and the author of the work from the creation of the work. Any full-time employee of an ad agency or corporation or commercial art studio who creates ad copy, a script, a jingle, a photograph, a drawing, or any other copyrightable work in the course of performing his or her employment duties has created that work as a work-for-hire.

Works created by free-lance creatives cannot be works-for-hire unless certain requirements are met. There must be a written document in which both the creator of the work and the person commissioning it agree that it is to be considered a work-for-hire and it must fall into one of the nine classes of works which are enumerated in the copyright statute as kinds of works which may be works-for-hire if specially ordered or commissioned from an independent contractor, that is, a free-lancer who is not a regular employee of the commissioning party.

A work commissioned for use as a contribution to a collective work (such as a photo or article prepared specifically to be included in a magazine or a corporate annual report), as a part of a motion picture or other audiovisual work (such as a musical composition written to be used as the soundtrack for a television spot or a slideshow presentation), as a translation, as a supplementary work (such as a chart or graph used to illustrate a chapter in a book), as a compilation (such as research data compiled from a survey for publication as a reference book), as an instructional text (such as a pamphlet instructing the consumer in the proper method for assembling a bicycle or other product), as a test, as answer material for a test, or as an atlas may be a work-for-hire even if it is prepared by a free-lancer.

Many free-lancers object to work-for-hire agreements. They feel that, in most circumstances, work-for-hire agreements are unfair to free-lance creative people. This problem stems in part from lack of information; many ad agency personnel, for example, don't realize that it is not necessary to acquire a free-lancer's work as a work-for-hire in order to secure the rights of copyright they need. There are other ways to acquire the right to use a copyrighted work.

May I See Your License? An "assignment" of copyright is like a sale of the copyright; the author and original copyright owner sells all or some of his or her exclusive rights of copyright ownership for the entire term of copyright or a shorter period. Copyright assignments are also called "transfers" of copyright. Anyone who acquires any right of copyright by assignment can, in turn, sell that right to someone else.

A "license" to use a copyrighted work is like a lease of the copyright or a part of it; a copyright owner can grant as many overlapping or identical licenses, or permissions to use, as he or she wants. In the case of an exclusive license, the author and original copyright owner grants to another person the sole right (that is, that person is the only person who has the right) to exercise some or all of her or his exclusive rights of copyright ownership for a specified time but maintains ownership of the copyright itself. A copyright owner can assign or license as many or as few of the exclusive rights of copyright for as short or as long a time, in whatever geographic area and for whatever purpose, he or she wishes. Like assignments, copyright licenses can ordinarily also be sold to someone else after acquisition.

Any time a copyright owner assigns or licenses to someone else an exclusive right of copyright there must be a written agreement to that effect, signed by the copyright owner. If a copyright owner grants a non-exclusive license, that is, grants to someone else the right to exercise some or all of the exclusive rights of copyright but not exclusively (that is, that person is not the only one the copyright owner permits to exercise those rights) the license does not have to be in writing. Any such assignment or exclusive license agreement may be recorded in the Copyright Office in order to document that the particular right(s) transferred or licensed exclusively are owned by someone other than the person who created the copyrighted work; recording an assignment or license is a very good idea in the case of any creative work of more than temporary significance.

Never Die in a Skirmish

In recent years in the advertising world a battle over work-for-hire has been fought between free-lance photographers and ad agencies and other companies, such as design studios, which rely on free-lance photographers to produce photos used in clients' ads. The photographers object to being asked to sign work-for-hire agreements under any circumstances; ad agencies and design studios want to acquire as much control as possible over the photographs they commission. Like most disputes, this one has two sides. Luckily, there is also an almost overlooked middle ground where everyone involved can meet, if only they will come out of their corners long enough to investigate a compromise.

Photographers believe that no matter what the contribution of designers or ad agency creative personnel it is *their* skill, equipment, and talent that produce the photographs. They also feel that they are being paid primarily for their services and, although they anticipate that the photographs they produce will be used by a client of the design studio or agency which hires them, they do not feel that the payment they receive for their services and that use is adequate to permanently vest all rights in the photographs in the studio or agency.

Further, they feel violated by work-for-hire, since the commissioning party — the design studio or agency — is considered to be the creator or "author" of the photographs for copyright purposes. That means not only no photo credit for the woman or man behind the camera but also no control over the future use of the photo and no further compensation for any such future uses, no matter how much money the agency or studio makes from them.

Designers and ad agencies are often irritated by these attitudes of photographers. They feel that when agency or design studio personnel come up with the concept for the photograph, specifying in detail the subject matter of the photo and supplying the props, models, wardrobe, and location or studio background to be used, supply sketches for the composition of the photograph, carefully arrange the props and models, and specify and approve lighting and other technical aspects involved in the creation of the photograph, it is unconscionable that the photographer should be the sole owner of the copyright in it. Further, they know from experience that their clients are impatient with the fine points of copyright and will balk at any necessity for seeking any permission from a photographer for an additional use of a photo, or for paying anything additional for that use. All this also applies to illustrators, who have fought the work-for-hire battle alongside photographers.

In That Case, What Is the Question?

Who's right? Everybody is, sort of. The positions of both the free-lancers and the agencies and design studios have merit, from a legal standpoint and from a practical standpoint. But that doesn't help matters, because commercial photographers (and illustrators) depend on design studios and ad agencies for a great part of their revenue, and design studios and ad agencies depend on free-lance photographers and illustrators to help them create their principal product, advertising. Fortunately, the solution to the work-for-hire dilemma is not deciding whose position has the most merit; that determination is beside the point. The solution is asking the right question. That question is not "Who owns the copyright?" but, rather "What use will be made of this photo?" (Or drawing.)

Metaphysics in Action

As we have seen, a photograph or drawing created by an independent contractor, that is, a free-lancer, is not considered to be a work-for-hire unless it (a) falls into one of the nine categories of works enumerated in the copyright statute and (b) is agreed to be a work-for-hire in a written document between the commissioning party (the design studio or the agency) and the free-lancer. Both (a) and (b) must be met or the copyright in the photo vests initially in the free-lance photographer or illustrator and must be transferred to the design studio or agency by assignment. Period. No argument. That is, the photograph or drawing cannot be made into a valid work-for-hire unless it is created for use in one of the nine ways listed, even if the free-lancer signs a work-for-hire agreement.

Now, only five of the nine categories enumerated in the copyright statute as proper subjects for works-for-hire are applicable at all to any sort of advertising; very few ad agencies or design studios ever produce a translation, a test, answer material for a test or an atlas for a client. Since many common uses of photographs and illustrations in advertising materials do not fall into one of the remaining five work-for-hire categories, one photo or drawing planned for several uses in an ad campaign (magazine ad, billboard, customer pamphlet, and annual report cover) could fall both within and outside of the permitted work-for-hire categories, depending upon the various uses planned for it.

All this hair-splitting means that if agencies routinely ask free-lancers to sign work-for-hire agreements, regardless of the circumstances, the validity of those agreements will often be dubious. And many highly professional free-lancers are angered and become recalcitrant when asked to sign work-for-hire agreements, which raises their blood pressure and that of the designers or agency creative directors who hire them.

What to Do, What to Do?

If a free-lancer does not sign any written agreement regarding a photo or illustration he or she creates, even if it is specially commissioned, the only right conveyed to the agency by the photographer's or illustrator's action in delivering the photograph or drawing to the agency is the right to use that work under a non-exclusive license. That is, the free-lancer is under no obligation to refrain from granting a similar license or even selling the copyright in the photo or drawing to someone else. This means that design studios and agencies should always acquire a written agreement from free-lancers specifying the scope of the studio's or agency's rights to any photo or drawing produced for it. In most cases, this agreement should be an assignment of copyright rather than a work-for-hire agreement.

An assignment of all copyright rights makes an agency or design studio the owner of the copyright in a photograph or illustration in just about the same way that a valid work-for-hire agreement does. The major pertinent differences are that with an assignment the free-lance photographer or illustrator can elect to terminate the transfer of copyright rights between the thirty-fifth and thirty-sixth year of the term of copyright; under a work-for-hire agreement, the agency or design studio is considered the "author" of the photo or drawing from its creation and owns the copyright for the full term of copyright (seventy-five years from creation), with no possibility that the free-lancer can terminate that term midway.

Since thirty-five years is as good as forever as far as most advertising uses go, an agency or design studio which acquires an assignment of copyright in a photograph or drawing is well-protected from any use of that photo or drawing which conflicts with its client's use or is otherwise objectionable.

Now or Forever   And an assignment, or sale, of copyright does not have to be for the full term of copyright. Perfectly valid assignments can be made for one year or three years or twenty-five years — in short, for as long as you wish. This fact gives studios and agencies and photographers and illustrators (and other outside creatives, of course) the option of agreeing that the copyright in the photo or drawing (or other work) belongs to the studio or agency for the full period of time that the studio or agency believes it will want to use the photograph or drawing or needs to restrict any such use by any other party with whom the free-lancer might otherwise contract. At the end of that period, all rights in the creative work automatically revert to the free-lancer.

The other tool for avoiding work-for-hire standoffs is the exclusive license agreement, which gives the design studio or agency the right to use the photo or drawing for a stated period of time, which, again, can be a long or a short period of time and for all or only certain specified purposes, everywhere or within only a stated geographic are. For example, a photographer could agree to give a design studio the exclusive right to use within the United States his or her landscape photograph for ads for a client company for a period of five years but could reserve the right to sell the photo in Europe (to a magazine, perhaps) during the five years and to anyone anywhere for any use thereafter. In most cases, an exclusive license is all a studio or agency needs to get its money's worth and protect its client from seeing specially commissioned elements of its ad campaign used for someone else's poster or ads or billboard.

An assignment of copyright generally gives an ad agency or a design studio the right to use a freelancer's creative work in any way that the agency or studio sees fit during the period of the assignment. A copyright license usually specifies a more limited scope of permitted use. It is to the advantage of the agency or studio to include in an assignment or license language that allows the agency or studio to edit or crop the photo or modify the drawing or otherwise alter the creative work to accommodate its intended use. It is to the free-lancer's advantage that the agency or studio agree, in any such document, to pay a re-use fee whenever the photo or drawing or other work is used.

Use the Right Fork

Now that you understand the differences between copyright licenses and assignments and work-for-hire agreements, you can gauge which is appropriate and fair in any given situation. It's simply a matter of considering the rights conveyed by each in light of the practical aspects of the situation.

Since an assignment is like a sales contract by which the free-lancer transfers all copyright rights in a creative work to the design studio or agency, the free-lancer can negotiate a "sales figure" that adequately compensates him or her for his or her services in creating the work and for the sale of the copyright for the period of time agreed upon.

With an exclusive license, the free-lancer also negotiates both the term of the license (the "lease period") and a fair amount for giving up the rights of copyright for that time period and to compensate him or her for his or her services, but further bases his or her price on the scope of the exclusive license; that is, he or she considers the rights retained as well as those bargained away.

A work-for-hire agreement, which really should be used only in situations that fit the copyright statute's requirements for independent contractor's work-for-hire, is, of course, the most exhaustive way of vesting rights in an agency or design studio, since the free-lancer, with a work-for-hire agreement, forfeits not only any ownership of the copyright in the creative work but also any right to further payment for any use of the photo or drawing or other work. He or she has no say as to how the work is used and cannot even demand credit if it is displayed or published. Fair-minded advertising production people will demand work-for-hire agreements only when they are really necessary and will be prepared to pay the free-lancer enough to compensate her or him appropriately under all the circumstances of the situation.

Get Smart

In any business situation involving intangible property rights like copyrights, it's smart for all parties to have a very good idea, in advance, of their respective rights and obligations. In the past, the law accommodated the assumption that any specially commissioned work was prepared as a work-for-hire; this is not now the case and the advertising industry, probably as much or more than any other industry, must adjust and leave less to unvoiced assumptions.

Advertising is business. Presenting a photographer (or other free-lancer) with an agreement which transfers specified copyright rights is not unfair or over-reaching. Inquiring of ad agency or design studio personnel what rights are wanted before quoting a fee is not objectionable. Figuring out your "deal" in advance is businesslike. Failing to do so is risky. Refusing to do so is unprofessional.

In the Appendix section of this book there are three examples of photographer/ad agency agreements. One is a license, one an assignment (for the full term of copyright, as given, although shorter assignments are possible), and one is a work-for-hire agreement. The language of the three agreements is essentially the same except for the paragraphs which specify what rights are conveyed. If you read these agreements you should understand better how the rights in photographs are properly granted by photographers to agencies (and design studios, since a design studio would acquire the rights it needs in precisely the same manner).

Most of What You Need To Know About Written Agreements

Anatomy of a Contract

A contract is set of legal rights and responsibilities created by the mutual agreement of two or more people or business entities—the "rules," so to speak, by which a particular business relationship is to be run. A contract is the agreement itself, not the paper document that memorializes the agreement. In fact, many contracts don't even have to be in writing to be valid; although, as we shall see, written contracts are almost always a good idea.

Except in old movies, written contracts do not depend for their effectiveness on complicated legal language. The goal of a good contract lawyer is to "draft," or write, a document that sets out in completely unambiguous language the agreement reached between the parties. This generally means that the more clearly a contract is written the more effective it is as a contract, but eliminating ambiguity may also require more detailed language than most people are accustomed to using and may result in a much longer written agreement than the contract lawyer's client thinks is necessary. However, in a skillfully drafted agreement *every* provision is necessary. Even in the case of an apparently simple agreement, a good contract lawyer will write an agreement that not only provides what happens when the agreement is working but also what happens when it stops working.

There is no particular "architecture" required to make a written document a contract. What determines whether a document is a binding agreement is the content of the language, not the form in which the language is arranged in the document. However, there are certain standard sections into which formal written agreements are customarily divided.

The introductory section of a formal written agreement gives the names, and sometimes the addresses, of the parties to the agreement, indicates their legal status (an individual doing business under a trade name, a partnership, or a corporation), gives the short terms by which the contracting parties will be referred to in the agreement ("Robert Williams Wilson, hereinafter referred to as the 'Writer'...") and specifies the date the agreement is made or is agreed to become effective.

The "premises" section of a formal written agreement sets out, sometimes after the word "Whereas," the set of circumstances upon which the agreement is founded, or "premised." This section makes certain representations about the facts which have influenced the parties' decision to enter the agreement and, although it may look like excess language to non-lawyers, in reality sets out information which could be important if, in a lawsuit based on the agreement, a court had to "construe," or interpret, the written agreement in order to rule on the intent of the parties when they entered the agreement.

In the body of the written agreement, most contracts

enumerate the various points of agreement between the parties in a series of headlined paragraphs, each of which sets out one facet of the agreement and all of which probably use the word "shall" to indicate the mandatory nature of the action expected from each party.

Besides all the major points of the agreement, a formal contract will also contain what are sometimes entitled "miscellaneous provisions" and what lawyers often call "boilerplate." These provisions look unnecessary to most non-lawyers, since, among other things, they set out methods for handling various contingencies which may never occur, but they can be crucially important. For example, one standard miscellaneous provision provides that any lawsuit based on the agreement will be brought in the courts of a specified state or city and that any dispute will be decided according to the laws of a specific state. This sort of provision can determine whether you sue to enforce your agreement in your home state or, at increased expense, in a distant city.

Get It in Writing No lawyer can include any provision in any written agreement that will compel ethical conduct from a dishonest person. The best any lawyer can do is to include provisions in the written agreement that prescribe penalties for failure to abide by the terms of the contract, and even this will not ensure that a dishonest person does not act dishonestly. Your best protection against truly dishonest people is to avoid entering agreements with them, since a true renegade has little fear of lawsuits. In any event, having to go to court to obtain what, by rights, you were due under the terms of the agreement you made is an expensive, time-consuming, and frustrating experience.

Many business people, especially those in the creative fields, assume that written contracts between people who know and trust each other are unnecessary and that having lawyers prepare a written agreement in such a case is an avoidable expense. Neither of these assumptions is true. Even if you enter a business agreement with another ethical person, a written agreement is necessary, for precision and for documentation.

Honest but Poor

Even honest and knowledgeable business people sometimes fail to communicate to each other all the terms of their agreement. Putting an agreement in writing lets both parties "see" their agreement and provides an opportunity for them to negotiate points of the agreement they have previously omitted from their discussions. Further, a written agreement serves as a memorial of the terms of the agreement throughout the life of the business arrangement. Human memory is fallible; even honest people can forget the precise terms of their agreements if they are not written down. And a written agreement can be crucial to proving the existence of the agreement if one of the people who originally made the agreement leaves his or her job for another company or, in the case of an individual, dies.

Generally, then, the more complex the terms of the agreement and the longer its duration, the more it should be documented in writing. Further, while it may be desirable and good business practice to reduce most agreements to writing, some sorts of agreements are not valid or enforceable unless they are in writing. For example, the United States copyright statute requires transfers and exclusive licenses of copyrights to be in writing and provides that no creation of an independent contractor can be a work-for-hire unless there is a written agreement to that effect. And contracts which may not be performed within a year are required, almost everywhere, to be in writing.

Get a Lawyer

All these are good reasons for consulting a lawyer when you enter an agreement of any importance. A good contract lawyer who is familiar with your business and your concerns can not only help you define and document your agreement, but can advise you concerning the law that governs your business relationship and suggest contract provisions that can help you reach your business goals and avoid disputes.

Consulting a lawyer can be just as important, or even more important, when the written contract was drafted by lawyers for the other party. In any business agreement it is important to remember that there are actually two sorts of possible written contracts documenting the relationship — their version and your version.

This is especially true when the contracting parties are not equal in power, such as when free-lancer, an individual designer or illustrator or photographer, is presented with an agreement drafted by a design studio or advertising agency; or when a design studio or small agency is negotiating with a larger and richer client. Having a lawyer on your side in a situation like this can help you feel less like David confronting Goliath. Your lawyer can explain complex contract provisions to you and, by negotiating on your behalf, turn the offered agreement into one that allows you more control, gets you paid more quickly, and is generally more favorable than the un-negotiated contract you were offered originally.

However, your lawyer must know the business before he or she can do an effective job for you. If you take a work-for-hire agreement to your friend the real estate lawyer and he says "Great! I've always wondered what one of these things looked like," it's time to consult another lawyer.

Intangible but Valuable

Nobody ever fights over an unsuccessful project. The more successful your book or poster or business venture, the more important it is to have the agreements concerning it reduced to unambiguous writing. This is true in most areas of business, but it is especially true with regard to intellectual property; copyrights and trademarks and the personal services of creative people are intangible, but they are valuable, and their ownership and the business arrangements surrounding them should be in writing, on paper, in contracts.

The Basics of Trademark Law

Chapter 5

Understanding Trademarks

This is a short chapter because, past knowing what a trademark is, as you must already know if you live in the United States, and how trademark ownership arises, which is not a very long story, the main thing you need to know about trademarks is how not to infringe them. We'll get to that just as soon as you really do understand trademarks.

Capitalist Tools In a free enterprise society, trademarks are everywhere. Trademarks are the guideposts of commerce; they embody the commercial reputation of products or services in the marketplace. Manufacturers use trademarks to communicate to consumers the origin of the products they market. Consumers use trademarks to help them find the particular products and services they want. As long as you can't thump a television set like a watermelon to decide whether to buy it, but must rely instead on what you know about the television manufacturer, trademarks will be an important part of life in America.

We all rely on trademarks every day. Almost everything you use, from the coffee you drink in the morning to the mattress you sleep on, was bought by brand name, which is another way of saying "trademark." Nobody shows up with a checkbook at the nearest auto dealer and asks, simply, to buy "a car"; you drive a Toyota Camry or a Ford Escort or a BMW, and you bought your car by name because of the reputation, for reliability or economy or prestige, which attaches to that car by its name. Any trademark represents the commercial reputation of the product or service it names. We avoid products we dislike, by name, and we seek out the ones we want, by name.

Use It or Lose It In the United States, a trademark owner gains rights in a particular name or logo for a product or service by using the name or the logo in the marketplace. ("Logos," short for "logotypes," are simply design trademarks, as opposed to names, which are verbal trademarks. Trademarks can also be combinations of names or words and designs or logos. Service marks are the variety of trademarks which name services. For simplicity's sake, the general term "trademark" or simply "mark," will be used here to refer to both the names or symbols for services and those for products.)

It is very important to understand that in this country trademark rights are gained by use of a mark, not by registration of it. State or federal registration of a trademark enhances the rights of the owner of the trademark and serves as notice to others of ownership of the mark, but a business which uses a trademark in the marketplace owns the right to use that mark *because* of that use — unless some other business has a better claim to it through longer and/or wider use — whether or not the mark is ever registered.

The reverse is also true; if a trademark owner ceases for too long to use a trademark in the marketplace, that owner can lose all ownership rights in the mark, regardless of whether the mark has been registered.

Trademark ownership is also determined by priority of use. That is, to own a trademark, you must do more than simply use it in the market, you must also be the *first* to use the mark. Trademark rights are always roughly commensurate with the degree of use of the mark. The longer you use a mark and the more widely you use and advertise it, the "stronger" the mark and the more extensive your rights in it; that is, the greater your ability to keep others from using the same or similar marks on the same or similar products or services.

Anyone who is involved in the marketing process knows what enormous effort and expense go into developing and publicizing new products. Trademark law allows companies which spend time and money developing their market shares to reap the benefits of that effort. Trademark law lets you enjoy the benefits of your own commercial reputation and prohibits anyone else from taking a free ride on your commercial coattails. It also protects consumers by allowing them to spend their money only on the products and services they have grown to trust.

Look For the Union Label

Almost anything can be a trademark so long as it is used on a product or in advertising a service to indicate the origin of the product or service. In other words, who made the product and who renders the service? All of the following can and do serve as trademarks because consumers came to associate them with the products and services they are used to market. (Throughout this section of the book, upper-case letters are used for word trademarks to indicate the precise verbal content of the marks.)

- Words (ACE bandages, PLEDGE furniture polish)

- Names (WATERMAN fountain pens, HART-MANN luggage)

- Designs (the embroidered Jordache jeans hip pocket design, the famous Coca-Cola "dynamic ribbon device")

- Slogans ("SEE THE U.S.A. IN YOUR CHEV-ROLET," "WHEN IT RAINS, IT POURS")

- Drawings (Prudential's Rock of Gibralter logo)

- Logos (the AT&T globe logo, the National Cotton Council "cotton boll" logo)

- Likenesses of fictitious people (BETTY CROCKER, the Quaker Oats Quaker man)

- Likenesses of living people (Paul Newman's image used as a logo for NEWMAN'S OWN salad dressing)

- Likenesses of deceased people (Colonel Harlan Sanders' image on KENTUCKY FRIED CHICKEN containers)

- Literary characters (all the main characters in *Star Wars* are also trademarks for a variety of goods)

- Initials (IBM, CBS, A&W)

- Music or songs (the "Sesame Street" television show theme song)

- Package designs (the well-known Chanel perfume bottle shape)

- Architectural features of businesses (the McDonald's golden arches)

Population Explosion

Graphic designers and advertising creative people encounter trademarks in perhaps the most critical period of their existence — their birth. Most designers and advertising people are asked pretty regularly to create new corporate logos or design trademarks or name new products or services for their clients. When this happens, they are being asked to "incubate" brand new trademarks.

Cute Little Fella, Ain't He?

Designing a new corporate logo or design trademark for a client is one of the most important functions you will undertake. Naming a product well is nearly as challenging as naming a new baby. Either task is also risky, perhaps more so than any other of your creative activities.

That's because we are running out of trademarks. That is, we have more trademarks than ever before bombarding us, seeking to attract our attention in magazine and television and billboard ads. What we are running out of is material for new trademarks; with applications for registration of more than fifty thousand new trademarks filed each year in the U.S. Trademark Office and more than half a million currently valid United States trademarks registered there, it is easy to understand why it has become very difficult to avoid stepping on an existing trademark when you design a new logo or name a new product. It can be done, however, and the next chapter will tell you how.

Chapter

6

Trademark Infringement and How To Avoid It

I Didn't Know the Gun Was Loaded
A trademark represents the commercial reputation of a product or service in the marketplace. Trademark owners often expend enormous amounts of money in establishing and promoting their trademarks. Once established, a trademark may be one of the most valuable assets owned by a company. Consequently, trademark owners act quickly against anyone who encroaches upon their trademarks. Adopting the wrong trademark can land you in a lawsuit for trademark infringement, even if you had no knowledge when you chose your trademark that it might infringe another trademark. This means that care in choosing a name for a new product or service is very important. Unfortunately, trademark selection in this country is, for the uninformed, a little like Russian roulette.

Trademark Trouble
Imagine this scenario. After you've made three separate presentations to them and long after you've given up hope of landing the account, the marketing department of The Mega Corporation calls to say they have chosen your agency to handle all their U.S. advertising. Seems they were impressed with your proposals and decided to give their business to an agency in your city, where they have their home office. They are happy with their decision. You are happy with their decision. You and your partners hire a new media

buyer, two more artists, and a copywriter and get to work on your first big Mega assignment, developing an ad campaign to break their new product, a universal television VCR remote control that will work with all Mega Electronics products and with the products of most other manufacturers as well.

But before you can advertise the new remote, you have to name it, so you and your three best creative people retire to your conference room late one afternoon to think of the perfect name. After several loud arguments, two six-packs, and more than three hours of intense brainstorming, you and your creative staff reach a consensus.

Full Steam Ahead!

Everyone likes the name UNI-TROL. So do the Mega marketing people, when you present the name to them. They give you the go-ahead on the whole project and, simultaneously, a tight deadline. They want to have their product in the stores before the beginning of the new fall television season and they authorize you to do whatever is necessary to complete on time all the packaging and advertising materials they need. You roll up your shirtsleeves, work a lot of late nights, and meet their deadline.

The new product is a hit. There is no other product like it that is as inexpensive or as simple to operate. Sales are through the roof. You start thinking of buying a new car. Then, out of the blue, you get an outraged call from the Mega marketing department head. He's just learned that The Mega Corporation has been sued in federal court for trademark infringement by a big New York law firm representing a German corporation which owns a U.S. trademark registration for the name you thought was *your* creation and Mega thought *they* owned.

It seems that the German corporation, Unicorp, markets various sorts of electronic equipment around the world under various trademarks, all of which begin with UNI. They are asking the court for an award of money damages and the profits from Mega's marketing of the UNI-TROL remote, plus an injunction which would force Mega to recall all its remotes previously distributed under the UNI-TROL name, to destroy all packaging and advertising materials which use or bear the offending name, and to cease using, immediately and forever, the trademark by which the public knows the new product, UNI-TROL. There is no joy in Mudville.

The only people who are not unhappy about the trademark infringement lawsuit are the lawyers hired by the Mega Corporation to defend it. They know that some of the money you thought Mega would spend with your agency is now going to be consumed by *their* legal fees.

Man the Lifeboats! The saddest news of all is hearing that Mega's lawyers have said that Mega's use of the UNI-TROL mark does infringe the Unicorp marks and that, under the circumstances, the best thing for Mega to do is to cut its losses and immediately voluntarily pull all the UNI-TROL television and print ads and stop distributing the remotes completely until a new name and new packaging and promotional materials can be developed. Which, of course, means that what Mega's dealers will remember about Mega's innovative remote control product is that (a) somebody goofed in naming it and (b) that goof destroyed the momentum the product initially gained in the market, cutting their profits. And what Mega will remember, regrettably, is that you proposed the name that is causing all the trouble.

None of this had to happen. In almost every case, trademark infringement problems can be avoided by the proper attention at the right time to a few simple considerations.

Had you been better informed, you would have

made some effort to check on the availability of the UNI-TROL mark when you proposed it to Mega, by recommending to Mega that it have a trademark search conducted or by commissioning one yourself, on behalf of Mega.

Look Before You Leap

A "full" trademark search, that is, a search of United States federal and state registrations as well as of data regarding valid but unregistered marks, would have turned up the "family" of UNI- marks owned by Unicorp and registered in the United States for various electronic products. The lawyer interpreting the trademark search report would have picked up the phone and called you and recommended that you go back to the drawing board for the new Mega mark. The whole process would have taken no more than ten business days and cost about $600 or $700, lawyer's fees included; an expedited search could have been done, for an increased fee, in as little as twenty-four hours.

You could have chosen another good name for the remote. Mega could have liked it. The lawsuit might still be in the back pocket of the Unicorp lawyers. And all those carefully produced UNI-TROL ads and materials could be winning you Addy awards instead of gathering dust in a Mega warehouse somewhere.

But perfect hindsight is poor consolation. What you really need is to know enough about trademark infringement to avoid it. Lots of trademark disputes arise because trademarks are chosen solely on the basis of artistic merit and the image they will create in the advertising media. Those are, of course, important considerations; coming up with a name that fits the new product and will attract consumers is a hard thing to do. However, the other hard part of naming a new product or service is finding a name that doesn't infringe an established mark. That part of the process can make you wish you'd gone to dental school.

I'm Confused   Trademark infringement usually results because someone has chosen for a new product or service a name which is the same as or is very similar to a mark which has been used longer for the same or a similar or related product or service.

The test courts apply in determining infringing similarity between marks is "likelihood of confusion"; that is, would consumers confuse the new name with the older, established trademark because of the similarity of the marks? The similarity between marks is gauged by what is called the "sight, sound, and meaning test." That means you want to avoid choosing for a new mark any word and/or design that looks so much like and sounds so much like and has a meaning so like an established trademark which represents a similar product that consumers will mistake the new mark for the established mark. If there are enough similarities between the marks that the average buyer is likely to confuse the products or services the marks represent or believe that the new product or service is somehow related to the owners of the older mark, the new mark infringes the older mark.

Generally, infringement occurs only when similar or identical marks name similar or related products or services. However, this is not always true in the case of "strong" trademarks. "Strong" marks, because they have achieved broad reputations, enjoy broad protection from upstart imitators who try to capitalize on their fame and distinctiveness by associating themselves with the famous marks. KODAK, COCA-COLA and LEVI'S are examples of strong verbal marks; the "woolmark" design logo of the International Wool Secretariat, the "Morton Salt girl" character trademark, and the Shell Oil Company logo are examples of strong trademarks which consist largely or only of design or visual elements. It is a very good idea to give famous trademarks a wide berth when naming any product or service, even if the new product or service is very different from those named by the famous marks, since most owners of widely advertised and well-known marks protect their trademarks vigorously.

All this sounds a lot harder than it usually is. Since "confusing similarity" is evaluated as if through the eyes and/or ears of an average consumer, members of your own creative staff can function as a sort of built-in first line of defense against choosing a trademark that infringes another trademark. In other words, if you think it might, you're probably right.

They Remind Me of Each Other A few examples of "confusing similarity" will give you a feel for the degree of trademark similarity which constitutes confusing similarity.

BEARCAT for trucks will infringe BEARCAT for boats or tires or travel trailers, but not for, say, bicycles or hunting boots or police scanner radios.

TWINKLE TOYS for a child's building block set will infringe the famous TINKER TOYS trademark. Call your new block set TWINKLE BLOCKS, though, and you're probably safe.

ZESTA for saltines does not infringe SHASTA for soft drinks. Calling any food item the exact same name of any other food item, however, is asking for a lawsuit, no matter how different the two varieties of food. The reasoning behind this rule is that consumers can reasonably assume that a manufacturer of one food item has begun marketing another under the same trademark.

This sort of association confusion as to the origin of a product is a variety of a trademark infringement. For example, the manufacturer of GOLD MEDAL flour might not like having its commercial reputation confused by being mistakenly believed to be the maker of GOLD MEDAL ice cream, even if the ice cream is a very good ice cream.

Bear in mind that the categories of products or services named by the marks are very important in making any evaluation of possible infringement. A breakfast roll named BON JOUR probably won't infringe the mark of a department store named BON JOUR, because rolls are far removed from department store services, both in their consumers and in the channels of trade in which they are offered.

However, as we have seen, "strong" marks transcend the boundaries between categories of products and services. BON JOUR for a brand of breakfast rolls could infringe the trademark rights of the owners of a famous restaurant named BON JOUR, for a combination of the reasons just mentioned; that is, because consumers, familiar with the reputation of the famous restaurant, might believe that breakfast rolls were a new product of the restaurant.

Generally, infringement results when the inherent similarity between two marks is "multiplied" by the degree of similarity of the products or services the marks name and the fame of the established mark. At some point, these factors reach a critical mass and ignite into a trademark infringement lawsuit.

Confused Again In the case of logos or pure design marks with no verbal content, the standard for judging confusing similarity is the same as that used to evaluate the similarity between word trademarks, with the exception, of course, that a mark without any words has no "sound when spoken." With logos or design marks you must carefully compare the appearance of the proposed logo or design mark with that of all other marks that name similar products or services, including marks that are combinations of words and design elements. You must also consider the implications of the design elements of your proposed mark; that is, will your "star" logo infringe an existing mark for a similar product named STAR?

Judging similarity between logos or the design elements of marks is often more difficult than judging similarity between verbal marks because the evaluation of similarity between trademark visual elements may be much more subtle and difficult to make.

I Resemble That Mark

It is hard to talk about design trademarks in print, but a few examples of confusion between design trademarks and logos are possible.

Any white-on-red or red-on-white curve at all similar to the famous Coca-Cola double-curve design trademark used for any soft drink will infringe Coke's famous trademark. However, a similar curve, perhaps in another color combination, used for, say, a brand of farm equipment, might escape challenge.

Similarly, any design of any deer or deer-like animal used for insurance services or related services, such as financial services, would probably infringe the famous hundred-plus-year-old Hartford Insurance Company standing-stag design trademark. Use your deer for ice cream, however, and you are safe.

Any clown design or character used to advertise a fast food restaurant, whether like McDonald's Ronald McDonald trademark character or not, would probably be viewed by McDonald's as infringing upon its famous clown-trademark. If your clown design or character was very different from our friend Ronald (say a female clown named Pandora who wears a yellow wig and dresses all in pink) you could safely use her picture and an actress dressed like her to advertise and promote children's shoes.

Employ any depiction of a tipped cup perpetually losing the "last drop" of your client's coffee and you will run afoul of Maxwell House. You may even get into trouble by using such a depiction in signage for a chain of coffee shops, since consumers could believe that the shops serve or otherwise have some association with MAXWELL HOUSE coffee. Set your coffee cup upright on its saucer, however (O.K., so it's not a new idea), and you are probably safe.

The famous Columbia Broadcasting System "eye" symbol is as effective today as it was when first designed in 1958. That means that any abstract or realistic eye design used for any product or service that is even remotely connected with broadcasting or television or film production is going to be challenged by CBS as soon as it leaves your design studio. You can use a dissimilar, realistic depiction of the human eye as the logo for franchise optometry shops, however, without looking over your shoulder to see if CBS is watching.

Trademark Two-Step

The first step in avoiding infringing an established trademark is to consciously avoid choosing for your client's new product or service a name or design that is identical or closely similar to another trademark that is already in use for a similar or related product or service.

This seems too obvious to mention, but it needs to be said. More than a few trademark infringement lawsuits have been filed because someone mistakenly thought that, because a name or design worked for someone else, it could work for him or her, too. This means that when you are asked to develop a new trademark, you should ask anybody who proposes one where it came from. Ignorance of trademark law will not save your client from a trademark infringement lawsuit if you step on the toes of a trademark owner determined to protect its established mark.

And it doesn't matter that you came up with the proposed new trademark without the knowledge of the established mark that it infringes; if it infringes the older mark, the source of your proposed mark is irrelevant. Nor will changing a few letters or design elements in an existing mark or spelling it differently or even combining it with other words or symbols save you from a charge of infringement, unless the changes you make are so significant that they eradicate the confusing similarity between the old and new marks.

Take Two

The second important way to avoid trademark disputes is the trademark search, which is a search made by a professional trademark search firm to locate any established trademarks which are similar enough to your proposed mark to be confused with it. The trademark search firm will examine federal and state trademark registration records and data on unregistered but currently used marks and will compile data on marks similar to the proposed mark in a trademark search report.

Because this data needs interpretation, which is not furnished by the trademark search firm, you really need a lawyer for a trademark search, contrary to what you will hear occasionally from even reputable trademark search firms. A lawyer will properly instruct the search firm as to the direction and scope of the search when commissioning it, will evaluate the raw data in the search report, and will give a legal opinion assessing the degree of risk, if any, involved if the proposed mark is adopted by your client.

And not just any lawyer will do; trademark law is a narrow area of the law about which most lawyers are content to remain ignorant, because it is confusing and sometimes even infuriating and resembles semantics more than it does other areas of the law. This means that you need a trademark lawyer, whom you can hire on behalf of your client, or whom your client can contact after you have narrowed your proposals to two or three possibilities.

Be prepared to find out that your favorite proposed mark is already being used by someone else; it happens every day to some designer or advertising creative person who spent weeks developing what she or he believed to be a unique new mark. The good news is that it is much easier and much less expensive to discard a proposed mark before any money is spent advertising it than to abandon a new trademark six months into the first big promotion of it.

Pages from two trademark search reports conducted to clear the name for a hamburger restaurant, along with the opinion letters written by the lawyer who evaluated the searches, are reproduced in the Appendix section of this book. Since trademark search reports are often forty to fifty pages long, the only pages reproduced from the reports are the search summary pages, which list briefly only the federally registered trademarks located by the search.

These search reports and opinion letters illustrate the process of elimination that occurs during trademark clearance. YESTERYEAR'S was the first name searched; it proved to be unavailable for use because of both previously registered marks and marks which were unregistered but in use and therefore valid. A second search, for THE SOUTHERN BURGER COMPANY, turned up no obvious conflicts and that name was adopted and used for two years, until the restaurants were gobbled up in a corporate merger and renamed something else. (O.K. That's not what actually happened and all the names except the proposed trademarks are made up to protect client confidentiality, but otherwise things were just as they are presented.)

Twist Their Arms Of course, you can't compel your clients to hire trademark searches or authorize you to hire them on their behalf, but you can make sure that you formally recommend to them, in writing, that they conduct searches to "clear" the marks you suggest. Your job is to help your client choose a mark that works for the new product or service and, above all, doesn't cause problems. At the very least, you want to avoid being blamed for any problems that may result from the new mark. If you routinely recommend trademark searches to your clients, you won't lose accounts because of what they perceive to be your negligence.

Although it is not your legal responsibility to determine that any mark you propose to a client will not infringe someone else's mark, a client who has been hit with a trademark infringement suit may fail to make that distinction. Advertising clients will always be fickle, but trademark searches give them one less basis for deciding that you should be replaced.

All this is true for in-house creative people, too, except that for them the stakes are higher. If you work for a company and are asked to name a new product or service, failing to recommend a trademark search could cost you your job. Unless you know that your company's legal department, if there is one, or an outside law firm is handling a search, recommend one at the very beginning of the trademark selection process. The least that will happen is that you will look like you are doing your job; the best result of your recommendation may be that you save your employer a great deal of money by averting an avoidable problem.

Most experienced marketing people view trademarks searches as a necessary part of the process of launching new products or services. If your clients have a different view, it's your obligation to point out the pitfalls inherent in ignoring the fact that their actions can get them in hot water, even if their intentions are innocent.

Help Yourself   Even though you need a lawyer to interpret the raw data in a trademark search report, there is one way that you can, by yourself, conduct a preliminary trademark search to eliminate early in the trademark selection process some marks that are very obviously unavailable. This is the trademark directory. A trademark directory lists trademarks which are registered and therefore already in use by someone else. Marks are listed alphabetically, according to the category of product or service they name.

By consulting a trademark directory at the point in the trademark selection process when you have narrowed your choices for the new mark to three or four names, you can eliminate any marks that are already registered in the United States. This saves the expense of conducting a full trademark search for every possible name and speeds up the selection process by halting your further consideration of marks that are already in use and registered for a product or service similar to the one for which you are selecting a name or design mark.

Using a trademark directory correctly takes a little practice and requires a basic knowledge of what constitutes trademark infringement, but anybody who can use a dictionary can learn to do it as effectively as a lawyer. A directory is most useful in the case of word marks; there are two major directories of word marks. However, a directory that collects design marks can also be helpful, and there is also one of those.

The Trademark Register of the United States and *The Trademark Design Register of the United States* are both published by a company called The Trademark Register. *The Compu-Mark Directory of U.S. Trademarks* is a similar directory, published by a company called Compu-Mark U.S., which offers quarterly updates in addition to the basic directory. All these directories are expensive, the Compu-Mark directory especially so. However, for any agency or design studio or company that creates even one or two new trademarks a year, these directories can save more than they cost. Information on ordering these publications is included in the Resources section of this book.

Also listed in the Resources section are a couple of publications which are more in the nature of compilations of selected design trademarks than actual comprehensive trademark directories. These books can also be used to eliminate some unavailable design marks and are much less expensive than the trademark directories.

It is very important to realize that looking up a proposed trademark in a trademark directory and failing to find it listed as an already-registered mark does *not* necessarily mean that the mark is available. The absence of a mark in the directory only means that you should proceed to the next step in the trademark clearance process, which is the full trademark search commissioned and interpreted by a lawyer. A trademark directory only short-circuits further pursuit of unavailable marks; it cannot finally clear a mark for use.

More Trademark Trouble

There are other ways to infringe a trademark besides adopting a name for a product or service that is confusingly similar to an established mark for a similar product or services. Advertising creative people need to know that use in an ad of a trademark belonging to some company other than their client company can, depending on the nature of the use, also constitute trademark infringement.

Comparative advertisements can safely make use of competitors' trademarks if they are carefully constructed. Using a photo of another company's product or mentioning the product by name in an ad that compares the client's product to the products of other companies is not an infringement of the trademark rights of the other companies if the ad truthfully compares the products named by the trademarks and if the character and arrangement of the photo elements and the content of the ad copy do not create any likelihood that consumers will somehow mistakenly believe that the product being advertised has some relation to the other products that are pictured.

This means that advertising creative people should write and design such comparative ads very carefully and should probably have any comparative ad previewed by a lawyer knowledgeable about the law of advertising. Further, in any ad where the product or trademark of another company is depicted or mentioned, a "footnote" should be used. That is, a short statement should be included somewhere along the bottom margin or up the side margin of print ads and at the bottom of the screen in television commercials to the effect that "CRUNCHIES is a trademark of the Toasted Oats Company and is not owned or licensed by the makers of SWEETIES brand cereal." Because not just any such disclaimer will suffice, any such ad and proposed disclaimer should be reviewed before the ad is published by a lawyer who can evaluate the possibility that the ad will result in an infringement lawsuit.

Dilutions of Grandeur

The second sort of advertising use of trademarks that can create problems is the use of well-known products as visual elements in ads. Clever ad people sometimes come up with clever ads that use a famous trademark or a photo of a familiar product to make the ad work. An ad with the headline, "Any way you spell it, Enrico's is the last word in fine dining," and a photo of a Scrabble board with the names of various menu items spelled out with Scrabble tiles or an ad for a real estate broker using a photo of a Domino's pizza box under the headline, "We deliver," will be scrutinized by the owners of the famous marks.

Any ad like this is very likely to prompt a nasty letter from lawyers representing the owner of the parodied mark. The reason is this: even though the mark belonging to the other company is not used on a product or service, its use in an ad is seen by the trademark owner, and could be held by a court, to be a "dilution" of the famous mark or could be construed by readers of the ad to represent some sort of sponsorship or approval by the owners of the famous mark of the product advertised .

All this is easier to understand if you remember that what a trademark represents is the reputation of the product or service it names and that that reputation, especially for marks famous enough to be effectively used in an ad of this sort, was earned at great expense, often over the course of many years. When you look at it this way, it isn't hard to see why trademark owners are sometimes over-vigilant in acting to protect their marks from even small encroachments.

Cheated Death Again

This is not to say that it is never possible to use a trademark in an ad without being sued; many have done so and lived to tell the tale. However, before attempting any such use of a trademark that does not belong to your client, you should call up the aforementioned trademark lawyer for an opinion as to how mad the ad is likely to make the owner of the other trademark. Really. Even if you are absolutely sure that your ad will not cause problems.

Unfortunately, more than one trademark infringement lawsuit has been brought simply because the trademark owner was aggravated and felt like doing something about it, regardless of the existence of grounds for a suit. And if this doesn't scare you, consider the fact that owners of famous trademarks have whole platoons of trademark lawyers who have to justify their existence by periodically going after evildoers. If they are short of true malefactors this month, you and your ad may look like very good targets. When it comes to using someone else's famous trademark in an ad without permission, discretion really is the better part of valor.

Hate Mail

The letter reproduced on pages 113 and 114 is an example of that dreadful beast, a "cease and desist letter." Names have been faked to protect the guilty, but this is essentially the text of an actual letter sent in circumstances very similar to those mentioned.

ROMANO AND TORTELLINI, ATTORNEYS
715 Eleventh Street, N.W.
Olympia, Idaho 61495

October 26, 1990

VIA CERTIFIED MAIL

Mr. Charles Abbott, President
Mountain Properties, Inc.
1248 East Mountain View Drive
Adamsville, Colorado 89342

Dear Sir:

This firm represents Brown Management Corporation of Blair, Colorado. Brown Management owns three resort hotels in Colorado, the Brown House Hotel in Denver, the Greenview Hotel in Blair, and the Brownstone Inn in Hopewell, which is, as you know, just over the county line from Adamsville. It is with regard to the Brownstone Inn that I am writing.

Brown Management Corporation has owned and operated the Brownstone Inn since 1954. Over the years Brown Management has expended a great deal of money to advertise the Brownstone Inn and to ensure that the services and facilities there are the finest available. Consequently, the Brownstone Inn has an excellent reputation, both within Colorado and nationally, as a luxury hotel. Brown Management is the owner of two service marks, both of which have been registered in the United States Patent and Trademark Office. These service marks are the famous "Brownstone Inn" name, which is the subject of federal registration 1,894,002, and the well-known "Brownstone Inn" script logo, which is the subject of federal registration 1,899,035. Copies of these two registration are attached to this letter as Exhibits A and B.

It has come to the attention of our client that your corporation has begun construction on an Adamsville time-share condominium development which you intend to call and, indeed, are already calling in advertisements in national travel magazines and in publicity of other kinds, "the Brown Stone Community." Your use of the name "Brown Stone Community" for your resort condominium development constitutes infringement of our client's registered service marks and unfair competition, since consumers may mistake your condominiums for our client's famous hotel or mistakenly believe that your condominiums and our client's hotel have the same owners or that your development is sponsored by or affiliated with Brown Management Corporation or the Brownstone Inn. Further, your use of "the Brown Stone Community" for your development dilutes the strength of our client's famous marks and damages the business reputation and diminishes the good will of the Brownstone Inn, all of which were developed and acquired by our client at great expense and effort.

You should be aware that the United States trademark statute (15 U.S.C. 1051 et seq.) provides in part that:

> When a violation of any right of the registrant of a mark registered in the Patent and Trademark Office shall have been established in any civil action arising under this chapter, the plaintiff shall be entitled...to recover (1) defendant's profits, (2) any damages sustained by the plaintiff, and (3) the costs of the action.

Mr. Charles Abbott
October 26, 1990
Page Two

The law also allows the court to award treble damages and reasonable attorney's fees to the prevailing party. In addition, the court may order that all labels, signs, packaging, and advertisements in the possession of the defendant which bear the registered mark or a colorable imitation thereof be delivered up and destroyed.

Therefore, on behalf of our clients, we hereby demand that you immediately cease any uses of the name "Brown Stone Community" or any other imitation or version of our client's registered marks in connection with any present or projected condominium development. Our client will require destruction of any printed advertising or promotion materials bearing the infringing name, including brochures and signage. In addition, your corporation must agree to cease giving out any news stories or causing any advertisements to be published or promulgating any materials connected with the offering of your condominiums which contain any reference to those condominiums as "the Brown Stone Community" development.

Due to the serious nature of your infringing conduct, we require your response to our demands not later than ten days after your receipt of this letter. If you agree to our terms, we will forward an appropriate settlement agreement for execution by an officer of your corporation. If we do not hear from you within ten days or if you refuse to comply with our demands, we are authorized by our client to commence an action in federal court on behalf of Brownstone Management Corporation seeking an injunction, damages, your profits, our costs and attorneys' fees, and all other relief allowed by law, without further notice to you.

Although we are hopeful that we can obtain satisfaction for our client without litigation, this letter is written without prejudice to our client's rights and remedies, all of which are expressly reserved.

Sincerely,

ROMANO AND TORTELLINI, ATTORNEYS

HUBERT ROMANO

HR/tb

Confusion in the Courts

**Too Close
For Comfort**

The following trademarks were held to be confusingly similar when used in conjunction with identical or similar products.

AMS and MS-2

COMSAT and COMCET

MEDI-ALERT and MEDIC ALERT

SLAGCRETE and SAKRETE

HINT O'HONEY and HIDDEN HONEY

SONIQUE and MONIQUE

DENBAG and BENDAG

CINTEL and KINTEL

HUVILON and UVINUL

JOCKEY and ROCKÉ

BREW MISER and COFFEE MISER

ULTRA VELVET and ULTRA SUEDE

ENDAL and INTAL

DRAMAMINE and BONAMINE

SYROCOL and CHERACOL

PLEDGE and PROMISE

MOUNTAIN KING and ALPINE KING

BLUE SHIELD and RED SHIELD

CYCLONE and TORNADO

OXON ITALIA and EXXON

ARISE and AWAKE

FACE TO FACE and CHEEK TO CHEEK

KEY and a picture trademark in the form of a representation of a key

CHAT NOIR and BLACK CAT (foreign language equivalent meanings can constitute infringing similarity)

DERNIERE TOUCHE and THE FINAL TOUCH (ditto)

TORO ROJO and RED BULL (ditto)

MYSOLINE and MYOCHOLINE

DAN RIVER, DAN MASTER, DAN TWILL, DAN TONE, DAN and DANFRA (a new mark that is even somewhat similar to an established "family" of marks can infringe those related marks by being mistakenly believed to be merely a new addition to the "family")

Close, But No Cigar

Think you've got the hang of it? Maybe not. The following trademarks were held not to be confusingly similar when used in conjunction with identical or similar products.

REJUVA-NAIL and REJUVIA

MATCH and MACHO

TACO TOWN and TACO TIME

CAR-X and EXXON

THUNDERBOLT and THUNDERBIRD

TRUSS-SKIN and TRUSCON

MUGS UP and 7 UP

MOTHER BESSIE'S and MOTHER'S BEST

SUMARK and MARK

WINTERIZER and WINTERSTAT

HELICARB and HELI COIL

DAWN and DAYLIGHT

GREEN LEAF and BLACK LEAF

SATIN QUICK and SUDDENLY SATIN

We Are Not Amused

Last Laughs   The exceedingly clever people who came up with the following parodies of famous marks were a big hit around the office but not with the owners of the very valuable famous marks parodied, who sued, claiming a long list of infractions, all of which boil down to the disparagement of the valuable reputation embodied in the famous mark because of the (usually) derogatory, unsavory, or obscene parody. Humorous parodies of famous trademarks almost always result in suits, which are almost always lost by the wiseguy parodist, especially if the parody mark somehow tarnishes the famous mark. The following is a short list because most defendants in cases of this sort recognize a lost cause when they see one and have the good sense to settle out of court.

- WHERE'S THERE'S LIFE...THERE'S BUGS was used as a slogan by an insecticide manufacturer, to the chagrin of Anheuser-Busch, Inc., which did not like the connotations of the parody of their famous slogan WHERE THERE'S LIFE...THERE'S BUD. Busch sued and won.

- The Coca-Cola Company was not happy that an oh-so-clever poster company both imitated and altered its famous ENJOY COCA-COLA trademark by publishing a poster with the parody slogan, in the distinctive Coca-Cola script, ENJOY CO-CAINE. Guess who lost in court.

- Those reserved folks at the General Electric Company were not happy that a small novelty company began marketing men's tee shirts and briefs emblazoned with the parody trademark GENITAL ELECTRIC and a monogram similar to the GE logo. Somebody ended up with a warehouse full of unsaleable underwear, if it was not ordered by the court to be destroyed.

- The Girl Scouts didn't think that it was funny that somebody published a poster depicting a very pregnant young woman wearing a regulation Girl Scout uniform with the headline "Be Prepared." Score one for the Girl Scouts, who know how to sue to protect themselves from disparagement, as well as how to sell cookies.

- However, when Johnny Carson sued to enjoin the use of HERE'S JOHNNY on portable toilets, the court held that the use was not trademark infringement because no one would believe that the toilets were associated with Carson. The court ruled, though, that the use of the slogan so widely associated with Carson was an infringement of his right of publicity. (More about right of publicity in Chapter Nine.)

Chapter 7

Trademark Registration and Protection

Naming Names   In addition to determining that your proposed new trademark will not infringe an established trademark, it is important to consider whether the name you choose for your client's new product or service will be eligible for federal trademark registration.

There are two sorts of trademark registration, state trademark registration, which is cheap and easy to obtain and confers some benefits, and federal trademark registration, which is not easy to obtain, but which confers much greater benefits. Since most trademark owners will want to be able to register their marks federally, that is, with the U.S. Patent and Trademark Office, federal registration is the sort of registration discussed in this chapter.

The federal trademark statute, which governs trademark registration, imposes certain restrictions on which marks can be granted federal registration. The inherent characteristics of the mark determine whether these restrictions will prevent the eventual registration of the trademark. That means that the problem of these restrictions can be largely eliminated by careful avoidance of a few varieties of names that can cause the Trademark Office to deny a registration application.

There are ten reasons the Trademark Office will deny federal registration to a trademark (other than defects in the form of the application or some other procedural problem). They are:

Twins Again   The mark is confusingly similar to a trademark which is already federally registered. (This is in addition to any liability that may be incurred by the infringing use of the previously registered mark.)

It Doesn't Work   The word or, more usually, symbol for which registration is sought does not function as a trademark, that is, does not act in the marketplace to identify the source of the goods or services to which it is applied. This basis for refusing federal registration is most often cited in applications for design marks which the Trademark Office believes are being used on goods merely for purposes of ornamentation rather than in any way that indicates the source of the products. In other words, the famous JORDACHE jeans hip pocket embroidery designs may not have achieved federal trademark registration if they had not become "distinctive of the goods," that is, if they had not begun to function to indicate to consumers that the jeans which bore them were manufactured by Jordache.

I'm Shocked   The mark is "immoral, deceptive or scandalous." Some marks which are slightly *risqué* make it to registration, but none which are really off-color or offensive will be granted registration.

Heaven Forfend   The mark disparages or falsely suggests a connection with persons, institutions, beliefs, or national symbols, or brings them into contempt or disrepute. For example, if you try to register HARVARD for scholastic aptitude tests, your employer had better be the famous university, and if you name candy, in the form of white chocolate crucifixes, IMMACULATE CONFECTIONS, don't expect the Trademark Office to allow you to register the mark.

Salute!   The mark consists of or simulates the flag or coat of arms or other insignia of the United States or of a state or municipality or a foreign nation. The American flag and other symbols of the sort named are owned by every citizen of the particular state or nation; the Trademark Office won't grant to any one person or company, by virtue of a federal trademark registration, the exclusive right to use such a symbol.

Bubble Trouble   The mark is the name, portrait, or signature of a particular living individual who has not given his or her consent for use of the mark or is the name, signature, or portrait of a deceased president of the United States during the life of his or her surviving spouse, unless that spouse has given consent to use of the mark.

For obvious reasons, the Trademark Office cannot grant exclusive rights in a name or likeness of a real live person without the consent of that person or, in the case of a deceased president, without the consent of his or her widowed spouse. Otherwise, you might find one day that someone is marketing bubblegum using your portrait and the government has given them the exclusive right to do so, without your permission. (More about this sort of thing later, when we talk about the rights of privacy and publicity.)

Bronx Cheers   The mark is "merely descriptive" of the goods or services it names. Many creative and marketing people hate this restriction and make rude noises when their trademark lawyers remind them of it, since they believe that the more a new product name describes the product or service it names, the better a trademark it is. If you think about it, you will realize that this is not true.

Tickle Your Fancy   In actuality, the best trademarks are fanciful, that is, they don't mean anything much, they just capture the imagination and come to signify the particular product they name rather than being equally applicable to any product of the same kind, which is the case with marks that are descriptive. Think of KLEENEX or EXXON or WISK; none of those marks mean anything as ordinary English words, but they each immediately bring to mind the specific products marketed under them.

Besides this important consideration, there is the fact that the Trademark Office almost always disallows an application to register a descriptive mark; it will not allow, by virtue of a federal trademark registration, one company to bar all others from using what are simply ordinary words to describe a product or service. If you ask yourself whether a proposed mark would tell consumers what a product or service is, or, in the case of publication names, by whom the publication is intended to be read, you can ferret out descriptive marks before they are adopted by your client and, later, turned down for federal registration.

Now, it must be said that there are many trademarks which are very descriptive that are currently registered in the U.S. Patent and Trademark Office. These marks, for the most part, started out as unqualified for registration because of their descriptiveness but later, because of the fame that attached to them as the products or services they named became well-known, came to signify to consumers the products or services of their particular companies. In short, after awhile the Trademark Office will reconsider allowing registration of descriptive marks which have achieved some fame. But at the trademark selection stage in the history of a product, this exception to the descriptiveness restriction shouldn't make any difference to you, whose job it is to come up with a new mark that doesn't need to work at becoming capable of federal registration.

Little Lies

The mark is "deceptively misdescriptive" of the goods or services it names. This restriction on registration is akin to some of the ones mentioned above which are designed to deter the adoption of misleading or distasteful trademarks by denying registration to them. "Deceptively misdescriptive" means a mark that falsely suggests that a product or service has some characteristic that it does not indeed possess.

For example, LAPIS for a line of blue glass-bead jewelry would not be granted registration, since the Trademark Office would hold that the word "lapis," when used for blue jewelry not made of the semi-precious stone lapis lazuli, was a "deceptively misdescriptive" name which could mislead consumers. Ditto for, say, TOP GRAIN for vinyl luggage and SILKSHIRT for a line of women's polyester blouses.

Bigger Ones   The mark is "primarily geographically descriptive or deceptively misdescriptive" of the goods or services it names. When the name of a product or service includes a geographic term, if that geographic term is an actual place name or name of a river or mountain range, etc., and either tells where the product comes from or suggests falsely that it comes from a place that it does not, that name will run afoul of this restriction when the trademark owner seeks to make a federal registration for it.

The general rule has long been that if the Trademark Office can find the geographic term in any mark in an atlas or gazetteer, registration for that mark will be denied; the thinking behind this rule is that if the product comes from the geographic region named, marble from Italy named CARRARA STONE, for instance, registration would deny all the other marketers of marble quarried from the famous deposits at Carrara the right to truthfully call their stone "Carrara stone" and if the product does not actually come from the region named but is rather, in this example, marble taken from less famous quarries, the name CARRARA STONE is deceptively misdescriptive and is misleading to consumers.

Now bear in mind that you can make up fictitious place names all day long and register them as trademarks; EMERALD CITY for mobile homes or BIG ROCK CANDY MOUNTAIN for sugar cubes would be registrable. And you can use actual place names in purely fanciful ways, because then no one will be likely to believe that they are used to actually indicate the origin of a product or service; both KENYA for safari-style sport clothing and BLUE DANUBE for a china pattern would be registrable.

The Name Game   The mark is primarily a surname. Personal names have long been considered not to be inherently distinctive when used as trademarks, which is another way of saying that they are "descriptive" or "generic" and can't, in and of themselves, point to a particular source for a product.

Think of this example: there are four zillion people in the United States named Smith, so the source of SMITH'S SOCKS for children could be anyone in the country whose name is Smith. Further, until one SMITH'S SOCKS became well-known enough to transcend the anonymity of most surname marks, all of the Smiths in the United States could market socks using their mutual surname without infringing each other's trademark rights.

Now, obviously there are many famous surname trademarks that have been granted federal trademark registration by the Trademark Office. That is because WATERMAN for fountain pens, SMITH BROTHERS for cough drops, CAMPBELL'S for soups, LIPTON for tea, WILSON for sporting goods, HOOVER for vacuum cleaners, and CRANE for stationery are all trademarks that have risen above anonymity by virtue of having achieved strong reputations in the market-place. Since a trademark represents in the market the reputation of a product or service, this is just a way of saying that these surname marks achieved trademark status, or what the Trademark Office calls "secondary meaning," sufficient to persuade the Trademark Office to allow their registration.

Words and Pictures

It is important to remember that all the restrictions on registration listed above can also apply to design trademarks or trademarks which combine graphic elements and words. You may be able to get away with registering BON VIVANT for a *"parfum"* which is actually manufactured in New Jersey without running into the "geographically misdescriptive" restriction on registration, but use a map of France as the background for the words BON VIVANT on the perfume bottle labels and the Trademark Office will reject the application to register the mark.

Similarly, although ASTRONAUT for children's underwear would be, alone, registrable, your use, in conjunction with the word ASTRONAUT, of sketches of Alan Shepard and Sally Ride, without permission from them, would cause the registration application to be rejected (and would probably result in a suit for the infringement of the astronauts' right of publicity, which we will discuss in Chapter Nine).

If all these kinds of trademarks are unregistrable, how do you find a trademark that will work? Easy. Simply think of a name that has never existed before or use a common word in an uncommon way. Nobody had ever heard of OREOS or EXCEDRIN or CRAYOLA until somebody named cookies and pain reliever tablets and crayons those now-famous names. And APPLE once meant only a kind of fruit; now we know it also means a particular famous brand of computer.

Or look at the forms and shapes of nature and geometry for inspiration for a new logo; the Texaco star logo is one of the simplest commercial designs on the cultural landscape, but it has also outlasted a lot of fussier, more pretentious logos and has for a long time signified only that company and its products to most Americans.

Then there are the kinds of marks that are what the Trademark Office calls "suggestive," which is not the kind of "suggestive" you think; these are marks which call to mind an association related to the product they name. They imply strength or softness or freshness or flavor, depending on the product; they are subtle marks, created by marketers and ad people who were very skilled at their jobs. Think of TORO lawn mowers, DOWNY fabric softener, IRISH SPRING deodorant soap, and ZESTA saltine crackers.

The Saurus and Other Dinos

Any method for coming up with new trademarks that works, works. Use a thesaurus to suggest appropriate words. Read Shakespeare (that's where Toyota got CRESSIDA) or mythology. Ask your mom. Look through dictionaries. Use free association. Read the *Brittanica*. Study heraldry or the symbols of ancient cultures or origami. Ask your child's classmates to draw their ideas for a new corporate logo. Haunt art galleries.

If all else fails, suggest the given name of the C.E.O.'s child, but only as a last resort; SARA LEE cakes and WENDY's hamburgers immortalized those two little girls, but not even Ford likes to think about EDSEL autos anymore.

A caveat. Despite having a whole book of written-down rules to operate by, the Trademark Office, like God, often moves in mysterious ways. This means that all of the above statements about what are and are not registrable trademarks are subject to some Trademark Office exceptions, whims, and inconsistencies. Use the list of restrictions on registration as a guideline in selecting marks to propose to your client and leave the final opinion as to the registrability of any proposed mark to someone who pays for malpractice insurance, your client's (or company's) trademark attorney. You don't have to function as a trademark lawyer in order to do your job, but you can forestall a great many problems for the owner of the new trademark if you know a little about what you are doing when you propose it.

Washington Again

Once your client or marketing department has settled on a mark, chosen from a list you propose after careful consideration of the aforementioned dreaded Ten Pitfalls of Trademark Selection, and has conducted a trademark search to make sure that the mark is available for use, the next step is the registration of the trademark. Most clients who are serious enough about a new mark to spend any time or money developing and clearing it for use will want to file as soon as possible for federal trademark registration, which means registration of the trademark in the U.S. Patent and Trademark Office, in Washington. (Ignore the fact that the name of the office includes the word "patent"; the Trademark Office and the Patent Office are entirely separate government departments which were mistakenly joined at the hip before you were born by a Congress which got confused and thought that they had something to do with each other, which they do not.)

Once upon a time in America, it was necessary for trademark owners to have used their trademarks in interstate commerce before applying for federal trademark registration, and trademark rights began to accrue from the date a trademark owner actually began to use a mark in the marketplace. Now, however, and just since November 16, 1989, a trademark owner can apply for registration before actually beginning to use the new trademark, so long as the trademark owner has a "bona fide intent" to begin to use the mark in interstate commerce within six months of the date the registration application is filed. (The period of time for beginning use of the mark may be extended, in six-month increments and upon making the proper filings, up to a total period of thirty-six months.) Registration may then be granted after use of the mark is made in interstate commerce.

**You Have
No Reservation**

This system of registration represents a big change in the law. It is not quite the same as the system that exists in certain European countries which allows marketers to "reserve" a trademark for use before actually adopting it, but it is close, since now U.S. companies can put everyone on notice that they intend to use a mark before they actually do so. This change should eliminate the situation that formerly existed, where two companies, which had to begin using their new marks before they applied for trademark registration, began to use the same mark for similar products— each discovering the existence of the other only upon filing their applications, after they had expended the time and money necessary to launch a new mark. In this situation, only one of the two companies could end up owning and registering the mark — the company that began using it first.

Now, when a company files an "intent-to-use" application to register a mark, stating that it will begin using the mark within six months, its intentions become part of the official records maintained by the Trademark Office and are included in the data searched by trademark search firms. This means that when a second company conducts a search to ascertain the availability of the mark, the first company's application for that mark, indicating that the first company has already "staked a claim" to the mark, will appear in the search and warn the second company away from the mark.

The Dating Game The new intent-to-use applications confer one other new benefit on trademark owners; when a registration is eventually granted to an intent-to-use applicant, the date of the applicant trademark owner's rights in the mark are deemed by the new rules to date from the filing date of the application to register, rather than just from the date of the applicant's first actual use of the mark. This means that early filing of a trademark application can now give additional months or even years of ownership rights, on the front end of the ownership period, to a trademark owner who had not even begun to use the mark on the date of filing.

Boiling Point All this complicated stuff boils down to this for advertising creative people and graphic designers: you should know and should mention to your clients that it is possible to file for federal trademark registration just as soon as a search has cleared a new mark for use. Speed is important because the earlier the date of filing, the sooner the ownership rights in the mark will be, eventually, deemed to have begun. In addition, early filing removes some of the danger that two marketers will be competing for registration and ownership of the same mark.

It is one thing to know federal trademark registration is desirable and something about the registration process, but filing for federal trademark registration is, like searching a trademark to clear it for use, not a do-it-yourself project. The Trademark Office allows trademark owners to file their own applications for registration, without the help of a lawyer, but satisfying the complicated filing requirements imposed by the Trademark Office is not easy and filing without the help of a trademark lawyer is likely to result in the rejection of the application. Lawyers do have their uses; filing for trademark registration is one of them.

Like copyright registration, federal trademark registration offers several important advantages to trademark owners. A marketer that registers its trademark in the U.S. Patent and Trademark Office is in a much better position to quash infringers than if its mark were not registered, since federal registration affords immediate access to a federal court, where a federal registrant can obtain an injunction with nationwide effect to stop infringers.

Even better, federal trademark registration helps companies avoid the necessity of bringing suit to stop trademark infringers, in two important ways. First, once a trademark is registered in the Trademark Office, any other companies which conduct searches to clear proposed new marks will know that the registered mark is already in use for the goods and services it names and will stay clear of it or any confusingly similar mark. Secondly, even if some company other than the owner of a federally registered trademark does infringe the mark, it is likely to agree to stop using the mark immediately upon the receipt of a cease and desist letter from the trademark owner's lawyer, since the infringer will know that the owner of the registered mark does have the clout to prevent the continued infringing use of the mark.

® You Registered?

Once a trademark is registered federally, and this means registered in the U.S. Patent and Trademark Office, not simply registered in one or more states or in another country, the trademark owner is allowed to use, and should use, a trademark registration notice in conjunction with the registered mark, to warn others that the mark is registered and that ownership of it is claimed by the owner, and to gain the advantages that are granted when such a notice is used.

The most familiar trademark registration notice is the "circle R" symbol, or ® ; the ® symbol should be used "on the shoulder" of the registered mark or in the subscript position very near it. Alternate forms of notice are "Registered in the U.S. Patent and Trademark Office," or "Reg. U.S. Pat. & Tm. Off."; these alternate forms of notice should be used with an asterisk placed close to the registered mark and a corresponding asterisk preceding the notice itself, which usually appears in a footnote position on the package or label or in the ad, etc.

It is important to know that the forms of trademark notice specified above are the only forms of notice that have the legal effect of proper trademark registration notice. You can't, in short, make up your own.

Not using the ® symbol (or one of the other prescribed forms of trademark registration notice, although they are generally used less often and may, in fact, be less likely to be recognized as notice of registration than the familiar ® symbol) in conjunction with a federally registered trademark will not invalidate the registration, but it can deprive the trademark owner of some very important advantages in the event that the registered mark is infringed.

There's a Hole in My Doughnut If the Rounder Doughnut Company registers its trademark HOLE IN ONE for packaged doughnuts sold in grocery stores, everyone else in the world who wishes to adopt and use in the United States a confusingly similar trademark for doughnuts is presumed by law to have notice that HOLE IN ONE is owned by Rounder, even if they do not conduct a trademark search and discover Rounder's federal registration. If Burgerama, Inc., adds to the breakfast menu for its fast food restaurants a doughnut it calls HOLE IN ONE, the Rounder Doughnut Company will sue Burgerama, since consumers could easily confuse the fast food restaurants' doughnuts with those marketed by Rounder. By virtue of its federal registration, Rounder will be entitled to an injunction from the court ordering Burgerama to cease use of HOLE IN ONE.

But if Rounder also wants to be awarded an amount of money representing the damages it has suffered because of Burgerama's infringement or the profits of Burgerama (attributable to Burgerama's sale of its doughnuts under the HOLE IN ONE name), resulting from Burgerama's actions before its receipt of Rounder's cease and desist letter saying "Cut that out. We have a registration for HOLE IN ONE," Rounder must have used the ® symbol (or another prescribed form of notice) on its packaging in conjunction with its registered trademark. If Rounder did not use a trademark registration notice with its mark, the court is allowed by law to award only damages or profits which resulted from actions of Burgerama after Burgerama received actual, specific notice that the HOLE IN ONE mark was registered.

Now all this may sound like mumbo-jumbo, but it's not. It may seem unlikely that something that an art director does or does not do in pasting up the artwork for a new cereal box or an ad for a vacuum cleaners can determine how much money a federal court can award to the cereal manufacturer or the vacuum cleaner company, but that is precisely the case.

It is not your legal responsibility to find out whether a client's trademark is registered and to make sure that a trademark registration symbol is used, and properly, with that trademark. That responsibility belongs ultimately to the trademark owner. However, if you want to keep your clients and keep them happy you must be at least conversant with the basics of proper usage of trademark registration symbols and notations, since usage so directly effects valuable rights of your clients.

I'm Proper, ® You?

An important related consideration is the *improper* use of the ® symbol (or another of the prescribed forms of trademark registration notice). If trademark registration notice is used in conjunction with a trademark that is not federally registered, or used with a trademark appearing in advertising for or in conjunction with goods or services for which it is not registered, serious consequences can result, including the loss of the trademark owner's right to recover for trademark infringement or to register the mark federally.

Many people, even people who should know better, think that the "TM" symbol they often see printed next to trademarks is the equivalent of the ® symbol and has some legal effect. In reality, it does not. "TM" is sometimes used by a trademark owner as a "no trespassing" sign to indicate that someone is claiming ownership of the mark. It has no real legal effect but can be useful, since there are no requirements to be met before it can be used and there really is no such thing as misuse of it. In addition, many trademarks are not yet federally registered, or have been denied federal registration or cannot be federally registered for one reason or another. Use of the "TM" symbol, which usually appears in the same locations as those used for placement of the ® symbol, can warn others that the owners of these names consider them to be trademarks and claim ownership of them.

Similar to the "TM" symbol is some statement such as "The name DENTAL ASSISTANT'S QUARTERLY is a trademark of the Dental Assistance Association of America." Statements of this sort have exactly the same effect (some) and uses (several) that the "TM" symbol does; that is, they are another variety of informal trademark notice.

Dead Trademarks

Trademarks, whether registered or not, can theoretically last perpetually. As long as someone markets goods or services under a name, it has a legal existence as a trademark. However, trademarks "die" every day.

A trademark's demise can occur in two ways. One of the ways a trademark dies is by "abandonment"; that is, the owner of the mark ceases using it. This ordinarily happens to trademarks which name unsuccessful products or services and, of course, is a result of a decision by the trademark owner to abandon the mark.

The other way a trademark dies is almost the converse of the first situation, because such deaths often befall very famous trademarks and always occur against the will of the trademark owner. This form of trademark death results when a trademark becomes "generic," that is, when the word which formerly served as a trademark comes to signify to the general public the kind of product or service it names rather than representing a particular brand of that product or service. This form of trademark extinction should be of great interest to advertising creative people and graphic designers, since loss of a trademark through its becoming generic is always a great financial loss to trademark owners. Designers and advertising creative people are the first line of defense against that unhappy event.

You Snooze, You Lose

"Escalator," "cellophane," "aspirin," and "linoleum" all once named particular products of particular companies; they were trademarks rather than, as now, the generic terms for whole classes of goods. Because they became generic, that is, because they lost their status as the names of particular products of particular companies, they are now anyone's to use.

In the case of the former trademark "escalator," a court held that because consumers thought of all moving stairways as "escalators," ESCALATOR had lost its ability to point only to products of the Otis Elevator Company. In the decision that cancelled Otis' fifty-year-old trademark registration for ESCALATOR, the court stated the fact that Otis itself had used in its own ads ESCALATOR as "escalator," that is, as a generic term for a class of products, supported the contention that the mark had become generic. Otis, and its ad agency, goofed, and they paid the price by losing one of Otis' most valuable assets, its famous trademark ESCALATOR.

Similar scenarios surrounded the ends of the other former trademarks mentioned above, and others. Ironically, it is the names of unique and innovative products that are most at risk of becoming generic. This is because the name of the first version of a ground-breaking product can come to mean that type product in the minds of consumers, who may refer to all products of the same sort by the trademark of the first one they encountered. XEROX is one trademark that is presently in danger of becoming a generic term (for photocopy machines and photocopies). LEVI'S, FORMICA, WALKMAN, and TUPPERWARE are similarly endangered.

How the Mighty Have Fallen! In some cases, a company may be virtually powerless to prevent its trademark for a unique product that captures the public's imagination from falling into common usage as the name of the *type* of product rather than the name of one particular *brand* of that product. "Nylon," "yo-yo," and "linoleum" may have been marks that no amount of care could have preserved from genericness. However, in almost every case a company can at least put up a fight to halt the fall of its marks into genericness, by care in its use of them and, when necessary, by ads which promote the names as trademarks.

Anyone who creates ads and marketing materials for a trademark owner is very much involved in the fight against trademark genericness. Like using the ® symbol, proper use of a company's trademark can have very real dollars-and-cents consequences for the trademark owner. Trademarks are often considered to be among the most valuable assets of the companies that own them because they often represent a certain steady share of the market for the products they name. If a trademark becomes generic (and therefore available for use by anyone), that market identity and share are lost.

By the Book

Proper trademark usage, crucial for protecting the exclusive ownership of a trademark, involves a few rules of "trademark grammar" that all advertising people should know and use. Remember that:

- A trademark is always an adjective, never a noun. It is "SUDSY laundry powder" or "SUDSY brand detergent," never simply "SUDSY"; hence "Get your clothes clean with SUDSY laundry detergent." Think of "HEINZ sauces," "TOTES umbrellas," "HOLIDAY INN hotels," and "POLAROID film."

- A trademark is a proper adjective. It is "COKE adds life." never "I'll have a coke." Think of "LEVI'S jeans," "EGG MCMUFFIN breakfast sandwiches," and "CHANEL perfumes."

- A trademark is always singular, never plural. It is "SNAZZY shoes," never simply "SNAZZIES." Think of "CRAYOLA crayons," "APPLE computers," and "KLEENEX tissues."

- Trademark variations should be avoided. Trademarks should never be made possessive, i.e., it is never "FIZZY'S great taste" but is, rather, "The great taste of FIZZY cola." And if the mark is registered or ordinarily used in one typeface or format, don't change its customary appearance without direct authority from the owner of the mark; otherwise, how will consumers recognize their old friend? Similarly, avoid changes in the verbal content of the mark at all costs; it is "Fried to a crisp with FRY COOK all-vegetable shortening!" not "FRY COOKed to perfection again!"

The Rest of the Story

Proper use of trademark registration notice and proper trademark usage are broader topics than can conveniently be covered here. There is one clearly written little book that deals with both subjects and important related topics in detail. This is the book *Trademark Management*, written for non-lawyers and full of practical information, published by the Clark Boardman Company. Do yourself a favor and invest in this inexpensive book. Information on ordering it is included in the Resources section of this book.

Condemned to Anonymity

Has-Beens

The following terms were held by the Trademark Office or a court to be incapable of serving as indicators of particular sources for the goods and services they named because they had become, in the minds of consumers, generic terms for those products or services. After being declared to be non-trademarks, these terms became free for anyone to use in describing such products or services and ceased to be the exclusive property of their originators.

AL-KOL for rubbing alcohol

ASPIRIN for acetyl salicylic acid

BABY OIL for mineral oil

BATH OIL BEADS for bath oil, water softener, and perfume

BODY SOAP for body shampoo

BRASSIERE for women's bras

BUNDT for a type of ring coffee cake

CELLOPHANE for transparent cellulose sheets

COLA for a soft drink

COMPUTER LEARNING CENTER for computer courses

CONSUMER ELECTRONICS MONTHLY for a magazine for electronics enthusiasts

COPPERCLAD for copper-coated conductors

CUBE STEAK for tenderized steaks

DRY ICE for carbon dioxide in solid form

EASTER BASKET for an Easter floral basket

ESCALATOR for moving stairways

EXPORT SODA for an exported soda cracker

FLOR-TILE for wooden flooring

FLOWERS BY WIRE for intercity floral delivery services

FLUID ENERGY for hydraulic/pneumatic equipment

HAIR COLOR BATH for a hair coloring preparation

HARD TO FIND TOOLS for a tool mail order service

HOAGIE for sandwiches

HONEY BAKED HAM for honey-glazed hams

JUJUBES for gum candies

LIGHT BEER for a light-bodied beer

METALOCK for a metal repair method

MONOPOLY for a real estate trading board game

MONTESSORI for an education method and associated toys

MULTISTATE BAR EXAMINATION for a bar examination given in several states

MURPHY BED for beds which fold into a wall or closet for storage

POCKET BOOK for paperback books

PRIMAL THERAPY for a type of psychotherapy

PROM for programmable "read only memory" computer systems

RUBBER ROPE for an elasticized rubber rope product

SAFE T PLUG for electrical plugs

SHREDDED WHEAT for baked wheat biscuits

SOCIOGRAPHICS for a technique of management consulting

SOFTSOAP for liquid hand soap

SUPER GLUE for rapid-setting cyanoacrylate adhesives

SURGICENTER for a surgical center

THE COMPUTER STORE for retail computer sales services

THE PILL for oral contraceptives

THERMOS for vacuum-insulated bottles

TRAMPOLINE for rebound tumbling equipment

VIDEO BUYERS GUIDE for a magazine for videotape buyers

WORK WEAR for industrial clothing

YO-YO for return tops

(Reprinted by permission of the Xerox Corporation.)

Libel, Privacy, and Publicity Law

Chapter *8*

Libel Defined

Chocolate or Vanilla

Defamation is the name for the harm that results when someone's reputation is damaged by an untrue statement. Defamation comes in two flavors, "libel" and "slander." Libel once referred only to printed defamation, slander only to spoken defamation. The advent of radio and television made the traditional libel/slander distinction outmoded.

Now most jurisdictions in the United States regard defamatory statements made over the airwaves as libel. It is more logical to treat such statements like libellous articles in newspapers and magazines, because they are disseminated over wide areas and are therefore capable of causing great harm, rather than like slander, which historically has meant a defamatory statement spoken by one person to others and which is less likely to do the harm that a widely disseminated libellous statement can do.

The libel/slander distinction is important primarily because the penalties for libelling someone are more severe than those for speaking the same defamatory statement. Since any defamation that advertising creative people have to worry about is likely to result from a print or radio or television ad, and that sort of defamation will be, legally, most likely libel, we will refer only to libel throughout this chapter.

The coming of radio and television did more than complicate the definitions of defamation. They, and the proliferation of other kinds of mass communications media, like the news magazines and tabloids that are printed and circulated in weekly press runs that would have dwarfed the yearly circulation of most of the famous magazines and newspapers of the early part of this century, have also "multiplied" the law of defamation. In other words, one zillion copies of *The National Enquirer* equals X angry celebrities equals Y libel suits.

Many of those libel suits result in court decisions that become part of the case law of the state where they were brought or, often, of federal case law. Graphic design studios and advertising agencies haven't had a lot to do with creating this enlarged body of libel law, which has mostly resulted from disputes involving the legitimate (and, sometimes, illegitimate) press, but advertising creative people, like any other citizens who create and disseminate any communications, need to know enough of it to avoid libelling anyone.

Avoiding libel is, like virtue, its own reward. No one gives out medals, or Addys, for clean libel litigation records, but the truth is that if you are sued you may not be around long enough afterwards to win an Addy and you sure won't be getting any medals. Libel lawsuits make even the plaintiffs unhappy and the defendants are usually left miserable, sometimes broke, and maybe unemployed.

Elementary, My Dear

Because of the variations between state laws, it is difficult to make any general statements about United States libel law that are not also somewhat misleading. However, boiled down to their common elements, U.S. statutes generally provide that libel is:

- a false statement;

- which is "of and concerning" the plaintiff;

- made as a statement of fact (that is, is not just someone's opinion, stated as such);

- which causes harm to the plaintiff by injuring her or his reputation or subjecting her or him to shame and ridicule in the community; and

- which is the result of some omission or fault of the defendant.

We will look at each of the elements of libel in detail, below.

Man Speaks With Forked Tongue

A "false statement" can be almost anything that can be broadcast, printed, or displayed and need not be a verbal statement. A photograph or drawing can libel someone just as surely as a printed verbal statement. True statements are *never* actionable for libel (although you may want to remember that even publishing the truth can get you in trouble for invasion of privacy, as we will see in the next chapter). However, you had better be able to *prove* the truth of any unflattering statements you make, because if you cannot, you may be found guilty of libelling someone in spite of the fact that *you* know you did not.

Are You Referring to Me, Perchance?

A statement "of and concerning" the plaintiff means a statement that can be reasonably understood to refer to the plaintiff. Obviously, this includes statements that name the plaintiff and photographs that include face shots of the plaintiff. It also means that even if the plaintiff is not named in the statement itself (or recognizably depicted in the photograph), if by either some outside facts known by some people who see the statement or some implication contained in the statement itself, the plaintiff can be identified, then the plaintiff has been libelled.

For example, if a public service ad promoting racial harmony uses a photograph of a young black lynching victim under the headline "In 1955, the men of Greentown, Mississippi, murdered Hiram Edwards because he wanted to vote," any man who lived in that small town in that year who had not been convicted of the lynching would be libelled by the imputation inherent in the ad that he had been a part of committing that heinous crime, even though there was no photograph of him or any mention of him by name.

The implication of the headline would be that all adult male citizens of the town were guilty. It would obviously be unlikely that every such man participated in the hanging, but the friends and acquaintances of each man who lived in the town in 1955 would think only of that particular man when reading the ad and his reputation would be damaged. (This sort of example only works where the class of people to whom the defamatory statement applies is small. You might pause to consider if an acquaintance from the very small town of Greentown, Mississippi, which had sixty-two adult male citizens in 1955, could be guilty of lynching; you probably would not wonder if your friend from Chicago was one of the "Chicago gangsters" referred to in a political ad touting a candidate's illustrious record as a crime-busting D.A.)

The requirement that a libellous statement be "of and concerning" the plaintiff before it is actionable also includes even mistaken identifications. For advertising creative people, supposedly fictitious names used in ads are a pitfall of this sort, since there may be a real Harrison P. Adams out there somewhere who objects heartily to being named in an ad as a satisfied user of a certain brand of condoms.

However, mere name-sameness is generally not enough to support a libel suit. There must be more than a simple coincidental use of someone's name to get you in real trouble. However, if Harrison P. Adams thinks hard enough he may be able to come up with some other similarities between your Harrison P. Adams and himself. (The man pictured in the ad has grey hair, Harrison P. Adams has grey hair. The man in the ad is dressed as a business executive, Harrison P. Adams is a business executive. And so on.) And being innocent of libelling someone will not always prevent that person's filing a suit; unfortunately, some people threaten to sue or do sue when they believe they can extort a settlement payment, regardless of the fact that they cannot win in court.

Spreading Lies The requirement that the libellous statement be communicated by the defendant to at least one other person besides the plaintiff is called the "publication" requirement. Here, "publication" does not necessarily mean publication in the ordinary sense of the word but, rather, means something like "dissemination by any means." If you think about it, it is obvious that no harm can result to the plaintiff's reputation (the heart of a libel claim) unless someone besides the defendant and the plaintiff see the libellous statement or photograph. And you can't disclaim responsibility for disseminating a libellous statement just because someone else published it first unless you have acted responsibly to investigate and verify, independently, the truth of the statement.

For example, if you publish in a campaign ad a photograph of the other candidate accepting money from a furtive-looking man in a windbreaker and baseball cap who, it turns out, has a criminal record, and imply in the ad copy that the opponent candidate is accepting a bribe, you are not relieved from responsibility for your reckless charge just because the photographer who shot the photo told that version of events to the campaign manager for your client, who already published the photograph and similar copy in a campaign flyer. If it turns out that the opposing candidate is innocent of accepting any bribe and that he was, in fact, simply giving cash to a parking lot attendant about whom he knew nothing, you (and the campaign manager and his candidate) could be in big trouble.

In My Opinion The general rule is that only a statement of fact can be libellous and that an expression of opinion cannot. This rule, like many legal standards, is simple in theory and confusing in practice, since courts often have a hard time distinguishing between statements that are in the nature of opinions and therefore not libellous and those that are presented as fact and therefore defamatory. The many rules and magic formulas that exist in various parts of the country for determining what statements are non-defamatory opinions and what statements are actionable statements of fact are too numerous for anyone but libel lawyers to really understand and are, in any event, too complicated to remember and apply in the real live daily circumstances in which most advertising creative people work.

This really doesn't matter because most of these fine distinctions only come into play in litigation, and your whole aim should be to avoid lawsuits in the first place. This means that discretion is the better part of valor; you should simply stay away from any photograph or copy that may insult or anger or embarrass anyone enough to result in a libel lawsuit unless such a statement is one made in an area where *only* opinions are possible, such as matters of personal taste, literary criticism, religious beliefs, moral convictions, political views, and social theories.

If you make the statement in an ad (as someone did) that "The Wet Look Is Dead!" you are announcing a new trend in personal grooming; makers of hair oil may not like what your ad implies, but they can't sue you (or your employer or your client). Try saying "Only geeks use Oilcan Hair Oil!", however, and you may be sued by The Oilcan Company.

This distinction points up an important truth about advertising, one that relates to the opinion/statement distinction and also has broader application. Generally, saying something positive about your client's products or services ("The French cuisine at Chez Richard is the finest on the Eastern seaboard") is much safer from a libel standpoint than any negative statement about your client's competitors ("The 'French' chef at Pierre's couldn't find France on a map").

How Humiliating! To be libellous, a statement or photograph must cause harm to the plaintiff by injuring her or his reputation or subjecting her or him to shame or ridicule in the community. The more subtle applications of this standard can be hard to understand, but past court decisions give us a long list of kinds of statements that, unless they are true, almost always result in judgments of libel.

It is libellous to make an untrue statement that:

- someone engages in criminal activities or has a criminal record ("Beauregard is a felon");

- someone is dishonest ("Carmen lied to her boss when she said she was ill last Tuesday");

- someone is unethical ("Angela has the ethics of a weasel; she taught her son how to cheat at cards");

- someone is incompetent or unskilled at his or her trade, business, or profession ("Orville is a very bad accountant");

- someone engages in conduct that renders him or her unfit or incompetent to engage in his or her profession or occupation (This often depends on what conduct and which profession. Stating "Dr. Ortiz drinks on the job," if it is untrue, implies that Dr. Ortiz's behavior renders her unfit to practice medicine. Stating falsely that a bartender drinks on the job may not be libel, however, because of the differing professional requirements and standards for bartenders and doctors.);

- someone drinks to drunkenness or is an alcoholic or uses illegal drugs or abuses legal drugs ("Geraldine drank like a fish at the museum benefit and passed out behind a statue");

- someone engages in immoral behavior or, especially a woman, is "unchaste" ("Hermione may be a brilliant scientist, but she sleeps with her best friend's husband whenever she has the opportunity." Stating that anyone, man or woman, is an adulterer or otherwise engages in any sexual conduct of which your grandmother would not approve is very dangerous but, partly because most men are less likely than women to challenge untrue statements about their sexual prowess and mostly because defamation law has historically held that women are in a special category when it comes to their reputations for sexual chastity, libelling a woman is much more dangerous than making the same libellous statement about a man.

  In light of the greater equality with which the law treats women and men today, this distinction may no longer be valid, but you'd rather find that out in a later edition of this book than argue it in a libel lawsuit. Be wary of imputing anything less than Sunday school behavior to anyone, especially women, unless you know your statement is a true statement. Then, beware of a suit for invasion of privacy.);

- someone has a "loathsome disease." (Historically, this usually has meant leprosy or one of the "traditional" venereal diseases. Since, regrettably, we now know that there are many dangerous *virii* circulating in singles bars, other sexually transmitted diseases may perhaps now be included in the list. Stating, without foundation, "Lawrence caught herpes from that woman he met at Arnoldo's" is just as actionable as stating that he has syphilis.); or

- someone is mentally deficient ("Xavier has Alzheimer's disease." This does not include statements of mental deficiency that are really in the nature of mere epithets, which are not, strangely, actionable, probably because the law presumes that people will not believe "Xavier is a peabrain" to be the literal truth, as they would believe a more particular statement.)

The categories of false statements listed above are all sure-fire ways to start libel lawsuits, but they are not by any means the only ones. Many successful (for the plaintiffs) libel lawsuits are brought because of statements that are much less obviously dangerous than, say, stating that someone is incompetent at his or her job or has a venereal disease. This very often happens because of statements that are, in themselves, relatively innocent but which are libellous when coupled with some extrinsic fact known to some of the people who see the false statement and know the plaintiff.

For instance, stating falsely that Edgar won $1,000 at the blackjack tables during a convention he attended in Las Vegas is not, in itself, defamatory. However, because Edgar's friends know that he is an official in a church that sternly prohibits gambling of any sort and that the convention was a church convention, held in Las Vegas for the express purpose of converting gamblers into former gamblers, the statement libels him. Similarly, stating, falsely, that Anastasia married Harold last Saturday afternoon seems harmless enough unless you know that Anastasia is still Mrs.

Ricardo Brown, since her divorce has not yet been granted, and that the reported marriage last Saturday would have made her a bigamist.

Bad Business You should also know that corporations (as well as unincorporated businesses) can be defamed. Corporations don't have many of the rights to sue for libel that an individual has, since corporations don't have reputations for chastity or sobriety to protect, for example, but corporations can and do sue for libel on account of false and damaging statements made about their credit or property, corporate honesty, efficiency, and business performance. And since most corporations have more money tied up in their reputations in these areas than most individuals and, perhaps, more money to spend protecting their reputations, libellous statements about them can be very dangerous. In other words, if you step on the toes of a competitor company, make sure that it is only because the products you are selling out-perform the ones it is marketing. Libel lawsuits brought by corporations are just as tedious as those brought by individuals.

A caveat. Lawyers and judges evaluate libel according to some standards that we aren't even going to peek at. That is, they make important distinctions between statements that are inherently libellous and those which are not and between the kinds of harm which result from various types of defamation, and generally engage in a lot of hairsplitting that we will forego, because all these permutations are really of no concern to you.

The metaphysics of libel vary widely from state to state. The only time you will ever worry about these finer points of libel law is when you are sued for making some defamatory statement, and then you (or rather, your lawyer) will be worried only about the law of the particular jurisdiction where the suit is brought.

Your job, really, is simply to know enough about U.S. libel law generally to avoid being sued in the first place. Since most of the materials a design studio or an advertising agency creates are disseminated beyond or outside the state in which the studio or agency is located, it is really almost a matter of luck, anyway, in which state the person who believes she has been libelled by your television spot lives; that state is where she will bring suit and its laws will determine what law applies to that suit. It is far more productive to spend your time figuring out how to sidestep libel altogether than to worry about the differing consequences and standards of proof that apply in one state or another.

It's My Fault   The requirement that a false statement must owe its falsity to some omission or fault of the defendant before the defendant can be held accountable offers defendants only some protection from the consequences of their blunders. The point is not whether you meant to libel someone but, rather, whether the libel could have been avoided by your taking what would have been, in that particular situation, proper measures to ensure the accuracy of the statement you publish. (In fact, in some circumstances, a "strict liability" standard may apply; that is, if you publish a false statement about someone that harms his or her reputation, the law provides that you will not be relieved of responsibility even if you were not at fault.)

Since the circumstances giving rise to libel lawsuits are never precisely the same from one suit to another, the best the law can do is offer vague guidelines for the amount of care necessary to relieve you of any responsibility for making an otherwise libellous statement about someone. To make it even more complicated, there are different sets of vague guidelines for different plaintiffs and contexts. The two ends of the spectrum for libel plaintiffs are the private citizen plaintiff who has been libelled by a false statement which concerns some matter that has no bearing on public welfare, and the public figure plaintiff who has been libelled by a false statement touching upon some matter of urgent public concern. In short, you can get away with saying a lot more untrue things about the president of the United States regarding his performance of his official duties, especially if you do not actually know that statements you published are false, than you can say about the sexual proclivities of Miss Turnipseed down the street, who keeps to herself and has never inserted herself into any public dialogue or run for public office.

Since even commercial speech (like ads or annual reports or sales brochures or billboards) is protected by the First Amendment, the fact that a false statement is made in an ad should not subject you to greater liability for libel than if it is made in a newspaper editorial. However, in the real world and with juries, it just doesn't work that way. Whatever the law books say, juries and judges are more likely to find that a false statement made in an ad is libel than the same statement made in a newspaper column.

Which brings us to a very important point. The standard of care required to defeat a claim of libel, that is, how careful you have to be in order to wiggle out of responsibility for making a false statement that harms someone, is in the nature of a "defense" to libel. That is, it is one of the first areas that your lawyer will inquire into after you are sued. ("Did you know or have any reason to know that Miss Turnipseed had never been in a male strip club, Mr. Cellini, before you superimposed a photo of her over a photo of the entrance to The Playgirl Club? What reason did you have to believe that she was a model who posed for the photo you used rather than a private citizen whose photograph was taken as she stood in front of her dentist's office? Had you found the photographer who brought you the photo of Miss Turnipseed to be reliable and truthful in the past?") Your care or lack of it will be a very important factor in any libel suit, but since defending even a libel suit that the plaintiff does *not* win will be very expensive and time-consuming for you, for your client, and for your employer, the very best thing to do, again, is to simply stay out of such suits.

Practice Makes Perfect

The best way to stay out of libel suits is to learn and use a few very simple rules. The following practices should be made a permanent part of your operating procedures and everyone who works for or with you should be made aware of the importance of these practices.

- Get releases for all photographs, including from any model who is paid for the use of his or her photo. Be careful never to "exceed" the permission given by any release. (For instance, if Miss Turnipseed posed, as a fundraising committee member, for an ad soliciting donations to the local children's hospital, you cannot simply locate that photo in your files whenever you need a photo of a funny-looking little old lady for an ad. That would be exceeding the consent to the use of her photo that Miss Turnipseed gave when she posed for the ad for the children's hospital.) A sample release is included in the Appendix section of this book and releases in general are discussed in the chapter on privacy and publicity rights, which follows this chapter.

- Be wary of making any statement or using any photo that would embarrass or anger or humiliate the person who is the subject of the statement or photo, even if you don't think your ad actually libels that person; 42.7% of all the troublesome, expensive libel lawsuits ever brought were brought more because someone was mad and wanted revenge than because his or her reputation had actually been harmed. Angry people want immediate revenge; a libel lawsuit, especially if you or your client or employer have enough money to fund a fat damages award, may look like the best alternative to punching you in the nose.

- Consider the implications of your ad copy, photos, and illustrations. Even if no one is named by name or actually pictured, could someone feel that he or she is, by some reference, included in some statement that is unflattering or embarassing?

- Never use first-and-last names, actual or fictitious, unless you are absolutely certain that you will not be offending the real, or another, Minnie P. Gonzales.

- Don't hurry production of your materials so much that any important proofreading is slighted or releases are not secured. An ounce of prevention is worth a pound of depositions.

- Finally, get yourself a lawyer. Having a lawyer knowledgeable about libel law "on tap" for quick opinions doesn't cost much now (and, if your client agrees, the lawyer's fee can be passed along to your client as a cost of production), but hiring one to defend a libel lawsuit will cost lots later.

Bob and Carl and Actual Malice One last cautionary comment about libel. Forget everything you learned about "freedom of the press" by watching movies about heroic investigative reporters; the standards for what they can say and get away with probably do not apply to you, partly because they are working journalists (maybe a court will feel that selling soap equates with saving the free world from Communism, but you don't want to find out with yourself as the guinea pig), partly because the people they write about are public figures subject to greater scrutiny and privileged with fewer rights to restrain what is said about them than private citizens, and partly because they are only movies, for goodness' sake. In short, try to be like Caesar's wife (above reproach) rather than like Woodward and Bernstein. You won't win any Pulitzers, but you may stay out of trouble.

Is It Libel?

Life Begins at Forty

To illustrate an ad for a local alcoholism treatment center you use a photograph of the group portrait of the graduating class from a 1959 high school yearbook that you bought at a yard sale, under the headline "By the time they were forty, 20 percent of these seniors had drinking problems." One of the former seventeen-year-olds (in fact, the person who sold you the yearbook), now a psychologist in private practice in your town, sues you, saying that you have libelled him by implying that he is an alcoholic. Is it libel?

Probably so. Although you did not name the man, you did publish his photograph, and even though he looks different from the way he looked when the graduation photo was taken, people who know him may recognize him. Since your ad says that 20 percent of "these seniors," a defined group of only the forty-three people pictured, developed drinking problems, it is not unreasonable to assume that someone will see your ad and believe that the psychologist is an alcoholic, even though he has been a strict non-drinker all his life, and perhaps, that he is unfit to practice his profession, which requires, of course, at least sobriety.

Further, the likelihood that someone who knows the psychologist will believe that he is an alcoholic because of the ad is, ironically, enhanced by the fact that the ad is for and sponsored by a recognized medical treatment facility for alcoholism, since that circumstance adds credibility to statements made in the ad. You'll also be found guilty of invading the good doctor's privacy by making unauthorized use of his photo, but you'll be so upset by the court's ruling in his favor on the libel charge that you may not even notice.

Don't Drink the Water

In a sales brochure for your client's in-home water purifying system you state that it is "the only in-home water purification system marketed in the United States that is capable of removing several common dangerous contaminants from tap water." Sales soar, but your client is sued by a competitor corporation which claims that because its purifiers do remove from tap water the contaminants your brochure says only your client's products remove, and it makes specific representations to its customers to that effect, you have defamed it as a corporation by, in effect, accusing it in your sales brochure of making false representations about its products. Is it libel?

Yes. If your statement that your client's purifiers are the only ones marketed in the United States which remove the named substances from tap water is untrue, then the other companies which truthfully claim their products do so have been defamed. It makes no difference that you did not name the plaintiff company in your brochure; the fact that there are only four companies that market purifiers of the sort your sales brochure advertises and the fact that the brochure states falsely that no other company's products can do what your client's products can do are sufficient to damage the competitor corporation's reputation.

A further damaging factor is the fact that the competitor corporation has been defamed before the very group whose good opinion it values, the consumers of home water purifier systems.

The competitor corporation will collect on the libel charge and, probably, also on a false advertising charge. And your water purifier client will permanently remove your name from its Rolodex (unless the information you used in the libellous ad was furnished to you by your client, in which case it is the guilty party here and you are off the hook, since it was not your negligence that caused all this trouble).

Hold the Lettuce

For a promotion for your fast-food drive-in restaurant client, you find an old photo of Bonnie Parker and Clyde Barrow and use it in a newspaper ad under the headline "Drive by Burger Biggie whenever you're on the run." The promotion, which features coupons printed "A burger and fries or I'll shoot" and take-out bags with the legend "Burger Biggie Bank," is a success. In fact, everybody loves Burger Biggie but the estate of one Eloise Fish, who was Clyde's sweetheart before he met Bonnie.

Seems the photo you found was a snap of Clyde and Eloise, who lived a blameless life and never robbed even one bank, not of Clyde and the infamous Bonnie. Eloise's estate is threatening to sue unless it is paid a Burger Biggie bag of money. Is it libel?

No. Sorry, Eloise. You were wronged posthumously, but the law says that since you are dead you cannot be defamed, no matter how scurrilous the false statements made about you. If you were alive, your lawyer could win a lifetime supply of hamburgers for you; because you have gone to your reward, no one can sue to protect your good reputation, which presumably you have taken with you to trade for a halo.

A Rose by Any Other Name

You prepare a newspaper ad for your client, the local chapter of the League of Liberal Voters. The ad consists of a slate of candidates in an upcoming local election which the local League supports, urges readers to vote for the listed candidates and concludes with a list of names of citizens who support the slate of recommended candidates. One name, "Carol Rose," appears as "Carroll Rose" because of a typesetter's error which your agency's proofreader failed to detect. Carol Rose is not too upset because her name is misspelled, but Carroll Rose calls the League in a very bad mood. It seems that he is upset because his friends may believe he is a League member when in fact he is a lifelong Republican and always votes for conservative candidates. He threatens to sue. Is it libel?

Probably not. Even if Mr. Rose's friends and associates believe that he lent his name to the League ad there is nothing defamatory in even a false representation that someone is participating in an honorable way in the political process. Further, even though Mr. Rose is a Republican who would be unlikely to support liberal candidates, he could have good reasons for doing so. The implication that someone supports liberal candidates is not inherently defamatory or, in this situation, defamatory because of extrinsic facts known to the plaintiff's friends and acquaintances. Further, because half the long list of people named in the ad are specifically identified as League members, there is little likelihood that anyone will believe that *every* name in the ad is that of a League member.

Lastly, the degree of fault attributable to your agency in failing to detect the typo that turned "Carol" into "Carroll" is not the sort of grievous negligence necessary for liability for libel in any context involving free speech and the political process. You're probably off the hook, but have a talk with your proofreader. If this had been an ad for N.O.R.M.L. or a pro-choice abortion rights group, Mr. Rose could probably win.

Photo Finish

In Trouble

Agatha and Lorenzo were, respectively, the creative director and head art director for a television station in a mid-size city in the southwest. They wanted very much to win an Addy, a goal that had eluded them for the past two years. They were excited when their station manager gave them the assignment of coming up with a full promotion — newspaper, TV spots, and radio — for a four-part public service series on the problem of teen pregnancy, scheduled to air during the fall ratings period.

They came up with one newspaper ad that they liked so well that they decided to use it as a centerpiece for the whole campaign. They planned to use a photograph of a diary, open to a page on which was written, in a teenage girl's handwriting, the entry "Dear Diary, today I found out that I am pregnant. What will I do now?" lying next to a snapshot of Lorenzo's younger brother hugging his old girlfriend Susan, under the headline "Guess what Mitzi found out today?" They used the elements of the newspaper ad to create a similar television spot and the headline of the newspaper ad as the hook for their radio spots.

Quick Delivery

The station manager and marketing director loved the ad and the television and radio spots that Agatha and Lorenzo developed, so much so that the station increased its planned media schedule for the campaign. The teen pregnancy series garnered a greater share of the audience than had been anticipated and Agatha and Lorenzo began filling out entry blanks for the local Addy competition. Then their bubble burst, simultaneously with the delivery of service of process for a lawsuit filed by Lorenzo's brother's former girlfriend, who sued the station for libel and invasion of privacy.

At trial, Susan's lawyer argued that Susan had been

libelled by the use of the snapshot in ads about a pregnant teenage girl. She testified that she had never had sex, with Lorenzo's brother or with anyone else, and had certainly never been pregnant. Susan's lawyer also argued that the use of the snapshot of Susan in the newspaper and television ads without permission from either Susan or her parents constituted an invasion of Susan's privacy.

The station's lawyers argued that even though the station's ads had used the snapshot of Susan, the ads had used the name "Mitzi" in referring to the fictitious pregnant teenage girl who was the subject of the ad and that therefore the ad was not "of and concerning" Susan and, further, that the snapshot used in the ads was merely an inoffensive photo of two young people hugging innocently and was not at all defamatory to Susan. Agatha and Lorenzo breathed easier when they heard the arguments of the station's lawyers; they felt they had been cleared, at least of the libel charge. Unfortunately for them, the court disagreed.

Two Counts

The court found for Susan on both the privacy and libel charges. It said that her privacy had been invaded by the use of the snapshot of her without her permission. And it dismissed out of hand the arguments of the station's lawyers that the ads had not libelled Susan. The judge said that the fact that Susan's name was not used in the ads was immaterial, since she could be easily identified by the snapshot and that a reasonable interpretation of the ads was that Susan was the pregnant teenager to whom they referred.

Career Moves

Then the judge awarded Susan enough money to send her through college, all at the expense of the television station. Agatha and Lorenzo did win an Addy for their newspaper ad, but it didn't matter much, because they were both out of advertising by then, having been fired by the station management shortly after the trial.

Agatha framed her award but hides it in a drawer among her other keepsakes. Lorenzo uses his for a dart board.

Chapter 9

The Rights of Privacy and Publicity

Rights and Wrongs

The right of privacy and the right of publicity are related rights by which, under United States law, individuals are allowed some control over the uses made in the media of their identities and of the facts concerning their lives, as well as the manner in which they are portrayed. Generally, private individuals possess and enforce the right of privacy and celebrities possess and enforce the right of publicity, although private citizens can also sue for infringement of their right of publicity and celebrities may sue for invasion of privacy. Although there are several important differences between the right of privacy and the right of publicity, the two rights are somewhat like fraternal twins, that is, they are not identical but they look a lot alike. We will consider both rights in this chapter, so you will learn to recognize each, so you will learn to tell them apart, and so you will never have to face down either evil twin in a courtroom.

Leave Me Alone

The right of privacy is the right everyone in this country has to live free from four kinds of invasion of privacy: invasion of privacy by being placed in a "false light" in the public eye ("false light invasion of privacy"), invasion of privacy by intrusion into some private area of life ("intrusion invasion of privacy"), invasion of privacy by public disclosure of private facts ("disclosure invasion of privacy"), and invasion of privacy by the unpermitted commercial use of name or image ("misappropriation invasion of privacy"). The best way to understand just what these four kinds of privacy invasion are, in an advertising context, is to consider examples of each.

Bad Light

False light invasion of privacy is very much like defamation. With false light invasion of privacy, however, the harm that the plaintiff claims is not that his or her reputation has been harmed, but that he or she has been portrayed falsely to the public and his or her dignity has been injured, with resulting mental suffering. Many statements that defame someone also constitute false light invasion of privacy, but defamation and false light invasion of privacy are not always found in pairs. The following examples illustrate false light invasion of privacy.

Sleeping Habits

You use, in an ad for a singles bar, a photo from your files showing well-dressed young professional men and women gathered around a bar, laughing and talking, under the headline, "Where Topeka's Singles Swing." One of the men pictured sues for invasion of privacy, claiming that your use of his photo in a magazine ad for a singles bar places him, a married man, in a false light and has embarassed him among his friends, causing him to lose sleep and avoid answering his phone. Your lawyer advises you to settle the suit, since your use of the man's photo did place him in a false light, injured his dignity, and caused him mental distress. (Your lawyer also tells you that you are lucky that the plaintiff did not also sue you for defamation, since, arguably, you have also defamed him by implying that his adherence to his marriage vows, an area of his morality, is less than wholehearted.)

Seeing Red

To advertise the wares of your women's clothing boutique client, you come up with the idea of a weekly newspaper ad which masquerades as a "fashion column." One week, you headline the column "Fashion Mistakes" and fill it with photos, shot on the street, of women whose fashion sense was on vacation the day their photos were taken. You obscure the eyes of the subjects with a black bar to conceal their identities, in the manner of a fifties detective magazine, and dissect, in print, the wardrobe of each, offering, of course, solutions available from the stock of your client.

The woman shown wearing a sweatsuit with scuffed high heels sues, stating in her complaint that you have invaded her privacy by suggesting that she is a person who has bad judgment about her grooming and wardrobe, when in fact she was voted "Best Dressed" by her college sorority last year. Further, she says that your efforts to disguise her identity failed to do so, since she is six feet tall and has a mane of flaming red hair, and that many of her sorority sisters have called to taunt her about the photo you used in your column, which has caused her great mental distress.

Your lawyer advises you to settle this one, but you are adamant that your efforts to obscure the identity of the plaintiff in the photo relieve you of any liability and refuse to make a settlement offer. You are sorry you were adamant when the judge makes his ruling. He says that your efforts to disguise plaintiff's identity were insufficient and therefore of no effect, since several young women testified at trial that they easily recognized the photo as being one of their red-haired friend on a bad day. Because you exposed the plaintiff (who was impeccably dressed during the trial) to the public eye in a false light, resulting in her humiliation, the court awards her enough money to continue to dress stylishly right through her last year of college. (The good news is that she didn't, because she couldn't, sue for libel, since the implications of your ad did not really amount to defamation.)

No Escape

For a poster to advertise the showing of the prize-winning documentary film *Escape from the Barrio*, you use a photo of a well-dressed Hispanic man walking along a downtown street carrying an expensive brief-case. The poster attracts a lot of attention, including that of the man portrayed in the poster photo, who sues for false light invasion of privacy. His complaint states that he has never resided in any *barrio*, that he has, in fact, always lived in nice neighborhoods, and that your use of his photo has exposed him to ridicule from the other physicians with whom he practices internal medicine and from his patients, who have not liked seeing someone for whose services they pay dearly portrayed as having "escaped" from neighborhoods into which they would never venture.

He is distressed; the only thing that could allay his distress is a nice fat settlement check from you. You pay up because you want to keep the adverse publicity concerning your agency to a minimum. The plaintiff "escapes" to the Bahamas during January, courtesy of you.

Am I Intruding?

Intrusion invasion of privacy involves some unreasonable intrusion upon the solitude and seclusion of someone or into her or his private affairs. In contexts other than advertising, intrusion invasion of privacy lawsuits often involve some physical invasion analogous to trespassing, such as a search by police without a warrant or entry into someone's home by journalists who employ false pretenses in order to get a story. Intrusion claims also quite often involve other sorts of unwelcome nosiness and pushiness, such as electronic eavesdropping, opening other people's mail, or photographs taken with a telephoto lens.

Jacqueline Kennedy Onassis' well-known suit against the *paparazzi* photographer Ron Gallella was an intrusion invasion of privacy suit and was brought because he followed her and her children around constantly, leaping from behind bushes and chasing them in cars, in order to take photographs of them. Just as false light invasion of privacy is related to and expands upon defamation law, intrusion invasion of privacy is related to and fills in some gaps left by the law of trespass.

As we have seen, intrusion invasion of privacy often involves some unauthorized entry onto someone's premises, which is trespass. The difference between trespass and intrusion invasion of privacy is that the harm for which a plaintiff sues in an intrusion invasion suit is not so much the physical trespass itself (which may be the subject of another part of the lawsuit), as the mental distress that results from the intrusion.

It is much less likely that a lawsuit for intrusion invasion of privacy will result from the activities of a graphic design firm or advertising agency than from those of, for instance, journalists (especially unscrupulous ones). However, the possibility, and danger, exists and advertising creative people must be aware of it in order to avoid it. The following examples illustrate some of the sorts of intrusion invasion of privacy that are possible in an advertising context.

Books and Their Covers

You publish as the illustration for an ad for a new "retirement village" a photograph of an old man sitting inside the front window of a shabby little house. He stares sadly out the window. Your ad emphasizes the advantages of living, in old age, among others in a community environment, and implies that the old man is alone, lonely, and neglected. He sues, claiming that the photograph of him was taken without his knowledge by a photographer who must have been standing on the sidewalk in front of his house, shooting through the window.

At trial, the photographer is forced to admit that those were precisely the circumstances surrounding the photograph. The court finds you (and the photographer and your client) guilty of intrusion invasion of privacy, and of false light invasion of privacy, since, despite appearances, the plaintiff is well cared-for by his daughter, who lives with him. You saved a model's fee by using an existing photograph that you could get cheaply from the photographer, but you lost the war.

If a Man Answers, Hang Up

You publish in an ad a photograph of a handwritten letter from a satisfied user of your client's product, a contraceptive jelly. The letter writer states in her letter that she has found the product to be superior to others on the market and has used it exclusively for three years. She also inquires whether your client manufactures the jelly in fruit flavors. The ad runs in several mainstream women's magazines, but also in some sexually-oriented periodicals that you would not leave lying on your coffee table.

The woman sues for intrusion invasion of privacy. It seems that you did not have her permission to publish her letter in an ad and that your use of the photograph of the actual letter, which included the woman's name and address, has led to a steady stream of unwelcome letters and anonymous obscene phone calls from men who saw the ad and who suggest to the woman various activities involving fruit-flavored contraceptive jelly. The trial judge is outraged by your (and your client's) carelessness and the frightening consequences of that carelessness. She awards a record amount in damages to the letter writer. You want your lawyer to appeal what you feel is the excessive amount of the award, but he tells you that you might as well pay up, because no appeals court is going to feel solicitous of your pocketbook after hearing the facts of the case.

Say "Cheese"   You use a photograph of a famous stage actress dining in a local restaurant in an ad for that restaurant under the headline "Where the Beautiful People Dine." She sues your restaurant client and you for invasion of privacy. The good news is that, because the photographer had entered the restaurant to have dinner, that is, with the permission of the owner of the restaurant, because the restaurant is a public place, and because the actress smiled for the photograph and generally cooperated in allowing her photo to be taken, the court rules that there was no "intrusion" into the actress' privacy. The bad news is that she wins with regard to her other claim, for infringement of her right of publicity (a subject we will consider later in this chapter).

Full Disclosure   Disclosure invasion of privacy involves some public disclosure of embarassing private facts about the plaintiff. It is the sort of invasion of privacy that most people think of when they hear "invasion of privacy." The elements of this sort of invasion of privacy are that the information disclosed must be of such a sort that its disclosure would be embarassing, objectionable, and offensive to a person of ordinary sensibilities and the information must not have been public prior to the complained-of disclosure.

Disclosure invasion of privacy differs from defamation in one very important way. To constitute defamation, the information published about the plaintiff must be untrue. There is no such requirement that the information involved in a disclosure invasion of privacy suit be false; in fact, it is the heart of a disclosure invasion of privacy suit that the information is true, but private. In a way, defamation and disclosure invasion of privacy are each the converse of the other. In other words, if you publish untrue information about someone and that information damages his or her reputation or humiliates him or her, you may be sued for defamation. If you publish the same information about the person but it is true, and private, and he or she can reasonably object to its publication and is embarassed by the disclosure of the information, you may be sued for disclosure invasion of privacy.

As with intrusion invasion of privacy, disclosure invasion of privacy suits result more from the activities of journalists than advertising creative people, but advertising creative people can get in big trouble with disclosure invasion of privacy claims just the same. A few examples of disclosure invasion of privacy will illustrate.

Over-Exposure To promote the annual state fair held each year in your city, you design a newspaper ad entitled "Fun at the Fair" and use an assortment of photographs of people who attended last year's fair. Among the photos you use is one of a young woman emerging from a midway funhouse who is prevented by the stuffed animals she carries from holding down the skirt of her dress when jets of air in front of the funhouse raise it, *a la* the famous Marilyn Monroe photograph. Her entire *derriere*, clad only in cotton undies, is exposed to the view of the camera and several young male bystanders, who are obviously having "fun at the fair" at the expense of the exposed woman. She sues when your ad is published, claiming disclosure invasion of privacy.

Your lawyer argues manfully at trial that since the photograph you used was taken in a public place, there were no "private facts" to disclose. The judge disagrees, stating that while the incident photographed did occur in a public place, you have increased exponentially the number of "bystanders" who witnessed the plaintiff's embarassment and, indeed, would have never published the photograph if it did not depict her exposure. You lose, and so does your client the state fair board.

Wrong Number In an ad promoting a new service of the largest hospital in your city, a clinic to treat impotence in men, you publish a list, furnished to you by the hospital, of names and phone numbers of men who are peer counsellors for the "Impotence Isn't Forever" support group that meets monthly at the hospital. The ad invites other impotent men to call one of these counsellors to discuss becoming a part of the support group. Unbeknownst to you, one of the counsellors whose name and phone number is published had not given his consent for his name and phone number to be included in the ad. He sues, you and the hospital, claiming disclosure invasion of privacy.

The hospital's lawyer says that you really don't have to hire your own lawyer, since you didn't do anything wrong, but later seems to you to have forgotten his promise to "take care of" you. Finally, you haul in your own lawyer, at some expense, and he is successful in convincing the plaintiff's lawyers that you would not be found guilty at trial of violating the rights of the plaintiff since you had no reason to believe that the hospital had erred when it told you that the men listed in the ad had all consented to the publication of their names. The hospital settles with the plaintiff, and you don't have to pay anything toward the settlement, but the director of marketing at the hospital is fired and replaced by another marketing director, who hires his brother-in-law's agency to replace yours.

Lost by a Nose   A local plastic surgeon hires you to help him put together a slideshow concerning his new technique for
rhinoplasty for presentation at a medical convention
in your city. Among the gory slides of nose surgery
in progress, there are some "before" and "after" photos, which you feel are the only really interesting parts
of the slideshow. A local beauty queen agrees. She
says in the complaint that she files for disclosure invasion of privacy that she had her nose "fixed" by the
good doctor several years ago. She is happy with her
new nose, but unhappy and embarassed that the fact
of the surgery has been made public by means of the
slideshow, especially since several of the plastic surgery residents in the audience are former college classmates of hers.

The court finds for the plaintiff. Both you and your
client are held liable. Your client is liable because even
though he told you that he did not have permission to
use some of the photos in his files, including the photos of the plaintiff, he is responsible for your actions
as his agent. You are liable because you employ the
art director who put the plaintiff's photos in the slideshow anyway, because he thought that they were the
most persuasive that the surgeon's techniques work
and believed that the woman pictured in them would
never find out anyway. You pay your lawyer's exor-
bitant fees and the fairly large damage award and
then, for revenge, you fire your errant art director.
However, not even that makes you feel much better
and you vow to avoid plastic surgeons forevermore.

Miss   If this lengthy account of all the varieties of invasion
Appropriation   of privacy is putting you to sleep, you should wake up
now, because we are going to consider the variety of
invasion of privacy that is most potentially dangerous
to advertising creative people, misappropriation invasion of privacy. Misappropriation invasion of privacy

involves the unauthorized use, for commercial purposes, of a person's name or likeness, with resulting
damage to the plaintiff's dignity and peace of mind.
In fact, any invasion of privacy suit involving any use
of the plaintiff's identity in an advertisement or in any
commercial context will be a misappropriation invasion of privacy suit, even if there are also other sorts
of privacy claims involved. If you will look back at the
examples of the other three sorts of invasion of privacy
which are given above, you will realize that, in addition to illustrating those sorts of invasion of privacy,
the examples also all illustrate misappropriation invasion of privacy. The following illustrations depict
situations in which only a misappropriation invasion
of privacy claim could properly be brought.

Oh, Susannah   Your client the furniture manufacturer names its new
line of fancy baby furniture the "Susannah" line. You
suggest that your client adopt a depiction of a pretty
little girl as the portrait of the fictitious "Susannah."
You survey all the photographs of pretty little girls you
can get your hands on and choose one, of whose little
girl you do not know, to give to your illustrator for
transformation into a nice line drawing logo for the
Susannah furniture line. The illustrator copies the
photo faithfully. You are very happy with the drawing and your client loves his new logo. Unfortunately,
the doting parents of "Susannah," whose real name is
Cynthia Ann, recognize their daughter as the original
of the Susannah logo and sue on behalf of their minor
daughter for misappropriation invasion of privacy,
saying that they would never have permitted your
client's use of their daughter's image and that they
want to stop the commercial exploitation of their child
because they believe it will damage her self-esteem.
Cynthia Ann wins. Your self-esteem is also damaged,
because you are in hot water with your client and out
a lot of money.

Shoe-In

The winner of your city's annual marathon crosses the finish line wearing a pair of running shoes manufactured by your client. You seize the opportunity and create a poster for distribution to all retail shoe stores which stock your client's running shoes. The poster uses a photo of the winner of the race, taken from a rear angle, which does not show the runner's face but prominently pictures the runner's shoes; the headline of the poster reads "Winners Wear Whizards" and the poster copy explains that the winner of the 15th annual Santa Fe marathon won wearing Whizard running shoes. The winner, an accountant by profession, sues for misappropriation invasion of privacy.

You are astounded when your lawyer tells you that the plaintiff can probably win his suit, because you believe the fact that the plaintiff's face was not shown in the photograph you used should eliminate the problem. It is news to you that, because the plaintiff can be identified as the runner in the photo by information in the poster other than the depiction of his face (he is the only person who won the 15th annual Santa Fe marathon), you have, as your lawyer says, "misappropriated his identity." Your lawyer recommends that you settle the case with a cash payment to the plaintiff. You know the rest of the story.

Self-Defense

A woman named Esmeralda Finnegan halts a bank robbery by using her karate skills on the two armed robbers who had taken her and seven other bank customers hostage. When interviewed after police arrived, she attributes her success in foiling the crime to the karate classes she took at Wong's Highway 96 Karate School. Wong's is your client. You reproduce the news story quoting Miss Finnegan in ads for Wong's. Even though neither Miss Finnegan's name nor photograph occurs in the ad other than the mention of her name in the reproduced news story, she sues for misappropriation invasion of privacy.

At trial your lawyer argues that you did not infringe the plaintiff's right of privacy because you merely reprinted a news story in your ad, did not say that the plaintiff recommended your client's school, and did not use any photograph of her. The court finds for the plaintiff, stating in its ruling that the use of the news story in an ad for Wong's constitutes an implication that Miss Finnegan endorses Wong's and is a misappropriation of her identity for commercial purposes. In other words, the plaintiff is right and you and Wong are wrong.

Publicity Stunts　If you are beginning to think that you cannot use the name or likeness of any living person in an ad without his or her consent, you are right. In fact, in some states and with regard to some people, you can't even use their names or likenesses in an ad when they are dead (without somebody's consent).

The right of publicity is very similar to misappropriation invasion of privacy. All the rights we have considered so far in this section of this book form a sort of progression, or chain, from defamation to false light invasion of privacy to intrusion invasion of privacy to disclosure invasion of privacy to misappropriation invasion of privacy to the right of publicity. Or maybe you would call it a vicious circle, because all these terms name rights that everyone has to keep you from doing a lot of things that you might assume are kosher, were you not now educated otherwise.

The last link in the chain, the right of publicity, differs from all the other rights named above in one basic way. Any of the sorts of invasion of privacy that we have discussed involve an assault upon someone's reputation or peace of mind or dignity. In contrast, when you infringe someone's right of publicity you infringe a property right, that is, you may be sued because you have infringed someone's legal right to be the only one who profits from the commercial value of his or her identity.

Private individuals have privacy rights and so do celebrities, though perhaps to a lesser extent, but in most ordinary circumstances only celebrities have the right of publicity. That is because generally only movie stars and sports figures and famous authors and retired politicians have the sort of name recognition that makes someone's identity valuable to advertisers. When a private person's identity is used without permission for commercial purposes, that person sues for misappropriation invasion of privacy, not for infringement of the right of publicity. The right of publicity otherwise looks pretty much like misappropriation invasion of privacy. That is, an infringement of someone's right of publicity occurs when that person's name or likeness is used for commercial purposes without his or her consent. The following examples of right of publicity infringements illustrate some of the features characteristic of right of publicity infringement disputes and suits.

Teed Off

You design packaging for a videocassette called "Golfing Tips of the Pros." You use photos on the cassette box of three famous golfers, Arnold Palmer, Jack Nicklaus, and Nancy Lopez. You neglect to ask anybody's permission to do so. You figure that all the famous golfers whose photos you used are public figures and you remember hearing something about public figures having less ability to control press coverage of their activities than private individuals. When the videocassette hits the market, the representatives of Mr. Palmer, Mr. Nicklaus, and Ms. Lopez call up the video distributor, threatening to sue the distributor if the videos are not pulled from store shelves and also to find out the address of your client, a video production company, in order to serve process in the lawsuits that are filed.

At trial your client is forced to admit that the "golfing tips" embodied in the videocassette are actually tips from the pros at the Sunnydale Golf Club and that the three famous golfers had nothing to do with creating the video. The lawyers representing the golfers argue that your use of their clients' photos on the video box implies that those are the pros whose tips are included on the video and constitutes an invasion of the right of publicity of the three golfers. Your client decides to cut his losses and settles the case after the plaintiffs present their case. Your lawyer tells you that you should be happy that the plaintiffs did not also claim that your actions constituted a Section 43(a) violation and that the video was pulled from store shelves before the Federal Trade Commission could find out that its packaging was materially misleading and commence a proceeding against your client for violation of its advertising regulations. You go home and think about what Shakespeare said about killing lawyers. (We will consider both private and FTC false advertising actions in the next chapter.)

All That Glitters

In an ad for "Glitter Gloves" you use a photo of the back view of Michael Jackson onstage, dressed in characteristic stage attire with one gloved hand raised in his familiar gesture. Well, actually, because you figured that Michael Jackson's fee for posing for your photo, if, indeed, he would consent to do such a thing, would exceed by far your glove manufacturer client's entire advertising budget, the photo is of a model carefully dressed and posed to appear to be Michael Jackson. Your client loves the ad. Michael Jackson doesn't.

Mr. Jackson's lawyers contact your client right after the ad appears in a national magazine, threatening to sue for what they say is your (and your client's) infringement of his right of publicity. They say that even though the photo is of a model dressed and posed to look like Michael Jackson and not Mr. Jackson himself, the intent and effect of the ad is to cause readers to believe that Michael Jackson is advertising Glitter Gloves.

You and your client consult an attorney, who tells you that Mr. Jackson's lawyers are correct in their assertions. Your lawyer says that your photo is so realistic that you have succeeded, regrettably, in appropriating Michael Jackson's "persona" without his participation or consent and that your use of the fake "Michael Jackson photo" is just as actionable as your use of an authentic photo of him without his permission. Your client pulls the ad, settles with Michael Jackson, and hires another agency. It also refuses to pay your last statement for your work on the "Michael Jackson" ad, leaving you holding the bag for all the production expenses and creative fees.

Elvis Sighting

You plan a "Fifties Days" promotion for all twelve locations of your restaurant client The Jukebox Cafe. The centerpiece of your promotion will be a weekly Elvis look-alike contest. You will also produce souvenir Elvis coffee mugs and tee shirts for sale at the restaurants' gift shops both during and after the promotion. For the mugs and shirts you plan to use a vintage photo of a skinny Elvis Presley in performance with the slogan "I Saw Elvis at the Jukebox Cafe."

The restaurant company marketing director loves the Elvis contest idea and the mug and tee shirt tie-ins, but he says he is worried that you need permission from somebody to use Elvis Presley's photograph and name in the promotion. You assure him that you remember reading that no dead person can be defamed and that, therefore, it is unnecessary to get permission from anyone before launching the planned promotion. All the locations of the Jukebox Cafe sell record quantities of cheeseburgers during the Fifties Days promotion and you have to reprint the Elvis tees twice during it in order to meet the demand.

You bask in glory until the day you get a call from the corporate legal department of the company that owns all the Jukebox Cafes. They say that they have been sued by the Elvis Presley estate for infringing Elvis Presley's right of publicity by producing and selling Elvis mugs and tee shirts. The suit asks for an injunction against further sales of the mugs and shirts, impoundment of all the unsold infringing mugs and shirts in your client's possession, your client's profits from sales of the items, and a substantial award of damages. You swallow your blue pencil and call a lawyer recommended to you by another graphic designer.

Your lawyer says that you are knee-deep in cheeseburgers because you have, indeed, run roughshod over the rights of the deceased Mr. Presley. You tell him that most people believe that Elvis Presley has been dead for years and ask him if he is one of those who think differently. He tells you that, for purposes of the lawsuit, it really doesn't make much difference, that under Tennessee law, the right of publicity, under some circumstances, survives the death of the celebrity and is owned and can be enforced by the celebrity's estate.

You tell him you did not know this. He says that it is obvious that you did not and that whether you knew what you were doing is immaterial. He advises you to do whatever you can to cooperate with the lawyers for your client and to settle the lawsuit. He also advises you that although only your restaurant client has been sued by the Presley estate, it is likely that you will, in turn, be sued by your client and thereby be brought into the same suit.

Your client settles the lawsuit quickly and agrees not to sue your company, but in return you have to agree to work for half your ordinary fees during the next year. You regret having to bite that bullet, but you feel as if you have escaped from a bad situation with as little harm to yourself and your pocketbook as possible under the circumstances. You are right.

Guessing Game Because right of publicity is a relatively new area of the law and has not been around long enough for all jurisdictions and courts and legal scholars to agree completely on its shape, right of publicity varies widely from one jurisdiction to another. About half the states expressly recognize the right, either by court decision or statute. It is likely that the right will be recognized in most states which have not at this writing recognized it just as soon as appeals court decisions are handed down in appropriate suits or forward-thinking legislators pass right of publicity statutes in states where there are none presently.

Because right of publicity law varies so widely from one state to another, and because you probably will not conduct an investigation prior to using a celebrity's identity to see just how much you can get away with under which statutes of which states, you are well-advised either to try to stay within the narrowest right of publicity restrictions that exist anywhere in the United States or eliminate the guessing game and get the celebrity's permission to use her or his name or likeness. You may be able to get away with using without permission the identities of some celebrities who live (or lived) in certain states and never run afoul of the law, but the only way to know for sure what you can do without permission is to do it and wait to see if a lawsuit shows up in your client's mail, which is no way to run an airline.

Twists and Turns There are some other twists to right of publicity law that you may not expect. One of the more interesting ones is the fact that, in some states, the right of publicity is a "descendable" right; that is, if you are famous, in some states and under certain circumstances your heirs can continue to exclusively control and profit from the commercial exploitation of your identity even after your death. This is unlike either the law of privacy or defamation. Your estate can't sue anyone for invasion of privacy or defamation if the alleged invasion or defamatory act occurred after your death; your rights in these areas die with you because you are presumed to be past caring, once you are dead, what anyone says about you. But a celebrity's right of publicity is a property right more like trademark ownership than a personal right to protect feelings from assault. Property can be passed to heirs and so can the right to protect the right of publicity after the celebrity's death.

How Peculiar   Another peculiarity of right of publicity law is the many ways by which a celebrity's right may be infringed. Generally speaking, the standard for identifiability is the same for right of publicity lawsuits as for invasion of privacy suits and libel suits. That is, if some people recognize the statement or photo or, even, fictitious depiction as referring to the plaintiff, the defendant is in trouble. However, since a celebrity is, by definition, a person whose appearance, voice, and personal habits are scrutinized and publicized so that they become very well-known, almost anything about a celebrity can identify him or her. This means that in the usual case, if you imitate any part of a celebrity's "persona," including his or her appearance, voice, singing voice, and nickname, sufficiently well that the ad which embodies the imitation "works," you have infringed that celebrity's right of publicity.

Think of it this way, if somebody is capitalizing on your hard-won fame by using your well-known nickname ("When you're 'The Greatest,' you fight in Slugger boxing shorts") or distinctive singing voice and style in an ad without your permission, you probably don't care whether it really is you in the ad or not, since what is being summoned up by the imitator, and stolen from you, is your reputation, not just your actual performance or image.

If the Suit Fits   The reason you need to know about the rights of privacy and publicity is, of course, so that you will be able to stay out of lawsuits. Many, and perhaps most, U.S. invasion of privacy lawsuits are filed because of transgressions by the news media, but that doesn't mean that non-media defendants are safer from invasion of privacy suits than newspapers and magazines or the broadcast media. In fact, because the courts don't allow defendants accused of invading plaintiffs' privacy in commercial contexts to plead the various defenses related to freedom of the press that are available to media defendants in such suits, non-media defendants are found liable for invasion of privacy in a higher percentage of privacy suits filed against them than are media defendants.

And practically all suits for infringement of the right of publicity are filed against defendants who are in the chain of people who market a product, lots of them ad agencies; First Amendment defenses are also generally unavailable in those suits. This means that you, as someone who creates ads, must pay special attention to privacy issues and to possible publicity claims, since if you invade someone's privacy or infringe his or her right of publicity in an ad, you can't get off the hook by "pleading the First."

Sometimes copyright and trademark infringement suits result from what are essentially business disputes; that is, two parties who have differing ideas of who is entitled to ownership of a copyright or a trademark can't work out their dispute between themselves and so resort to the courts for a resolution of the dispute. Libel suits and suits for invasion of privacy or infringement of the publicity right are seldom as dispassionate as even a fiercely fought copyright or trademark suit because, by definition, all involve somebody's stepped-on feelings or reputation or both.

Consider the fact that even lawyers, who usually speak in terms of "bringing an action" or "filing a complaint" have been heard to utter the phrase "slap those *!#@!* with a lawsuit" in contexts involving clients who have (choose any two of the following) squashed feelings, a damaged or misappropriated reputation, or a fat wallet and fire in their eyes. For any non-media defendant, there is simply nothing to be won in any of the sorts of lawsuits we have discussed so far in this section of the book. Further, these sorts of suits are typically fought by plaintiffs as grudge matches, long past the point where prudence would dictate that they let sleeping dogs lie. All this means that, with regard to privacy and publicity infringement suits (and, as we have seen, libel suits) an ounce of prevention beats a whole covey of lawyers for the defense. And prevention means releases.

Please Release Me

A release (also sometimes called a "consent" or "consent form") is simply a written document that evidences that someone has given his or her permission for his or her name or photograph or performance or other element of his or her identity to be used for the purposes specified in the release. Releases don't have to be long or complicated to do the job. In fact, in many cases a verbal release would actually do the trick, but most people don't want to rely on the memory and honesty of someone else to prove that a use of that person's name or photo was a permitted use.

Written releases should be a part of your standard operating procedure, a routine part of your business that you never neglect. There a few rules to remember in using releases.

Give Me Some Space

Have a lawyer prepare a release which is designed to work *for you*. Generally, the broader the release, the better. That is, the less specific your release in stating the uses to which your subject agrees his or her photo can be put, the more leeway you have later.

However, if the intended use for the photo is something that the model could object to if she or he is not made aware of it, such as use of the photograph on packaging for condoms or in an ad for guns or cigarettes, include the specific purpose contemplated in a handwritten addition to the general release. This handwritten addition should be made on the same piece of paper as the general release, preferably in a space reserved for such additions, even if it must be made on the reverse of the page, and should be initialed by the person who signs the release at the same time he or she signs.

Your release should give you permission to alter the photo, since only having permission to use it "as is" may make it unusable for your purposes. (The release reproduced in the Appendix section of this book may do the trick, but it also may need modification to work for you. Talk to your lawyer if you are in doubt about whether it will work in your situation.)

Have your release printed on your business letterhead and carry a supply of blank release forms with you so that you will have them whenever you need them. Make sure your employees and any free-lancers you hire know that you expect them to secure signed releases on your behalf.

Without Exception

Get a signed release from everyone who appears in any photo you may use in an ad or publication or in any other way. No exceptions. Even from people in the background of street or party or other group shots, unless their faces are not visible and their own mothers wouldn't recognize the set of their shoulders and the color of their hair. Even from paid models. Especially from private individuals who are not paid for their services.

And get mom or dad or a legal guardian, not just Aunt Linda or the child's agent or chaperone, to sign a release for anyone under twenty-one, the upper-limit age of majority (in some states), since the signature of a minor may invalidate the release.

Nothing Up My Sleeve

Never obtain a release by trickery or in any circumstances that could lead to a later challenge that the subject of the photograph was misled as to the use that would be made of it. If you don't tell the truth, or the whole truth, about the uses that will be made of the photograph of the person who signs a release, how can he or she validly agree to allow that use?

ABC's

Keep a central file of all releases you obtain, arranged alphabetically by the names of the people who sign releases and by year. Or, even better, keep one copy of each release with the negatives for the photos of the person to whom the release applies and one in a central file, for insurance against loss. It is also best to give a copy of the release to the person signing it, but that person probably won't keep his or her copy and, anyway, *you* are the one who needs proof that the release was signed, not the model or subject.

Make sure that you indicate, on the back of contact sheets or on negative envelopes or in some other reliable way, the name of each subject of each group of photos. Otherwise Jim may sue you for using his photo, because the only permission you had to use it was, in reality, a signed release from Chris.

March to the Scaffold

Never vary from your firm policy to obtain releases from everyone whose photo you take or hire taken. And never use a photo from a free-lancer without seeing and keeping a copy of the release from the subject of the photo. Never. Behead any employees who are lax with regard to obtaining releases. They can get you in a lot of trouble.

False Advertising Law

Chapter **10**

False Advertising Law

Coming and Going

There are two major ways a company can get into trouble for false advertising. One is a private suit under Section 43(a) of the Lanham Act; that is, a suit brought by an individual or another company for violations of that section of the federal trademark statute. The other is an investigation or litigation by an agency of the federal government, the Federal Trade Commission, because of a claimed violation of the Federal Trade Act or FTC Trade Regulation Rules. Generally speaking, an egregious enough misrepresentation in an ad will result in one or both of these varieties of false advertising trouble, along with headaches, enormous legal fees, and lots of time spent getting nowhere.

Truth in advertising is not, ultimately, entirely the responsibility of the company or person who creates the ad. As with trademark infringement suits, false advertising litigation is generally brought against the advertiser. However, it is not at all uncommon for an ad agency to be named in a false advertising suit and enjoined by the court from further actions that the court finds are violations.

Again, even being in the same room when an ad is created that is later the focus of a lawsuit can earn you demerits from your client, if not a pink slip. In an industry where more money is spent every year by ad agencies and design studios on client lunches and dinners and other forms of business ingratiation than some developing countries spend for running their armies, it only makes sense that, once they like you, you should do everything reasonably in your power to see that they don't change their minds. That means doing your best to keep your clients out of false advertising briarpatches.

It isn't all that hard, usually. All you have to do is squelch your cleverness long enough to ask yourself if Abraham Lincoln would say it or photograph it in the same way, had he been lucky enough to be you instead of the sixteenth president of the United States. Then you have to look at it through the eyes of a seventy-year-old widow living on a pension who is intimidated by the thought of not having enough insurance, or those of a four-year-old who believes everything he sees on television, or of (this one shouldn't be hard) a sophisticated survivor of the Eighties who never believes anything until *Consumer Reports* says it. If your ad passes these tests, you can send it to the printer. If it doesn't, call your lawyer.

In almost every case, the only goal for a defendant in either a Section 43(a) or an FTC suit is to get out of it as quickly as possible, which may be difficult. The only quick way to extricate yourself from false advertising litigation is to avoid it entirely in the first place. Avoiding trouble means knowing where the quicksand is. This chapter will serve as a map through the treacherous terrain of false advertising law.

Hidden Dangers

You might not expect to find a false advertising pitfall lurking in the middle of the federal trademark statute, but there it is. Section 43(a), the scourge of exaggerators and fabricators, was originally meant to provide a means of recourse against several forms of unfair competition, including false advertising. It allowed a company which had been harmed by some "false description or representation" made by a competitor about that competitor's goods or services to bring a federal suit to have the practice stopped. In other words, if your competitor lied about the merits of its products, you could sue to challenge the misrepresentations.

Section 43(a) has now been revised to enlarge the bases upon which a plaintiff can bring a Section 43(a) false advertising suit. Since late in 1989, it has also been possible for plaintiffs to sue competitors for making false statements of fact about the plaintiffs' products; this was not originally possible under the provision. This means that now Section 43(a) prohibits any advertising claim that misrepresents the nature, characteristics, qualities, or origin of anybody's goods, services, or commercial activities.

The revised text of Section 43(a) of the Lanham Act pertaining specifically to false advertising reads as follows:

> (a) Any person who, on or in connection with any goods or services, or any container for goods, uses in commerce any word, term, name, symbol, or device, or any combination thereof, or any false designation of origin, false or misleading description of fact, or false or misleading representation of fact, which. . . in commercial advertising or promotion, misrepresents the nature, characteristics, qualities, or geographic origin of his or her or another person's goods, services, or commercial activities shall be liable in a civil action by any person who believes that he or she is or is likely to be damaged by such act.

It is important to understand that a Section 43(a) suit is more than just a nuisance. Like a copyright or trademark infringement action, it is a suit that claims a violation of federal law and it is brought, and fought, in federal court, which is not small claims court. A winning plaintiff in a false advertising suit can recover the defendant's profits from the false advertising, the damages suffered by the plaintiff, the plaintiff's costs, and, sometimes, the plaintiff's attorneys' fees. In addition the court may enjoin further publication or broadcast of the offending ad and, sometimes, require corrective advertising.

So. The elements of a Section 43(a) claim are:

- a false statement of fact made (usually in an ad) by the defendant;

- about either the defendant's products or those of the plaintiff;

- which has actually deceived a substantial number of the people to whom the ad is addressed or has the capacity to deceive them; and

- which constitutes a material deception that is likely to influence purchasing decisions.

Except for a few particulars, which we will consider below, that's it.

That's a Fact
The requirement that a Section 43(a) false advertising claim be based on a statement of fact is like the defamation principle that opinions are not actionable. Nobody will sue your client for publishing an ad that quotes several satisfied consumers who sent fan letters about your client's new bathroom cleaner. However flattering the statements of those consumers, they are only opinions of those particular people and are not actionable even if they are incorrect.

But try stating that "98 percent of housewives surveyed prefer new Dazzle cleanser" when your research really reported that 98 percent of the housewives surveyed preferred Dazzle over Rustaway, but only 34 percent preferred Dazzle over Daisy, the other leading cleanser. Your client may find itself staring down the barrel of a Section 43(a) false advertising suit.

And remember that a "statement" can be visual or aural as well as verbal. In fact, given the power of visual representations and the great care with which advertising illustrations and photographs are constructed, visual statements may be potentially even more misleading than verbal ones. Designers and art directors must pay special attention to the implications of their visual representations of products to detect false implications.

Television spots are especially dangerous because they combine verbal, aural, and visual messages. Because television spots are so powerful, any misleading representation in a television spot is not likely to go unchallenged by competitors. One spot for an expensive car that ran a few years ago contained an implication that was so objectionable to the competitor of the sponsoring automaker that the competitor sued immediately. The spot was pulled from the air after only nine days, under a court injunction.

What's It All About?

A plaintiff in a Section 43(a) false advertising suit may sue because of false statements made either about the defendant's goods (or services) or those of the plaintiff. It isn't hard to figure out if the defendant made the statement about its own products or services; the ad itself tells you that.

It may be harder to tell if a false statement made in an ad is "about" the products or services of the plaintiff. Again, an analogy may be drawn to defamation law. A false statement about the plaintiff's products may be implied by an ad or may be seen to refer to them only by virtue of some outside facts not contained in the ad. "The only toothpaste sold in America scientifically proven to stop tartar!" implies that no other American toothpaste can stop tartar without ever mentioning any other toothpaste by name. Similarly, "Start-Up Batteries out-perform every other leading brand of auto batteries" includes in its scope, by reference, the other leading battery brands and is "about" them.

Ah, What a Tangled Web

The false statement must have actually deceived or have the capacity to deceive a substantial segment of the ad's audience. In other words, if only your gullible Uncle Mark and other bankers who don't get out much are going to believe that "Eating Crunchies for breakfast makes you handsomer!" the makers of Sweeties cereal will not have a valid ground for a Section 43(a) false advertising suit.

Obviously, most false advertising suits involve statements that are much more difficult to characterize as likely to deceive a substantial segment of the audience for the ad. People who design and write ads often use such subtle visual signals and language that evaluation of the possibility for deception is difficult.

The sophistication of the audience (or lack of sophistication) is a big factor in evaluating the possibility for deceptiveness. Certain groups, such as children and elderly people, are presumed to be more easily deceived than other groups. And the audience for any particular ad is not necessarily monolithic; one ad can aim at Mom and Dad *and* the kiddies. Further, even though ads accused of being misleading are evaluated according to whether the supposedly false statement concerns an important enough feature of the product (in other words, is "material") to influence a purchasing decision, the people who write the checks are not necessarily the audience for the ad that prompts them to do so.

Doting parents often make purchasing decisions because their tots have previously decided, due to a per-

suasive ad aimed at children, that they can't live another month without a glow-in-the-dark dinosaur
gumball machine. In situations like this, the parents
are not the audience for the ad even though they do
make the ultimate purchase. If your ad for the floures-
cent dino implies that the toy is a veritable perpetual
supply of tasty gumballs when in fact the gumballs are
not included, you may be in trouble with your competitors who want that segment of the dinosaur
gumball machine market for themselves and are will-
ing to sue to stop you from co-opting it by deception.

A Rock and a
Hard Place

It isn't always easy to gauge whether a statement in an
ad is "materially misleading." Materially misleading
statements come in two sizes, Plausible Falsehoods
and Stir-Fried Truth. Each variety of misleading statement represents a separate hazard for anyone who has
any role in creating advertising.

You don't have to worry too much about whether
you can get into trouble by employing a Plausible
Falsehood in an ad. You can. If you are so foolish as
to create an ad that contains any false statement of fact,
be it verbal or visual or aural, your client's competitor will file a suit, in federal court, accusing your client
of false advertising. Once again, good business judgment and garden-variety common sense dictate that
avoiding the issue is far preferable to having it decided
in court. That means scrutinizing the ads you create
to eliminate any false representation, made directly or
by implication, about either your own client's products or those of competitors.

This doesn't mean that you have to abandon the use
of humorous exaggeration or obvious tall tales.
Remember that your client can't be sued successfully
unless the false representation is a big one and is likely
to be believed. Courts look at what your ad actually
means to the people to whom it is addressed. Joe Izusu
told the biggest whoppers ever seen on TV outside of

political campaigns, but nobody sued Izusu because nobody believed Joe. And nobody in America has ever known how all those fancy cars are supposed to have landed on top of those picturesque western buttes, but no automaker has ever been sued for implying that its automobiles could fly there.

Hot Air

Further, what the law calls "puffery" in ads is not actionable. Puffery is flattering, sometimes exaggerated sales rhetoric that consumers are not likely to rely upon when making a purchase. ("The most generous auto dealer in Bangor!" or "Eat the biggest T-bones in Texas at Ethel's Surf and Turf Lounge.") But it is dangerous to rely too much on this exception to the "materially misleading statement" prohibition. "The most skilled auto mechanics in the world work for us" may be non-actionable puffery; "The best auto mechanics in Peoria" may not be. Since the burden of proving that an extravagant statement is puffery is on the defendant in a Section 43(a) suit, it is better to be safe than sorry.

The really hard part of avoiding Section 43(a) false advertising accusations is determining when a true statement can get you in trouble. Theoretically, telling the truth should never result in a false advertising suit. The tricky part is telling the truth in such a way that no one is misled. Otherwise, what you end up with is Stir-Fried Truth, which can land you in a lawsuit as quickly as any false statement.

In some cases, all this gets down to a matter of semantics and implications and interpretation. There is a line of cases known irreverently as "The Aspirin Wars" resulting from suits between two major American pharmaceutical companies over what most people would consider innocent representations of the relative merits of several brands of analgesics. These lawsuits were, and continue to be, fought so long and so fiercely that they, collectively, have worn out more

Ivy League lawyers than can dance on the head of a pen. Fresh teams of lawyers have replaced exhausted ones. Lawyers have grown old on the job. Some have thought about getting into real estate. All of them have taken a lot of aspirin. After more than eleven years of suits, the war continues. All because reasonable companies differ about the truth regarding their products.

I Failed Chemistry

The moral of this tale of life in a litigious society is that, past a point, determining the truth of statements made in ads is something that really is not in your bailiwick. You are not a research chemist, you did not conduct the survey, you did not test the product. You, personally, do not know if it does cut grease faster or is preferred by nine out of ten doctors or does last longer than any other comparably priced battery.

You must rely on your client for this information. And you must be very careful to present the information you receive from your client as accurately as possible, without implying that an ingredient of the sunscreen can prevent (rather than diminish the chance of) skin cancer, without exaggerating the amount of almonds in the cereal, without distorting the survey results by clever manipulation of the English language.

The following examples will help you understand a little better the kinds of advertising representations that can result in Section 43(a) lawsuits.

I'm O.J., You're O.J.

You create a snazzy television spot for your client the orange juice manufacturer, a company named Sunjuice. The spot features a well-known former Olympic swimming medalist, who squeezes fat oranges and pours the freshly-squeezed juice into a Sunjuice carton, all the while extolling the "wonderful fresh-squeezed taste" of Sunjuice orange juice. Two weeks after the debut of the ad Sunjuice's major competitor, the Liquid Gold Company, files a Section 43(a) suit, claiming that it has been harmed by Sunjuice's misrepresentation that Sunjuice's orange juice is fresh-squeezed orange juice, when in fact it is reconstituted from concentrate and is sometimes frozen before packaging.

Sunjuice's lawyers argue at trial that no one is likely to believe that Sunjuice orange juice is simply packaged fresh-squeezed juice and that therefore Sunjuice's spot is not actionable under Section 43(a). You were the creative director for the spot and, sitting in the Sunjuice cheering section in court on the day that Sunjuice makes this argument, you are hopeful that the judge will buy it. He doesn't.

The judge rules that the squeezing-pouring section of the Sunjuice spot, especially when coupled with the spokesman's comments, constitutes a material misrepresentation of fact by its powerful implication that Sunjuice sells fresh-squeezed orange juice in its cartons. He enjoins the further broadcast of the television spot. The Liquid Gold Company is happy. Sunjuice is very unhappy. So are you, because you lose the Sunjuice account.

Let's Be Frank   Your mail order marketing company client comes to you to get you to help him design materials to advertise and sell a "K-Tel" type collection of World War II-era pop music. Your client has obtained permission from the record companies which own the original master recordings of the 30 songs included in the two-cassette package to re-package and sell the recordings by mail. The cassettes include songs by various popular artists of the era, the most famous of whom is Frank Sinatra, who sings two selections.

You decide to capitalize on the fact that Frank Sinatra recordings are included when you create the

Sunday supplement newspaper ad for the package, which is called "Forties Favorites" Prominently displayed in the ad is the headline "Forties Favorites from Frank Sinatra (and Other Artists)." The "Forties Favorites" ad results in record sales and a federal lawsuit, filed by Frank Sinatra against your client's company.

Mr. Sinatra's complaint states that the use of his name in your client's ad was more prominent than the content of the cassette collection justifies and that this over-attribution of the "Forties Favorites" to Mr. Sinatra is material misrepresentation of the contents of the cassettes and constitutes false advertising under Section 43(a). The suit asks for an injunction against any further use of the misleading ad and damages for the previous publication of the ad.

Your client voluntarily pulls his ad, not wanting to add fuel to the flame by disputing Mr. Sinatra's claims, which include a claim for infringement of his right of publicity. Your client's lawyer tells him Mr. Sinatra's claims are justified and your client settles the lawsuit. You design a new, more accurate newspaper ad for your client but he stops returning your phone calls and hires another agency. (Section 43(a) claims often result from situations where the contribution or role of a famous person is over-stated in ads for some entertainment product. In such cases, they may be joined with right of publicity claims, which are similar, though not identical.)

Contented Italian Cows

You have a small dairy product manufacturer client, based in Wisconsin. Your client wants you to help it develop packaging for its new product, a packaged *gelatto*, produced in Wisconsin from authentic Italian recipes. You decide to emphasize the Italian angle, figuring that the *gelatto* will appeal to sophisticated buyers if it appears to be made somewhere besides the midwest.

You recommend to your client that the new product be called "Buono" and you design packaging for the gelatto that features the Italian flag prominently. As a further clever device, you also advise your client to print the label information in both English and Italian. Under the product name on the carton you use the slogan "A genuine Italian *gelatto*." Your client loves the name, the copy, and the packaging. The product is launched and breaks all sales records for the company within the first month of marketing in the three midwest states where it is introduced.

Then your client is sued by its competitor, who claims that the packaging for your client's *gelatto* is materially misleading in that it falsely represents that the product is made in Italy. Your client is outraged by the temerity of its competitor and fights the lawsuit, unfortunately to no avail.

The court says that your clever packaging is an obvious effort to lead consumers to believe that your client's *gelatto* is made in Italy. It ignores the arguments of the lawyers for your client that no sophisticated buyer of the product would believe this actually to be the case. It says that very few grocery shoppers are likely to know that the packaging for a real imported product would state that the product was manufactured elsewhere, and, in any event, that it is not reasonable to expect such a close reading of the label from a grocery shopper.

The plaintiff wins. Your client gets a lawyer who is knowledgeable about Food and Drug Administration labeling regulations and false advertising law to review the *gelatto* packaging. The lawyer makes a few copy changes and eliminates the Italian flag and Italian-language ingredients list. You find out all this by reading the new *gelatto* carton at the grocery store, because your client ditched you the day the court ruled in favor of its competitor.

Second Round   If you manage to steer clear of any violations of Section 43(a), you will probably also stay out of trouble with the Federal Trade Commission, affectionately known as the FTC. The FTC is the federal agency that enforces the Federal Trade Commission Act, which is another federal law that regulates, among other things, advertising.

The Federal Trade Commission Act prohibits unfair methods of commercial competition and unfair or deceptive trade practices and empowers the FTC to initiate proceedings to stop such methods or practices. One of the unfair methods of competition prohibited is false advertising, which the statute defines as follows:

> The term "false advertisement" means an advertisement, other than labeling, which is misleading in a material respect; and in determining whether an advertisement is misleading, there shall be taken into account (among other things) not only representations made or suggested by statement, word, design, device, sound, or any combination thereof, but also the extent to which the advertisement fails to reveal facts material in the light of such representations or material with respect to consequences which may result from the use of the commodity to which the advertisement relates under the conditions prescribed in said advertisement, or under such conditions as are customary or usual.

This short section of the statute is the basis for innumerable court decisions in suits brought by the FTC against advertisers accused of false advertising. This extensive body of case law is the source for almost all law which deals with compliance with the Federal Trade Commission Act.

The difference between being the defendant in a Section 43(a) suit and having the FTC investigate and prosecute you is the difference between the "plaintiffs" in these two sorts of actions. Your competitor can cause a lot of trouble and expense with its Section 43(a) suit, but it probably will not be able to wield the clout the FTC has, even if it wins.

It is possible that a company will be both sued by its competitors under Section 43(a) for false advertising and run afoul of the long arm of the FTC, but it doesn't happen much, at least not lately. One of the main reasons for this is that during the regime of Ronald Reagan the FTC's activities tapered off, and the formerly fierce consumer avenger left most American capitalists alone. It went after only the really bad guys and left a lot of the quibbling over the fine points of advertising language and visuals to the capitalists themselves, who enthusiastically filed Section 43(a) suits whenever one thought another had made an unfounded claim in an ad.

However, even though the FTC hasn't bitten as many advertisers lately as it did in the 1970's, it has by no means lost its teeth. This means that you need a good working knowledge of FTC false advertising standards in order to help your clients avoid FTC challenges to their ads. The first thing to know is the FTC's definition of a deceptive ad.

The FTC says that an ad is deceptive if it contains a material representation or includes a material omission which is likely, if reasonably interpreted under the circumstances, to mislead consumers and affect their decisions with regard to purchasing the product. If you think this sounds familiar, you get points for paying attention when you read the first part of this chapter, because the FTC standard for a deceptive ad is, with one notable exception, essentially the same standard as that for a Section 43(a) false advertising claim.

Like Section 43(a), the FTC considers false statements actionable if they are material. (A claim is "material" if it pertains to important characteristics of the product, such as performance, quality, cost, and function, so that the claim is likely to affect the consumer's purchasing decision.) And the FTC standard for "reasonable interpretation" of the ad is pretty much the same as that for Section 43(a) claims, that is, the FTC takes into account the sophistication of the audience for the ad and the likelihood that anyone will believe the false claim.

The difference is that the FTC will act to halt advertising that is deceptive because it omits information that would, if disclosed, affect the consumer's purchasing decision. There is no such provision in Section 43(a); those suits are brought because of specific claims. In other words, under Section 43(a) you can get into trouble because of what you say; you may incur the wrath of the FTC either for what you say or what you *don't* say.

There is one other important difference between FTC law and Section 43(a). The FTC requires that advertisers have "prior substantiation" for specific claims made in ads. A Section 43(a) defendant may try to prove at trial that the claims it made in the ad accused of being false are not false, but there is no requirement that a defendant have compiled evidence of the truth of the claim before making it. This is not the case with the FTC.

The FTC prior substantiation doctrine simply requires that an advertiser have a reasonable basis for making any important objective claims about its products before disseminating any ad containing those claims. Inability to supply such substantiation may result in even *true* statements being enjoined by the FTC. This only makes sense, if you think about it.

The FTC's whole goal with regard to its false advertising activities is to protect consumers from unscrupulous and less-than-careful marketers who make unfounded claims for their products. If the FTC allowed companies to try to verify their claims *after* making them in ads, consumers would be subjected to far more false advertising and the FTC would have to become an even bigger agency to handle the complaints that would result. The agency wisely decided to shut the barn door before the cow got out, by requiring companies to figure out in advance whether they were telling the truth and to be able to show the evidence of the truth of their claims later.

Generally speaking, the more specific and material the advertising claim, the higher the level of substantiation required by the FTC. "Claims" includes implied claims ("New, improved Sparkle window cleaner cuts grime 25 percent faster than before" implies that tests have been conducted that reached this determination). As with Section 43(a) claims, mere "puffery" is not actionable.

You don't have to become a window cleaner tester in order to do your job for your clients. The prior substantiation of advertising claims is your clients' responsibility. Your job is merely to let your clients know that they should be able to prove what they claim.

The alternative to complying with FTC advertising law is not a pretty sight. Acting on complaints from either consumers or your client's competitors, or on its own initiative, the FTC can, after an investigation, enter a "cease and desist order" against your client. A cease and desist order is in the nature of an injunction which prohibits an accused false advertiser from further dissemination of specified offending ads. Monetary penalties may be levied against companies which fail to abide by FTC cease and desist orders.

In addition to cease and desist orders, the FTC can ask, in federal court, for a whole laundry list of other remedies, including preliminary and permanent injunctions, civil and criminal penalties, and various forms of consumer relief, such as corrective advertising, refunds, and invalidation of contracts with affected consumers. Either before or after the FTC files a complaint in federal court, the FTC and the advertiser which is the subject of the FTC's investigation can enter a "consent decree," which is like a settlement agreement. More than 75 percent of all FTC investigations end with consent orders, probably because most accused advertisers know that the FTC is the government and they are not, and wisely settle.

The following examples of FTC cases will illustrate some of the features of these cases.

Bald Assertions

Your client Ernie tells you that he intends to begin marketing a baldness remedy through the mail, in addition to his other existing farfetched ventures. He brings you information that he wants included in a newspaper ad for his Hair Today Miracle Baldness Cure, which consists of an ointment that Ernie makes, from "all natural ingredients," in his basement. You produce the ad in time for him to mail it off to *The National Enquirer* and when he comes to pick it up you question his substantiation for a couple of the claims he makes in the ad copy. You ask him about "New Hair Growth in Only Seven Days!" and "Laboratory tests prove Hair Today works!" Ernie tells you that you worry too much and races to the post office with his ad.

Ernie's mail-order empire never gets off the ground. You hear in a few months that, after several consumer complaints, the FTC launched an investigation of Ernie and his baldness remedy. When Ernie couldn't supply the substantiation for his extravagant claims about Hair Today, he entered a consent decree with the FTC to forestall any further action by the agency. In the consent decree he promised, among other things, to cease making any unfounded claims for his product, which of course means no claims at all, since Ernie has no evidence and can't come up with any. In addition, since he failed to comply with the regulations of the Food and Drug Administration governing labeling for all sorts of products intended to be used on or in the body, including his ointment, he is in trouble with the FDA.

The last you hear, Ernie is thinking of re-labeling his garage full of ointment tins and selling the rejuvenated concoction as a shoe-waterproofing product.

Zapped

A local plastic products company comes to you for help in developing advertising and packaging materials for an addition to its line of toys. The new product is the "Space Cadet Ray Gun," which proves to be a sparkly silver plastic "space pistol" with a red lens in the end of the barrel and a flashlight battery to power the "death ray," which is activated when the trigger of the pistol is pulled.

You "test market" the toy by taking a pair of pistols to your nephews. They like the gun, but beef up its effect by yelling "Zap!" whenever they aim and fire.

You design a color ad for the gun which consists largely of a photo of young boys, dressed as spacemen, duelling with a pair of the toys. To emphasize the "death ray" feature of the gun, you retouch the photo to add red flares from the ends of the pistols. You also scatter a cloud of "Zap!" "sound effects" around the heads of the models, in the time-honored manner of super-hero comics. The packaging for the toy includes most of the same elements you used for the ad.

Your client loves the ad and packaging and sales of the toy are high. So, unfortunately, are complaints from parents of space cadets. It seems that a large percentage of children are very disappointed to find, upon receiving the gun, that it neither annihilates enemies with a red flare nor makes a "zap" noise when it does so. The next piece of bad news is that the FTC has sent your client a letter informing it that the FTC is considering beginning an investigation of it for misleading advertising.

Your client, on the advice of a lawyer it consults, immediately mails to all its dealers stickers for affixation to all "Space Cadet Ray Gun" packages. The stickers state that the gun has no red flare and makes no noise when "shot." You are called upon to alter the ad artwork and the artwork for future packaging of the toy. In the art for both, you eliminate the red flare retouching and replace it with a representation of a red glow from the end of the gun, which is a more accurate depiction of the product's abilities, and change the floating "Zap!" "sound effects" to cartoon-balloon dialogue from the models, clarifying the source of that sound effect.

The FTC is satisfied with your client's efforts to remedy the failings of your ad and packaging and enters a consent order with it. You don't lose your client because you are good at what you do. However, you are also more careful in future about the implications of the visual elements of your ads, especially those aimed at children, because you hope to avoid being zapped again by the FTC.

In the Soup A young entrepreneur named Sonia comes to you with an interesting assignment. After running a successful catering business from her home for several years, she has begun to sell some of her more popular recipes in grocery stores. She needs labeling and ads for her line of soups, called, of course, "Sonia's Soups," and wants you to design both.

Being efficient, Sonia has already arranged for guidance from a lawyer knowledgeable about the Food and Drug Administration's labeling regulations. You submit the label roughs and copy to him and begin on the newspaper ads for Sonia's Soups.

Sonia has supplied you with information about the nutrients in each variety of her soup. Since several of the soups are very high in fiber, you decide that this is a selling point and make this the focus of one whole segment of the ad campaign. Under the headline, "Sonia's Soups Are High in Healthy Fiber," you use a very nice photo of a bowl of Sonia's Soup. You had planned to use a bowl of navy bean soup, since that soup has a very high fiber content, but you couldn't come up with any way to make a bowl of it look interesting, so you use instead a tasty-looking bowl of *gazpacho*, with sprigs of parsley floating in it.

Sonia likes the ad. The state attorney general's office does not. It complains in a letter to Sonia that the ads are misleading because they make a claim (high fiber) that is not true about the soup illustrated. Sonia pulls the offending ad, at some cost and inconvenience, and also her account. She now has the fastest-growing business in the state, but you don't have any of it, because she also has a long memory.

Salute the Generals

As the last anecdote illustrates, the FTC and your client's competitors are not necessarily the only people who will pounce if your client's ads are not truthful. There are a lot of other politicos and bureaucrats scattered over the American landscape who also believe that free enterprise means fair competition. One of the most vigilant groups of late has been the National Association of Attorneys General (the NAAG), a group of law enforcers who bring false advertising suits under the consumer protection laws of their various states. (State consumer protection laws vary but generally seek to prevent the same unfair trade practices that aggravate the FTC.) Since the FTC's activities have been greatly diminished during the recent Republican administrations, the NAAG has become more active, acting as a clearinghouse for information about unfair trade practices, including false advertising, among its other multifarious activities. In short, if the feds don't get you, the "generals" will.

There are also a whole bowlful of alphabet-soup federal agencies which each regulate certain kinds of advertising. Some of these agencies are: the Bureau of Alcohol, Tobacco and Firearms (BATF); the Consumer Product Safety Commission (CPSC); the Department of Transportation (DOT); the Environmental Protection Agency (EPA); the Federal Communications Commission (FCC); the Federal Reserve Board (FRB); the Food and Drug Administration (FDA); the Securities and Exchange Commission (SEC); the Internal Revenue Service (IRS); and the U.S. Postal Service. The kinds of advertising these agencies regulate is, in the case of some, pretty obvious. Others are more surprising. The IRS, for instance, regulates some political advertising. Further, many of these federal agencies share jurisdiction with the FTC over the sorts of advertising they regulate.

Further, your clients' competitors may appeal to the standards divisions maintained by all the major television networks, or complain to the National Advertising Division of the Council of Better Business Bureaus, which is a self-regulatory group created by the advertising industry, if they don't like your client's ads.

Duty Calls

You have a responsibility to help your clients stay out of false advertising trouble of any sort. To start with, you can advise them that there is such a thing as false advertising. You can point out that making false claims about their own products or services can result in tedious and expensive lawsuits brought by their competitors or an investigation or litigation by the FTC or the NAAG. You can tell them that false statements about other companies' products or services are likely to result in Section 43(a) suits. You can let them know that even what they *don't* say can attract the attention of the FTC, if their omissions are serious ones. You can inform them that they have a legal responsibility to substantiate their important claims about their products or services before they begin making those claims in their ads. You can avoid turning the substantiated facts about their products into Stir-Fried Truth in the process of creating persuasive ads.

Good Reviews And you can tell them that even though you are familiar with the major features of the false advertising landscape, you are not a lawyer. The single most effective way to avoid false advertising claims of any sort, besides telling the truth, is to have a lawyer knowledgeable about false advertising law review ads for possible Section 43(a) and FTC problems, *before* publication. Not just any lawyer will do. Most real estate, divorce, and criminal lawyers know practically nothing about false advertising law and are content to leave things that way. You wouldn't hire a dermatologist to take out your appendix; recommend to your clients that they inquire about the primary areas of practice of any lawyer they propose to have review their ads. Or ask your client to allow you to hire a lawyer on its behalf.

You don't need to worry about every ad you produce. But any ad that makes specific claims about your client's or another company's products or is addressed to children or concerns any industry or product that is, or may be, regulated by the government or any state, should be reviewed. Legal fees are a necessary evil for many advertisers. With regard to some types of ads, those companies almost have no choice — they can either pay now, for ad review, or later, for litigation. You choose.

The Resources section of this book lists several publications which give more detailed information about avoiding false advertising. One of the very best of these publications is a free thirty-five-page booklet called "Advertising, Packaging, and Labeling" published by the Office of Consumer Affairs of the U.S. Department of Commerce. Addressed specifically to small and medium-sized businesses, this clearly-written booklet is also quite useful to ad agencies and graphic designers.

Appendix and Resources

LIMITED LICENSE FOR THE EXCLUSIVE
USE OF CERTAIN PHOTOGRAPHS

Agreement is made between _____
(hereinafter referred to as "Photographer") and _____
(hereinafter referred to as "Agency").

This Agreement is made with reference to the following facts:

A. That Photographer, an independent contractor, has prepared, at the instruction and under the direction of Agency personnel, certain Photographs (hereinafter referred to as "the Photographs").

B. That the Photographs may be described and identified as follows:
Subject(s) of Photographs:

_____

_____

_____

Date(s) on which Photographer shot Photographs:

_____

C. That the Agency, being engaged in the business of producing advertising materials and publications for use by its clients, wishes to employ the Photographs in the creation of certain of those advertising materials or publications.

1. That the Agency will pay to Photographer the sum of _____ Dollars ($_____), which amount it is agreed will constitute Photographer's entire fee and only payment for Photographer's services in preparing the Photographs and for the grant of rights made by Photographer herein, excluding reimbursement for such reasonable expenses as may be incurred by Photographer, within thirty (30) days after delivery by Photographer to the Agency of all existing physical embodiments of the Photographs, that is, all slides, transparencies, negatives, prints, etc., with the exception of a limited number of prints of the Photographs which Photographer may retain, with the Agency's consent (which consent may not be unreasonably withheld) for the sole purpose(s) of display in Photographer's professional portfolio or place of business or for entry in shows or competitions. Such slides, transparencies, negatives, prints, etc. shall be returned to Photographer upon request upon the expiration of the license granted herein; and

2. That Photographer grants to the Agency the sole and exclusive right to reproduce, publish, prepare derivative works of and from, incorporate into advertising materials and publications, display publicly and otherwise use, control the use of, and otherwise exploit the Photographs or

any of the Photographs for a period of _____ month(s) from the date written below. Photographer shall retain ownership of the physical embodiments of the Photographs, that is, slides, transparencies, negatives, prints, etc., but the Agency shall have possession of those embodiments except for such prints as Photographer may retain with the Agency's consent; and

3. That the Agency shall have the right to crop, edit, alter, or otherwise modify the Photographs to the extent that it, in its sole discretion, deems necessary to conform them to the style, design or physical dimensions of the advertising materials or publications into which they are incorporated or to suit them to such other use(s) as the Agency may choose to make of them; and

4. That Photographer warrants that he or she is the owner of copyright in the Photographs and possesses full right and authority to grant the rights herein granted. Photographer further warrants that the Photographs do not infringe the copyrights in any other works whatsoever, and do not invade any privacy, publicity, trademark, or other rights of any other person; however, such warranty by Photographer shall not relate to or include any specific, direct contribution(s) to the creation of the Photographs made by any employee or agent of the Agency. Photographer agrees to indemnify and hold the Agency harmless in any litigation or other dispute in which a third party challenges any of the warranties made by Photographer in this Paragraph; and

5. That this Agreement shall be governed by the laws of the State of _____ applicable to contracts made and to be performed therein and, shall be construed according to the Copyright Law of the United States, Title 17, Section 101, et seq., United States Code; and

6. That this Agreement shall enure to the benefit of and bind the parties and their respective heirs, representative, successors and assigns.

In witness whereof, the Agency and Photographer have executed this Agreement as of the _____ day of _____, 19_____.

PHOTOGRAPHER _____ AGENCY _____

Address _____ Address _____

_____ _____

Date of Birth _____ By:_____

Social Security Number _____ Title _____

-2-

ASSIGNMENT OF COPYRIGHT IN CERTAIN PHOTOGRAPHS

Agreement is made between _____
(hereinafter referred to as "Photographer") and _____
(hereinafter referred to as "Agency").

This Agreement is made with reference to the following facts:

    A. That Photographer, an independent contractor, has prepared, at the instruction and under the direction of Agency personnel, certain Photographs (hereinafer referred to as "the Photographs").

    B. That the Photographs may be described and identified as follows:
Subject(s) of Photographs:

_____

_____

_____

Date(s) on which Photographer shot Photographs:

_____

    C. That the Agency, being engaged in the business of producing advertising materials and publications for use by its clients, wishes to employ the Photographs in the creation of certain of those advertising materials or publications.

1. That the Agency will pay to Photographer the sum of _____ Dollars ($_____), which amount it is agreed will constitute Photographer's entire fee and only payment for Photographer's services in preparing the Photographs and for the grant of rights made by Photographer herein, excluding reimbursement for such reasonable expenses as may be incurred by Photographer, within thirty (30) days after delivery by Photographer to the Agency of all existing physical embodiments of the Photographs, that is, all slides, transparencies, negatives, prints, etc., with the exception of a limited number of prints of the Photographs which Photographer may retain, with the Agency consent (which consent may not be unreasonably withheld) for the sole purpose(s) of display in Photographer's professional portfolio or place of business or for entry in shows or competitions. Such slides, transparencies, negatives, prints, etc. shall be returned to Photographer upon request upon the expiration of the license granted herein; and

2. That Photographer hereby assigns, transfers and conveys to the Agency all right, title and interest in and to each and every Photograph described above together with the copyright(s) therein and the right to secure copyright registration therefor, in accordance with Sections 101, 204 and 205 of Title 17 of the United States Code, the Copyright Law of the United States. The above

assignment, transfer, and conveyance includes, without limitation, any and all features, sections and components of the Photographs, any and all derivative works derived therefrom, the United States and worldwide copyrights therein and any renewals or extensions thereof, and any and all other rights which Photographer now has or to which he or she may become entitled under existing or subsequently enacted federal, state, or foreign laws, including, but not limited to the following rights; to reproduce, publish, and display the Photographs publicly, to prepare derivative works of and from the Photographs, to incorporate the Photographs into advertising materials and publications and to otherwise exploit and control the use of the Photographs. The above assignment further includes any and all causes of action for infringement of the Photographs, past, present, and future, and any and all proceeds from such causes accrued and unpaid and hereafter accruing; and

3. That the Agency shall have the right to crop, edit, alter, or otherwise modify the Photographs to the extent that it, in its sole discretion, deems necessary to conform them to the style, design or physical dimensions of the advertising materials or publications into which they are incorporated or to suit them to such other use(s) as the Agency may choose to make of them; and

4. That Photographer warrants that he or she is the owner of copyright in the Photographs and possesses full right and authority to grant the rights herein granted. Photographer further warrants that the Photographs do not infringe the copyrights in any other works whatsoever, and do not invade any privacy, publicity, trademark, or other rights of any other person; however, such warranty by Photographer shall not relate to or include any specific, direct contribution(s) to the creation of the Photographs made by any employee or agent of the Agency. Photographer agrees to indemnify and hold the Agency harmless in any litigation or other dispute in which a third party challenges any of the warranties made by Photographer in this Paragraph; and

5. That this Agreement shall be governed by the laws of the State of _____ applicable to contracts made and to be performed therein and, shall be construed according to the Copyright Law of the United States, Title 17, Section 101, et seq., United States Code; and

6. That this Agreement shall enure to the benefit of and bind the parties and their respective heirs, representative, successors and assigns.

In witness whereof, the Agency and Photographer have executed this Agreement as of the _____ day of _____, 19_____.

PHOTOGRAPHER   AGENCY

Address   Address

Date of Birth   By:_____

Social Security Number   Title

-2-

PHOTOGRAPHER'S
WORK FOR HIRE AGREEMENT

Agreement is made between _____
(hereinafter referred to as "Photographer") and _____
(hereinafter referred to as "Agency").

This Agreement is made with reference to the following facts:

A. That Photographer, an independent contractor, has prepared, at the instruction and under the direction of Agency personnel, certain Photographs (hereinafter referred to as "the Photographs").

B. That the Photographs may be described and identified as follows:
Subject(s) of Photographs:

_____

_____

_____

Date(s) on which Photographer shot Photographs:

_____

C. That the Agency, being engaged in the business of producing advertising materials and publications for use by its clients, wishes to employ the Photographs in the creation of certain of those advertising materials or publications.

1. That the Agency will pay to Photographer the sum of _____ Dollars ($_____), which amount it is agreed will constitute Photographer's entire fee and only payment for Photographer's services in preparing the Photographs and for the grant of rights made by Photographer herein, excluding reimbursement for such reasonable expenses as may be incurred by Photographer, within thirty (30) days after delivery by Photographer to the Agency of all existing physical embodiments of the Photographs, that is, all slides, transparencies, negatives, prints, etc., with the exception of a limited number of prints of the Photographs which Photographer may retain, with the Agency consent (which consent may not be unreasonably withheld) for the sole purpose(s) of display in Photographer's professional portfolio or place of business or for entry in shows or competitions. Such slides, transparencies, negatives, prints, etc. shall be returned to Photographer upon request upon the expiration of the license granted herein; and

2. That the Photographs, including both negatives and prints, if any, and every other embodiment thereof, were specifically prepared for the Agency and comprise a work made for hire, as defined in Title 17, Section 101, et seq., United States Code, the Copyright Law of the United States.

Photographer further acknowledges that the Agency is considered the author of the Photographs and is the exclusive owner of copyright in the Photographs and of all rights comprised in copyright and that the Agency shall have the right to exercise all exclusive rights of copyright specified in 17 U.S.C., Section 101, et seq., the Copyright Law of the United States, for the full term of copyright and shall be entitled to register the copyright in and to the Photographs in the name of the Agency and to use the Photographs as it deems appropriate and necessary without further payment to Photographer; and

3. That this Agreement shall be governed by the laws of the State of _____ applicable to contracts made and to be performed therein and, with respect to the work-for-hire provisions of this Agreement, shall be construed according to the Copyright Law of the United States, Title 17, Section 101, et seq., United States Code; and

4. That this Agreement shall enure to the benefit of and bind the parties and their respective heirs, representative, successors and assigns.

In witness whereof, the Agency and Photographer have executed this Agreement as of the _____ day of _____, 19_____.

_____
PHOTOGRAPHER

_____
Address

_____

_____
Date of Birth

_____
Social Security Number

_____
AGENCY

_____
Address

_____

By:_____

_____
Title

-2-

⌨ Filling Out Application Form VA

Detach and read these instructions before completing this form. Make sure all applicable spaces have been filled in before you return this form.

BASIC INFORMATION

When to Use This Form: Use Form VA for copyright registration of published or unpublished works of the visual arts. This category consists of "pictorial, graphic, or sculptural works," including two-dimensional and three-dimensional works of fine, graphic, and applied art, photographs, prints and art reproductions, maps, globes, charts, technical drawings, diagrams, and models.

What Does Copyright Protect? Copyright in a work of the visual arts protects those pictorial, graphic, or sculptural elements that, either alone or in combination, represent an "original work of authorship." The statute declares: "In no case does copyright protection for an original work of authorship extend to any idea, procedure, process, system, method of operation, concept, principle, or discovery, regardless of the form in which it is described, explained, illustrated, or embodied in such work."

Works of Artistic Craftsmanship and Designs: "Works of artistic craftsmanship" are registrable on Form VA, but the statute makes clear that protection extends to "their form" and not to "their mechanical or utilitarian aspects." The "design of a useful article" is considered copyrightable "only if, and only to the extent that, such design incorporates pictorial, graphic, or sculptural features that can be identified separately from, and are capable of existing independently of, the utilitarian aspects of the article."

Labels and Advertisements: Works prepared for use in connection with the sale or advertisement of goods and services are registrable if they contain "original work of authorship." Use Form VA if the copyrightable material in the work you are registering is mainly pictorial or graphic; use Form TX if it consists mainly of text. **NOTE:** Words and short phrases such as names, titles, and slogans cannot be protected by copyright, and the same is true of standard symbols, emblems, and other commonly used graphic designs that are in the public domain. When used commercially, material of that sort can sometimes be protected under state laws of unfair competition or under the Federal trademark laws. For information about trademark registration, write to the Commissioner of Patents and Trademarks, Washington, D.C. 20231.

Deposit to Accompany Application: An application for copyright registration must be accompanied by a deposit consisting of copies representing the entire work for which registration is to be made.

Unpublished Work: Deposit one complete copy.

Published Work: Deposit two complete copies of the best edition.

Work First Published Outside the United States: Deposit one complete copy of the first foreign edition.

Contribution to a Collective Work: Deposit one complete copy of the best edition of the collective work.

The Copyright Notice: For works first published on or after March 1, 1989, the law provides that a copyright notice on a specified form "may be placed on all publicly distributed copies from which the work can be visually perceived." Use of the copyright notice is the responsibility of the copyright owner and does not require advance permission from the Copyright Office. The required form of the notice for copies generally consists of three elements: (1) the symbol "©", or the word "Copyright," or the abbreviation "Copr."; (2) the year of first publication; and (3) the name of the owner of copyright. For example: "© 1989 Jane Cole." The notice is to be affixed to the copies "in such manner and location as to give reasonable notice of the claim of copyright." Works first published prior to March 1, 1989, must carry the notice or risk loss of copyright protection.

For information about notice requirements for works published before March 1, 1989, or other copyright information, write: Information Section, LM-401, Copyright Office, Library of Congress, Washington, D.C. 20559.

PRIVACY ACT ADVISORY STATEMENT Required by the Privacy Act of 1974 (PL. 93-579)
The authority for requesting this information is title 17 U.S.C. secs. 409 and 410. Furnishing the requested information is voluntary. But if the information is not furnished, it may be necessary to delay or refuse registration and you may not be entitled to certain relief, remedies, and benefits provided in chapters 4 and 5 of title 17 U.S.C.
The principal uses of the requested information are the establishment and maintenance of a public record and the examination of the application for compliance with legal requirements
Other routine uses include public inspection and copying, preparation of public indexes, preparation of public catalogs of copyright registrations, and preparation of search reports upon request.
NOTE: No other advisory statement will be given in connection with this application. Please keep this statement and refer to it if we communicate with you regarding this application.

LINE-BY-LINE INSTRUCTIONS

1 SPACE 1: Title

Title of This Work: Every work submitted for copyright registration must be given a title to identify that particular work. If the copies of the work bear a title (or an identifying phrase that could serve as a title), transcribe that wording completely and exactly on the application. Indexing of the registration and future identification of the work will depend on the information you give here.

Previous or Alternative Titles: Complete this space if there are any additional titles for the work under which someone searching for the registration might be likely to look, or under which a document pertaining to the work might be recorded.

Publication as a Contribution: If the work being registered is a contribution to a periodical, serial, or collection, give the title of the contribution in the "Title of This Work" space. Then, in the line headed "Publication as a Contribution," give information about the collective work in which the contribution appeared.

Nature of This Work: Briefly describe the general nature or character of the pictorial, graphic, or sculptural work being registered for copyright. Examples: "Oil Painting"; "Charcoal Drawing"; "Etching"; "Sculpture"; "Map"; "Photograph"; "Scale Model"; "Lithographic Print"; "Jewelry Design"; "Fabric Design."

2 SPACE 2: Author(s)

General Instructions: After reading these instructions, decide who are the "authors" of this work for copyright purposes. Then, unless the work is a "collective work," give the requested information about every "author" who contributed any appreciable amount of copyrightable matter to this version of the work. If you need further space, request additional Continuation Sheets. In the case of a collective work, such as a catalog of paintings or collection of cartoons by various authors, give information about the author of the collective work as a whole.

Name of Author: The fullest form of the author's name should be given. Unless the work was "made for hire," the individual who actually created the work is its "author." In the case of a work made for hire, the statute provides that "the employer or other person for whom the work was prepared is considered the author."

What Is a "Work Made for Hire"? A "work made for hire" is defined as: (1) "a work prepared by an employee within the scope of his or her employment"; or (2) "a work specially ordered or commissioned for use as a contribution to a collective work, as a part of a motion picture or other audiovisual work, as a translation, as a supplementary work, as a compilation, as an instructional text, as a test, as answer material for a test, or as an atlas, if the parties expressly agree in a written instrument signed by them that the work shall be considered a work made for hire." If you have checked "Yes" to indicate that the work was "made for hire," you must give the full legal name of the employer (or other person for whom the work was prepared). You may also include the name of the employee along with the name of the employer (for example: "Elster Publishing Co., employer for hire of John Ferguson").

"Anonymous" or "Pseudonymous" Work: An author's contribution to a work is "anonymous" if that author is not identified on the copies or phonorecords of the work. An author's contribution to a work is "pseudonymous" if that author is identified on the copies or phonorecords under a fictitious name. If the work is "anonymous" you may: (1) leave the line blank; or (2) state "anonymous" on the line; or (3) reveal the author's identity. If the work is "pseudonymous" you may: (1) leave the line blank; or (2) give the pseudonym and identify it as such (for example: "Huntley Haverstock, pseudonym"); or (3) reveal the author's name, making clear which is the real name and which is the pseudonym (for example: "Henry Leek, whose pseudonym is Priam Farrel"). However, the citizenship or domicile of the author **must** be given in all cases.

Dates of Birth and Death: If the author is dead, the statute requires that the year of death be included in the application unless the work is anonymous or pseudonymous. The author's birth date is optional, but is useful as a form of identification. Leave this space blank if the author's contribution was a "work made for hire."

Author's Nationality or Domicile: Give the country of which the author is a citizen, or the country in which the author is domiciled. Nationality or domicile **must** be given in all cases.

Nature of Authorship: Give a brief general statement of the nature of this particular author's contribution to the work. Examples: "Painting"; "Photograph"; "Silk Screen Reproduction"; "Co-author of Cartographic Material"; "Technical Drawing"; "Text and Artwork."

3 SPACE 3: Creation and Publication

General Instructions: Do not confuse "creation" with "publication." Every application for copyright registration must state "the year in which creation of the work was completed." Give the date and nation of first publication only if the work has been published.

Creation: Under the statute, a work is "created" when it is fixed in a copy or phonorecord for the first time. Where a work has been prepared over a period of time, the part of the work existing in fixed form on a particular date constitutes the created work on that date. The date you give here should be the year in which the author completed the particular version for which registration is now being sought, even if other versions exist or if further changes or additions are planned.

Publication: The statute defines "publication" as "the distribution of copies or phonorecords of a work to the public by sale or other transfer of ownership, or by rental, lease, or lending"; a work is also "published" if there has been an "offering to distribute copies or phonorecords to a group of persons for purposes of further distribution, public performance, or public display." Give the full date (month, day, year) when, and the country where, publication first occurred. If first publication took place simultaneously in the United States and other countries, it is sufficient to state "U.S.A."

4 SPACE 4: Claimant(s)

Name(s) and Address(es) of Copyright Claimant(s): Give the name(s) and address(es) of the copyright claimant(s) in this work even if the claimant is the same as the author. Copyright in a work belongs initially to the author of the work (including, in the case of a work made for hire, the employer or other person for whom the work was prepared.) The copyright claimant is either the author of the work or a person or organization to whom the copyright initially belonging to the author has been transferred.

Transfer: The statute provides that, if the copyright claimant is not the author, the application for registration must contain "a brief statement of how the claimant obtained ownership of the copyright." If any copyright claimant named in space 4 is not an author named in space 2, give a brief, general statement summarizing the means by which that claimant obtained ownership of the copyright. Examples: "By written contract"; "Transfer of all rights by author"; "Assignment"; "By will." Do not attach transfer documents or other attachments or riders.

5 SPACE 5: Previous Registration

General Instructions: The questions in space 5 are intended to find out whether an earlier registration has been made for this work and, if so, whether there is any basis for a new registration. As a rule, only one basic copyright registration can be made for the same version of a particular work.

Same Version: If this version is substantially the same as the work covered by a previous registration, a second registration is not generally possible unless: (1) the work has been registered in unpublished form and a second registration is now being sought to cover this first published edition; or (2) someone other than the author is identified as copyright claimant in the earlier registration, and the author is now seeking registration in his or her own name. If either of these two exceptions apply, check the appropriate box and give the earlier registration number and date. Otherwise, do not submit Form VA; instead, write the Copyright Office for information about supplementary registration or recordation of transfers of copyright ownership.

Changed Version: If the work has been changed, and you are now seeking registration to cover the additions or revisions, check the last box in space 5, give the earlier registration number and date, and complete both parts of space 6 in accordance with the instructions below.

Previous Registration Number and Date: If more than one previous registration has been made for the work, give the number and date of the latest registration.

6 SPACE 6: Derivative Work or Compilation

General Instructions: Complete space 6 if this work is a "changed version," "compilation," or "derivative work," and if it incorporates one or more earlier works that have already been published or registered for copyright, or that have fallen into the public domain. A "compilation" is defined as "a work formed by the collection and assembling of preexisting materials or of data that are selected, coordinated, or arranged in such a way that the resulting work as a whole constitutes an original work of authorship." A "derivative work" is "a work based on one or more preexisting works." Examples of derivative works include reproductions of works of art, sculptures based on drawings, lithographs based on paintings, maps based on previously published sources, or "any other form in which a work may be recast, transformed, or adapted." Derivative works also include works "consisting of editorial revisions, annotations, or other modifications" if these changes, as a whole, represent an original work of authorship.

Preexisting Material (space 6a): Complete this space and space 6b for derivative works. In this space identify the preexisting work that has been recast, transformed, or adapted. Examples of preexisting material might be "Grunewald Altarpiece"; or "19th century quilt design." Do not complete this space for compilations.

Material Added to This Work (space 6b): Give a brief, general statement of the **additional** new material covered by the copyright claim for which registration is sought. In the case of a derivative work, identify this new material. Examples: "Adaptation of design and additional artistic work"; "Reproduction of painting by photolithography"; "Additional cartographic material"; "Compilation of photographs." If the work is a compilation, give a brief, general statement describing both the material that has been compiled and the compilation itself. Example: "Compilation of 19th Century Political Cartoons."

7,8,9 SPACE 7, 8, 9: Fee, Correspondence, Certification, Return Address

Deposit Account: If you maintain a Deposit Account in the Copyright Office, identify it in space 7. Otherwise leave the space blank and send the fee of $10 with your application and deposit.

Correspondence (space 7): This space should contain the name, address, area code, and telephone number of the person to be consulted if correspondence about this application becomes necessary.

Certification (space 8): The application cannot be accepted unless it bears the date and the **handwritten signature** of the author or other copyright claimant, or of the owner of exclusive right(s) or the duly authorized agent of the author, claimant, or owner of exclusive right(s).

Address for Return of Certificate (space 9): The address box must be completed legibly since the certificate will be returned in a window envelope.

MORE INFORMATION

Form of Deposit for Works of the Visual Arts

Exceptions to General Deposit Requirements: As explained on the reverse side of this page, the statutory deposit requirements (generally one copy for unpublished works and two copies for published works) will vary for particular kinds of works of the visual arts. The copyright law authorizes the Register of Copyrights to issue regulations specifying "the administrative classes into which works are to be placed for purposes of deposit and registration, and the nature of the copies or phonorecords to be deposited in the various classes specified." For particular classes, the regulations may require or permit "the deposit of identifying material instead of copies or phonorecords," or "the deposit of only one copy or phonorecord where two would normally be required."

What Should You Deposit? The detailed requirements with respect to the kind of deposit to accompany an application on Form VA are contained in the Copyright Office Regulations. The following does not cover all of the deposit requirements, but is intended to give you some general guidance.

For an Unpublished Work, the material deposited should represent the entire copyrightable content of the work for which registration is being sought.

For a Published Work, the material deposited should generally consist of two complete copies of the best edition. Exceptions: (1) For certain types of works, one complete copy may be deposited instead of two. These include greeting cards, postcards, stationery, labels, advertisements, scientific drawings, and globes; (2) For most three-dimensional sculptural works, and for certain two-dimensional works, the Copyright Office Regulations require deposit of identifying material (photographs or drawings in a specified form) rather than copies; and (3) Under certain circumstances, for works published in five copies or less or in limited, numbered editions, the deposit may consist of one copy or of identifying reproductions.

FORM VA
UNITED STATES COPYRIGHT OFFICE

REGISTRATION NUMBER

_____

VA   VAU

EFFECTIVE DATE OF REGISTRATION

_____

Month   Day   Year

DO NOT WRITE ABOVE THIS LINE. IF YOU NEED MORE SPACE, USE A SEPARATE CONTINUATION SHEET.

1

TITLE OF THIS WORK ▼   **NATURE OF THIS WORK ▼** See instructions

PREVIOUS OR ALTERNATIVE TITLES ▼

PUBLICATION AS A CONTRIBUTION If this work was published as a contribution to a periodical, serial, or collection, give information about the collective work in which the contribution appeared.   **Title of Collective Work ▼**

If published in a periodical or serial give: Volume ▼   Number ▼   Issue Date ▼   On Pages ▼

2

a

NAME OF AUTHOR ▼   **DATES OF BIRTH AND DEATH**
Year Born ▼   Year Died ▼

Was this contribution to the work a "work made for hire"?
☐ Yes
☐ No

AUTHOR'S NATIONALITY OR DOMICILE
Name of Country
OR { Citizen of ▶ _____
Domiciled in ▶ _____

WAS THIS AUTHOR'S CONTRIBUTION TO THE WORK
Anonymous? ☐ Yes ☐ No
Pseudonymous? ☐ Yes ☐ No
If the answer to either of these questions is "Yes," see detailed instructions.

NATURE OF AUTHORSHIP Briefly describe nature of the material created by this author in which copyright is claimed. ▼

NOTE

Under the law, the "author" of a "work made for hire" is generally the employer, not the employee (see instructions). For any part of this work that was "made for hire" check "Yes" in the space provided, give the employer (or other person for whom the work was prepared) as "Author" of that part, and leave the space for dates of birth and death blank.

b

NAME OF AUTHOR ▼   **DATES OF BIRTH AND DEATH**
Year Born ▼   Year Died ▼

Was this contribution to the work a "work made for hire"?
☐ Yes
☐ No

AUTHOR'S NATIONALITY OR DOMICILE
Name of country
OR { Citizen of ▶ _____
Domiciled in ▶ _____

WAS THIS AUTHOR'S CONTRIBUTION TO THE WORK
Anonymous? ☐ Yes ☐ No
Pseudonymous? ☐ Yes ☐ No
If the answer to either of these questions is "Yes," see detailed instructions.

NATURE OF AUTHORSHIP Briefly describe nature of the material created by this author in which copyright is claimed. ▼

c

NAME OF AUTHOR ▼   **DATES OF BIRTH AND DEATH**
Year Born ▼   Year Died ▼

Was this contribution to the work a "work made for hire"?
☐ Yes
☐ No

AUTHOR'S NATIONALITY OR DOMICILE
Name of Country
OR { Citizen of ▶ _____
Domiciled in ▶ _____

WAS THIS AUTHOR'S CONTRIBUTION TO THE WORK
Anonymous? ☐ Yes ☐ No
Pseudonymous? ☐ Yes ☐ No
If the answer to either of these questions is "Yes," see detailed instructions.

NATURE OF AUTHORSHIP Briefly describe nature of the material created by this author in which copyright is claimed. ▼

3

a

YEAR IN WHICH CREATION OF THIS WORK WAS COMPLETED This information must be given ◀ Year In all cases.

b

DATE AND NATION OF FIRST PUBLICATION OF THIS PARTICULAR WORK
Complete this information Month ▶ _____ Day ▶ _____ Year ▶ _____
ONLY if this work has been published.   ◀ Nation

4

See instructions before completing this space.

COPYRIGHT CLAIMANT(S) Name and address must be given even if the claimant is the same as the author given in space 2.▼

TRANSFER If the claimant(s) named here in space 4 are different from the author(s) named in space 2, give a brief statement of how the claimant(s) obtained ownership of the copyright.▼

APPLICATION RECEIVED

ONE DEPOSIT RECEIVED

TWO DEPOSITS RECEIVED

REMITTANCE NUMBER AND DATE

DO NOT WRITE HERE
OFFICE USE ONLY

MORE ON BACK ▶ • Complete all applicable spaces (numbers 5-9) on the reverse side of this page.
• See detailed instructions.   • Sign the form at line 8.

DO NOT WRITE HERE
Page 1 of _____ pages.

EXAMINED BY

FORM VA

CHECKED BY

☐ CORRESPONDENCE
Yes

FOR
COPYRIGHT
OFFICE
USE
ONLY

DO NOT WRITE ABOVE THIS LINE. IF YOU NEED MORE SPACE, USE A SEPARATE CONTINUATION SHEET.

PREVIOUS REGISTRATION Has registration for this work, or for an earlier version of this work, already been made in the Copyright Office?
☐ Yes ☐ No If your answer is "Yes," why is another registration being sought? (Check appropriate box) ▼
☐ This is the first published edition of a work previously registered in unpublished form.
☐ This is the first application submitted by this author as copyright claimant.
☐ This is a changed version of the work, as shown by space 6 on this application.
If your answer is "Yes," give: **Previous Registration Number ▼**   **Year of Registration ▼**

5

DERIVATIVE WORK OR COMPILATION Complete both space 6a & 6b for a derivative work; complete only 6b for a compilation.
a. Preexisting Material Identify any preexisting work or works that this work is based on or incorporates. ▼

6

See instructions
before completing
this space

b. Material Added to This Work Give a brief, general statement of the material that has been added to this work and in which copyright is claimed.▼

DEPOSIT ACCOUNT If the registration fee is to be charged to a Deposit Account established in the Copyright Office, give name and number of Account.
Name ▼   **Account Number ▼**

7

CORRESPONDENCE Give name and address to which correspondence about this application should be sent.   Name/Address/Apt/City/State/Zip ▼

Area Code & Telephone Number ▶

Be sure to
give your
daytime phone
◀ number

CERTIFICATION* I, the undersigned, hereby certify that I am the
Check only one ▼
☐ author
☐ other copyright claimant
☐ owner of exclusive right(s)
☐ authorized agent of _____
          Name of author or other copyright claimant, or owner of exclusive right(s) ▲

8

of the work identified in this application and that the statements made
by me in this application are correct to the best of my knowledge.

Typed or printed name and date ▼ If this application gives a date of publication in space 3, do not sign and submit it before that date.

_____ date ▶ _____

Handwritten signature (X) ▼

**MAIL
CERTIFI-
CATE TO**

Name ▼

Number Street Apartment Number ▼

**Certificate
will be
mailed in
window
envelope**

City State ZIP ▼

YOU MUST
• Complete all necessary spaces
• Sign your application in space 8
SEND ALL 3 ELEMENTS
IN THE SAME PACKAGE
1. Application form
2. Non-refundable $10 filing fee
   in check or money order
   payable to Register of Copyrights
3. Deposit material
MAIL TO:
Register of Copyrights
Library of Congress
Washington, D.C. 20559

9

* 17 U.S.C. § 506(e) Any person who knowingly makes a false representation of a material fact in the application for copyright registration provided for by section 409, or in any written statement filed in connection with the application, shall be fined not more than $2,500.

June 1989—100,000

U.S. GOVERNMENT PRINTING OFFICE: 1989—241-428 80.023

⧈ Filling Out Application Form TX

Detach and read these instructions before completing this form. Make sure all applicable spaces have been filled in before you return this form.

BASIC INFORMATION

When to Use This Form: Use Form TX for registration of published or unpublished non-dramatic literary works, excluding periodicals or serial issues. This class includes a wide variety of works: fiction, non-fiction, poetry, textbooks, reference works, directories, catalogs, advertising copy, compilations of information, and computer programs. For periodicals and serials, use Form SE.

Deposit to Accompany Application: An application for copyright registration must be accompanied by a deposit consisting of copies or phonorecords representing the entire work for which registration is to be made. The following are the general deposit requirements as set forth in the statute:

Unpublished Work: Deposit one complete copy (or phonorecord).

Published Work: Deposit two complete copies (or phonorecords) of the best edition.

Work First Published Outside the United States: Deposit one complete copy (or phonorecord) of the first foreign edition.

Contribution to a Collective Work: Deposit one complete copy (or phonorecord) of the best edition of the collective work.

The Copyright Notice: For works first published on or after March 1, 1989, the law provides that a copyright notice on a specified form "may be placed on all publicly distributed copies from which the work can be visually perceived." Use of the copyright notice is the responsibility of the copyright owner and does not require advance permission from the Copyright Office. The required form of the notice for copies generally consists of three elements: (1) the symbol "©", or the word "Copyright," or the abbreviation "Copr."; (2) the year of first publication; and (3) the name of the owner of copyright. For example: "© 1989 Jane Cole." The notice is to be affixed to the copies "in such manner and location as to give reasonable notice of the claim of copyright." Works first published prior to March 1, 1989, **must** carry the notice or risk loss of copyright protection.

For information about notice requirements for works published before March 1, 1989, or other copyright information, write: Information Section, LM-401, Copyright Office, Library of Congress, Washington, D.C. 20559.

LINE-BY-LINE INSTRUCTIONS

1 SPACE 1: Title

Title of This Work: Every work submitted for copyright registration must be given a title to identify that particular work. If the copies or phonorecords of the work bear a title (or an identifying phrase that could serve as a title), transcribe that wording *completely* and *exactly* on the application. Indexing of the registration and future identification of the work will depend on the information you give here.

Previous or Alternative Titles: Complete this space if there are any additional titles for the work under which someone searching for the registration might be likely to look, or under which a document pertaining to the work might be recorded.

Publication as a Contribution: If the work being registered is a contribution to a periodical, serial, or collection, give the title of the contribution in the "Title of this Work" space. Then, in the line headed "Publication as a Contribution," give information about the collective work in which the contribution appeared.

2 SPACE 2: Author(s)

General Instructions: After reading these instructions, decide who are the "authors" of this work for copyright purposes. Then, unless the work is a "collective work," give the requested information about every "author" who contributed any appreciable amount of copyrightable matter to this version of the work. If you need further space, request additional Continuation sheets. In the case of a collective work, such as an anthology, collection of essays, or encyclopedia, give information about the author of the collective work as a whole.

Name of Author: The fullest form of the author's name should be given. Unless the work was "made for hire," the individual who actually created the work is its "author." In the case of a work made for hire, the statute provides that "the employer or other person for whom the work was prepared is considered the author."

What is a "Work Made for Hire"? A "work made for hire" is defined as: (1) "a work prepared by an employee within the scope of his or her employment"; or (2) "a work specially ordered or commissioned for use as a contribution to a collective work, as a part of a motion picture or other audiovisual work, as a translation, as a supplementary work, as a compilation, as an instructional text, as a test, as answer material for a test, or as an atlas, if the parties expressly agree in a written instrument signed by them that the work shall be considered a work made for hire." If you have checked "Yes" to indicate that the work was "made for hire," you must give the full legal name of the employer (or other person for whom the work was prepared). You may also include the name of the employee along with the name of the employer (for example: "Elster Publishing Co., employer for hire of John Ferguson").

"Anonymous" or "Pseudonymous" Work: An author's contribution to a work is "anonymous" if that author is not identified on the copies or phonorecords of the work. An author's contribution to a work is "pseudonymous" if that author is identified on the copies or phonorecords under a fictitious name. If the work is "anonymous" you may: (1) leave the line blank; or (2) state " anonymous" on the line; or (3) reveal the author's identity. If the work is "pseudonymous" you may : (1) leave the line blank; or (2) give the pseudonym and identify it as such (for example: "Huntley Haverstock, pseudonym"); or (3) reveal the author's name, making clear which is the real name and which is the pseudonym (for example: "Judith Barton, whose pseudonym is Madeline Elster"). However, the citizenship or domicile of the author **must** be given in all cases.

Dates of Birth and Death: If the author is dead, the statute requires that the year of death be included in the application unless the work is anonymous or pseudonymous. The author's birth date is optional, but is useful as a form of identification. Leave this space blank if the author's contribution was a "work made for hire."

Author's Nationality or Domicile: Give the country of which the author is a citizen, or the country in which the author is domiciled. Nationality or domicile **must** be given in all cases.

Nature of Authorship: After the words "Nature of Authorship" give a brief general statement of the nature of this particular author's contribution to the work. Examples: "Entire text"; "Coauthor of entire text"; "Chapters 11-14"; "Editorial revisions"; "Compilation and English translation"; "New text."

3 SPACE 3: Creation and Publication

General Instructions: Do not confuse "creation" with "publication." Every application for copyright registration must state "the year in which creation of the work was completed." Give the date and nation of first publication only if the work has been published.

Creation: Under the statute, a work is "created" when it is fixed in a copy or phonorecord for the first time. Where a work has been prepared over a period of time, the part of the work existing in fixed form on a particular date constitutes the created work on that date. The date you give here should be the year in which the author completed the particular version for which registration is now being sought, even if other versions exist or if further changes or additions are planned.

Publication: The statute defines "publication" as "the distribution of copies or phonorecords of a work to the public by sale or other transfer of ownership, or by rental, lease, or lending"; a work is also "published" if there has been an "offering to distribute copies or phonorecords to a group of persons for purposes of further distribution, public performance, or public display." Give the full date (month, day, year) when, and the country where, publication first occurred. If first publication took place simultaneously in the United States and other countries, it is sufficient to state "U.S.A."

4 SPACE 4: Claimant(s)

Name(s) and Address(es) of Copyright Claimant(s): Give the name(s) and address(es) of the copyright claimant(s) in this work even if the claimant is the same as the author. Copyright in a work belongs initially to the author of the work (including, in the case of a work made for hire, the employer or other person for whom the work was prepared). The copyright claimant is either the author of the work or a person or organization to whom the copyright initially belonging to the author has been transferred.

Transfer: The statute provides that, if the copyright claimant is not the author, the application for registration must contain "a brief statement of how the claimant obtained ownership of the copyright." If any copyright claimant named in space 4 is not an author named in space 2, give a brief, general statement summarizing the means by which that claimant obtained ownership of the copyright. Examples: "By written contract"; "Transfer of all rights by author"; "Assignment"; "By will." Do not attach transfer documents or other attachments or riders.

5 SPACE 5: Previous Registration

General Instructions: The questions in space 5 are intended to find out whether an earlier registration has been made for this work and, if so, whether there is any basis for a new registration. As a general rule, only one basic copyright registration can be made for the same version of a particular work.

Same Version: If this version is substantially the same as the work covered by a previous registration, a second registration is not generally possible unless: (1) the work has been registered in unpublished form and a second registration is now being sought to cover this first published edition; or (2) someone other than the author is identified as copyright claimant in the earlier registration, and the author is now seeking registration in his or her own name. If either of these two situations applies, check the appropriate box and give the earlier registration number and date. Otherwise, do not submit Form TX; instead, write the Copyright Office for information about supplementary registration or recordation of transfers of copyright ownership.

Changed Version: If the work has been changed, and you are now seeking registration to cover the additions or revisions, check the last box in space 5, give the earlier registration number and date, and complete both parts of space 6 in accordance with the instructions below.

Previous Registration Number and Date: If more than one previous registration has been made for the work, give the number and date of the latest registration.

6 SPACE 6: Derivative Work or Compilation

General Instructions: Complete space 6 if this work is a "changed version," "compilation," or "derivative work," and if it incorporates one or more earlier works that have already been published or registered for copyright, or that have fallen into the public domain. A "compilation" is defined as "a work formed by the collection and assembling of preexisting materials or of data that are selected, coordinated, or arranged in such a way that the resulting work as a whole constitutes an original work of authorship." A "derivative work" is "a work based on one or more preexisting works." Examples of derivative works include translations, fictionalizations, abridgments, condensations, or "any other form in which a work may be recast, transformed, or adapted." Derivative works also include works "consisting of editorial revisions, annotations, or other modifications" if these changes, as a whole, represent an original work of authorship.

Preexisting Material (space 6a): For derivative works, complete this space and space 6b. In space 6a identify the preexisting work that has been recast, transformed, or adapted. An example of preexisting material might be: "Russian version of Goncharov's 'Oblomov'." Do not complete space 6a for compilations.

Material Added to This Work (space 6b): Give a brief, general statement of the new material covered by the copyright claim for which registration is sought. Derivative work examples include: "Foreword, editing, critical annotations"; "Translation"; "Chapters 11-17." If the work is a compilation, describe both the compilation itself and the material that has been compiled. Example: "Compilation of certain 1917 Speeches by Woodrow Wilson." A work may be both a derivative work and compilation, in which case a sample statement might be: "Compilation and additional new material."

7 SPACE 7: Manufacturing Provisions

Due to the expiration of the Manufacturing Clause of the copyright law on June 30, 1986, this space has been deleted.

8 SPACE 8: Reproduction for Use of Blind or Physically Handicapped Individuals

General Instructions: One of the major programs of the Library of Congress is to provide Braille editions and special recordings of works for the exclusive use of the blind and physically handicapped. In an effort to simplify and speed up the copyright licensing procedures that are a necessary part of this program, section 710 of the copyright statute provides for the establishment of a voluntary licensing system to be tied in with copyright registration. Copyright Office regulations provide that you may grant a license for such reproduction and distribution solely for the use of persons who are certified by competent authority as unable to read normal printed material as a result of physical limitations. The license is entirely voluntary, nonexclusive, and may be terminated upon 90 days notice.

How to Grant the License: If you wish to grant it, check one of the three boxes in space 8. Your check in one of these boxes, together with your signature in space 10, will mean that the Library of Congress can proceed to reproduce and distribute under the license without further paperwork. For further information, write for Circular R63.

9,10,11 SPACE 9, 10, 11: Fee, Correspondence, Certification, Return Address

Deposit Account: If you maintain a Deposit Account in the Copyright Office, identify it in space 9. Otherwise leave the space blank and send the fee of $10 with your application and deposit.

Correspondence (space 9): This space should contain the name, address, area code, and telephone number of the person to be consulted if correspondence about this application becomes necessary.

Certification (space 10): The application can not be accepted unless it bears the date and the **handwritten signature** of the author or other copyright claimant, or of the duly authorized agent of author, claimant, or owner of exclusive right(s).

Address for Return of Certificate (space 11): The address box must be completed legibly since the certificate will be returned in a window envelope.

FORM TX
UNITED STATES COPYRIGHT OFFICE

REGISTRATION NUMBER

	TX	TXU

EFFECTIVE DATE OF REGISTRATION

Month	Day	Year

DO NOT WRITE ABOVE THIS LINE. IF YOU NEED MORE SPACE, USE A SEPARATE CONTINUATION SHEET.

1

TITLE OF THIS WORK ▼

PREVIOUS OR ALTERNATIVE TITLES ▼

PUBLICATION AS A CONTRIBUTION If this work was published as a contribution to a periodical, serial, or collection, give information about the collective work in which the contribution appeared. **Title of Collective Work ▼**

If published in a periodical or serial give: **Volume ▼** **Number ▼** **Issue Date ▼** **On Pages ▼**

2

a

NAME OF AUTHOR ▼

DATES OF BIRTH AND DEATH
Year Born ▼ Year Died ▼

Was this contribution to the work a "work made for hire"?
☐ Yes
☐ No

AUTHOR'S NATIONALITY OR DOMICILE
Name of Country
OR { Citizen of ▶ _____
Domiciled in ▶ _____

WAS THIS AUTHOR'S CONTRIBUTION TO THE WORK
Anonymous? ☐ Yes ☐ No
Pseudonymous? ☐ Yes ☐ No
If the answer to either of these questions is "Yes," see detailed instructions.

NATURE OF AUTHORSHIP Briefly describe nature of the material created by this author in which copyright is claimed. ▼

NOTE
Under the law, the "author" of a "work made for hire" is generally the employer, not the employee (see instructions). For any part of this work that was "made for hire" check "Yes" in the space provided, give the employer (or other person for whom the work was prepared) as "Author" of that part, and leave the space for dates of birth and death blank.

b

NAME OF AUTHOR ▼

DATES OF BIRTH AND DEATH
Year Born ▼ Year Died ▼

Was this contribution to the work a "work made for hire"?
☐ Yes
☐ No

AUTHOR'S NATIONALITY OR DOMICILE
Name of country
OR { Citizen of ▶ _____
Domiciled in ▶ _____

WAS THIS AUTHOR'S CONTRIBUTION TO THE WORK
Anonymous? ☐ Yes ☐ No
Pseudonymous? ☐ Yes ☐ No
If the answer to either of these questions is "Yes," see detailed instructions.

NATURE OF AUTHORSHIP Briefly describe nature of the material created by this author in which copyright is claimed. ▼

c

NAME OF AUTHOR ▼

DATES OF BIRTH AND DEATH
Year Born ▼ Year Died ▼

Was this contribution to the work a "work made for hire"?
☐ Yes
☐ No

AUTHOR'S NATIONALITY OR DOMICILE
Name of Country
OR { Citizen of ▶ _____
Domiciled in ▶ _____

WAS THIS AUTHOR'S CONTRIBUTION TO THE WORK
Anonymous? ☐ Yes ☐ No
Pseudonymous? ☐ Yes ☐ No
If the answer to either of these questions is "Yes," see detailed instructions.

NATURE OF AUTHORSHIP Briefly describe nature of the material created by this author in which copyright is claimed. ▼

3

YEAR IN WHICH CREATION OF THIS WORK WAS COMPLETED This information must be given in all cases.
◄ Year

DATE AND NATION OF FIRST PUBLICATION OF THIS PARTICULAR WORK
Complete this information Month ▶ _____ Day ▶ _____ Year ▶ _____
ONLY if this work has been published.
◄ Nation

4

See instructions before completing this space

COPYRIGHT CLAIMANT(S) Name and address must be given even if the claimant is the same as the author given in space 2. ▼

TRANSFER If the claimant(s) named here in space 4 are different from the author(s) named in space 2, give a brief statement of how the claimant(s) obtained ownership of the copyright. ▼

DO NOT WRITE HERE OFFICE USE ONLY

APPLICATION RECEIVED

ONE DEPOSIT RECEIVED

TWO DEPOSITS RECEIVED

REMITTANCE NUMBER AND DATE

MORE ON BACK ▶ • Complete all applicable spaces (numbers 5-11) on the reverse side of this page.
• See detailed instructions. • Sign the form at line 10.

DO NOT WRITE HERE
Page 1 of _____ pages

EXAMINED BY

FORM TX

CHECKED BY

☐ CORRESPONDENCE
   Yes

☐ DEPOSIT ACCOUNT
   FUNDS USED

FOR
COPYRIGHT
OFFICE
USE
ONLY

DO NOT WRITE ABOVE THIS LINE. IF YOU NEED MORE SPACE, USE A SEPARATE CONTINUATION SHEET.

PREVIOUS REGISTRATION Has registration for this work, or for an earlier version of this work, already been made in the Copyright Office?
☐ Yes ☐ No If your answer is "Yes," why is another registration being sought? (Check appropriate box) ▼
☐ This is the first published edition of a work previously registered in unpublished form.
☐ This is the first application submitted by this author as copyright claimant.
☐ This is a changed version of the work, as shown by space 6 on this application.
If your answer is "Yes," give **Previous Registration Number** ▼   **Year of Registration** ▼

5

DERIVATIVE WORK OR COMPILATION Complete both space 6a & 6b for a derivative work; complete only 6b for a compilation.
a. **Preexisting Material** Identify any preexisting work or works that this work is based on or incorporates. ▼

b. **Material Added to This Work** Give a brief, general statement of the material that has been added to this work and in which copyright is claimed. ▼

6

See instructions
before completing
this space

—space deleted—

7

REPRODUCTION FOR USE OF BLIND OR PHYSICALLY HANDICAPPED INDIVIDUALS   A signature on this form at space 10, and a
check in one of the boxes here in space 8, constitutes a non-exclusive grant of permission to the Library of Congress to reproduce and distribute solely for the blind
and physically handicapped and under the conditions and limitations prescribed by the regulations of the Copyright Office: (1) copies of the work identified in space
1 of this application in Braille (or similar tactile symbols); or (2) phonorecords embodying a fixation of a reading of that work; or (3) both.
    a ☐ Copies and Phonorecords   b ☐ Copies Only   c ☐ Phonorecords Only

8

See instructions

DEPOSIT ACCOUNT If the registration fee is to be charged to a Deposit Account established in the Copyright Office, give name and number of Account.
Name ▼   **Account Number** ▼

9

CORRESPONDENCE Give name and address to which correspondence about this application should be sent. Name/Address/Apt/City/State/Zip ▼

Area Code & Telephone Number ▶

Be sure to
give your
daytime phone
◀ number

CERTIFICATION* I, the undersigned, hereby certify that I am the
Check one ▶
☐ author
☐ other copyright claimant
☐ owner of exclusive right(s)
☐ authorized agent of _____
of the work identified in this application and that the statements made   Name of author or other copyright claimant, or owner of exclusive right(s) ▲
by me in this application are correct to the best of my knowledge.

Typed or printed name and date ▼ If this is a published work, this date must be the same as or later than the date of publication given in space 3.

_____   **date** ▶ _____

Handwritten signature (X) ▼

10

**MAIL
CERTIFI-
CATE TO**

Name ▼

Number Street Apartment Number ▼

City State ZIP ▼

**Certificate
will be
mailed in
window
envelope**

YOU MUST
● Complete all necessary spaces
● Sign your application in space 10
SEND ALL 3 ELEMENTS
IN THE SAME PACKAGE
1. Application form
2. Non-refundable $10 filing fee
   in check or money order
   payable to Register of Copyrights
3. Deposit material
MAIL TO:
Register of Copyrights
Library of Congress
Washington, D.C. 20559

11

* 17 U.S.C. § 506(e): Any person who knowingly makes a false representation of a material fact in the application for copyright registration provided for by section 409, or in any written statement filed in
connection with the application, shall be fined not more than $2,500.

April 1989—200,000   ☆ U.S. GOVERNMENT PRINTING OFFICE: 1989—241-428/80,018

How to Investigate the Copyright Status of a Work

IN GENERAL

Methods of Approaching a Copyright Investigation

There are several ways to investigate whether a work is under copyright protection and, if so, the facts of the copyright. These are the main ones:

1. Examine a copy of the work (or, if the work is a sound recording, examine the disk, tape cartridge, or cassette in which the recorded sound is fixed, or the album cover, sleeve, or container in which the recording is sold) for such elements as a copyright notice, place and date of publication, author and publisher (for additional information, see p. 6, "Copyright Notice");

2. Make a search of the Copyright Office catalogs and other records; or

3. Have the Copyright Office make a search for you.

A Few Words of Caution About Copyright Investigations

Copyright investigations often involve more than one of these methods. Even if you follow all three approaches, the results may not be completely conclusive. Moreover, as explained in this circular, the changes brought about under the Copyright Act of 1976 must be considered when investigating the copyright status of a work.

This circular offers some practical guidance on what to look for if you are making a copyright investigation. It is important to realize, however, that this circular contains only general information, and that there are a number of exceptions to the principles outlined here. In many cases it is important to consult a copyright attorney before reaching any conclusions regarding the copyright status of a work.

HOW TO GO ABOUT SEARCHING COPYRIGHT OFFICE CATALOGS AND RECORDS

Catalog of Copyright Entries

The Copyright Office publishes the *Catalog of Copyright Entries (CCE)*, which is divided into parts according to the classes of works registered. The present categories include: "Nondramatic Literary Works," "Performing Arts," "Motion Pictures and Filmstrips," "Sound Recordings," "Serials and Periodicals," "Visual Arts," "Maps," and "Renewals." Effective with the Fourth Series, Volume 2, 1979 Catalogs, the CCE has been issued in microfiche form **only;** previously, each part of the *Catalog* was issued at regular intervals in book form. Each CCE segment covers all registrations made during a particular period of time. Renewals made for any class during a particular period can be found in Part 8, "Renewals."

Before 1978, the catalog parts reflected the classes that existed at that time. Renewals for a particular class are found in the back section of the catalog for the class of work renewed (for example, renewal registrations for music made in 1976 appear in the last section of the music catalog for 1976).

A number of libraries throughout the United States maintain copies of the *Catalog*, and this may provide a good starting point if you wish to make a search yourself. There are some cases, however, in which a search of the *Catalog* alone will not be sufficient to provide the needed information. For example:

- Since the *Catalog* does not include entries for assignments or other recorded documents, it cannot be used for searches involving the ownership of rights.

- There is usually a time lag of a year or more before the part of the *Catalog* covering a particular registration is published.

- The *Catalog* entry contains the essential facts concerning a registration, but it is not a verbatim transcript of the registration record.

3

Individual Searches of Copyright Records

The Copyright Office is located in the Library of Congress James Madison Memorial Building, 101 Independence Ave., S.E., Washington, D.C.

Most records of the Copyright Office are open to public inspection and searching from 8:30 a.m. to 5 p.m. Monday through Friday (except legal holidays). The various records freely available to the public include an extensive card catalog, an automated catalog containing records from 1978 forward, record books, and microfilm records of assignments and related documents. Other records, including correspondence files and deposit copies, are not open to the public for searching. However, they may be inspected upon request and payment of a $10-per hour search fee.

If you wish to do your own searching in the Copyright Office files open to the public, you will be given assistance in locating the records you need and in learning searching procedures. If the Copyright Office staff actually makes the search for you, a search fee must be charged.

SEARCHING BY THE COPYRIGHT OFFICE

In General

Upon request, the Copyright Office staff will search its records at the statutory rate of $10 for each hour or fraction of an hour consumed. Based on the information you furnish, we will provide an estimate of the total search fee. If you decide to have the Office staff conduct the search, you should send the estimated amount with your request. The Office will then proceed with the search and send you a typewritten report or, if you prefer, an oral report by telephone. If you request an oral report, please provide a telephone number where you can be reached during normal business hours (8:30-5:00).

Search reports can be certified on request, for an extra fee of $4. Certified searches are most frequently requested to meet the evidentiary requirements of litigation.

Your request, and any other correspondence, should be addressed to:
Reference and Bibliography Section, LM-451
Copyright Office
Library of Congress
Washington, D.C. 20559
(202) 287-6850

What the Fee Does Not Cover

Note that the search fee does *not* include the cost of additional certificates, photocopies of deposits, or copies of other office records. For information concerning these services, request Circular 6 from the Copyright Office.

Information Needed

The more detailed information you can furnish with your request, the less time-consuming and expensive the search will be. Please provide as much of the following information as possible:

- The title of the work, with any possible variants;

- The names of the authors, including possible pseudonyms;

- The name of the probable copyright owner, which may be the publisher or producer;

- The approximate year when the work was published or registered;

- The type of work involved (book, play, musical composition, sound recording, photograph, etc.);

- For a work originally published as a part of a periodical or collection, the title of that publication and any other information, such as the volume or issue number, to help identify it;

- Motion pictures are often based on other works such as books or serialized contributions to periodicals or other composite works. If you desire a search for an underlying work or for music from a motion picture, you must specifically request such a search. You must also identify the underlying works and music and furnish the specific titles, authors, and approximate dates of these works; and

- The registration number of any other copyright data.

Searches Involving Assignments and Other Documents Affecting Copyright Ownership

The Copyright Office staff will also, for the standard hourly search fee, search its indexes covering the records of assignments and other recorded documents concerning ownership of copyrights. The reports of searches in these cases will state the facts shown in the Office's indexes of the recorded documents, but will offer no interpretation of the content of the documents or their legal effect.

4

NOTE: Unless your request specifies otherwise, Copyright Office searches include records pertaining to registrations, renewals, assignments and other recorded documents concerning copyright ownership. If you want the office to search any other special records such as notices of use, or if you want to exclude specific records from your search, please make this clear in your request.

LIMITATIONS ON SEARCHES

In determining whether or not to have a search made, you should keep the following points in mind:

No Special Lists

The Copyright Office does not maintain any listings of works by subject, or any lists of works that are in the public domain.

Contributions

Individual works, such as stories, poems, articles, or musical compositions that were published as contributions to a copyrighted periodical or collection, are usually not listed separately by title in our records.

No Comparisons

The Copyright Office does not search or compare copies of works to determine questions of possible infringement or to determine how much two or more versions of a work have in common.

Titles and Names Not Copyrightable

Copyright does not protect names and titles, and our records list many different works identified by the same or similar titles. Some brand names, trade names, slogans, and phrases may be entitled to protection under the general rules of law relating to unfair competition, or to registration under the provisions of the trademark laws. Questions about the trademark laws should be addressed to the Commissioner of Patents and Trademarks, Washington, D.C. 20231. Possible protection of names and titles under common law principles of unfair competition is a question of state law.

No Legal Advice

The Copyright Office cannot express any opinion as to the legal significance or effect of the facts included in a search report.

SOME WORDS OF CAUTION

Searches Not Always Conclusive

Searches of the Copyright Office catalogs and records are useful in helping to determine the copyright status of a work, but they cannot be regarded as conclusive in all cases. The complete absence of any information about a work in the office records does not mean that the work is unprotected. The following are examples of cases in which information about a particular work may be incomplete or lacking entirely in the Copyright Office:

• Before 1978, unpublished works were entitled to protection at common law without the need of registration.

• Works published with notice prior to 1978 may be registered at **any** time within the first 28-year term; to obtain renewal protection, however, the claimant must register and renew such work by the end of the 28th year.

• For works that came under copyright protection after 1978, registration may be made at any time during the term of protection; it is not generally required as a condition of copyright protection (there are, however, certain definite advantages to registration; please call or write for Circular 1, "Copyright Basics").

• Since searches are ordinarily limited to registrations that have already been cataloged, a search report may not cover recent registrations for which catalog records are not yet available.

• The information in the search request may not have been complete or specific enough to identify the work.

• The work may have been registered under a different title or as part of a larger work.

Protection in Foreign Countries

Even if you conclude that a work is in the public domain in the United States, this does not necessarily mean that you are free to use it in other countries. Every nation has its own

5

laws governing the length and scope of copyright protection, and these are applicable to uses of the work within that nation's borders. Thus, the expiration or loss of copyright protection in the United States may still leave the work fully protected against unauthorized use in other countries.

OTHER CIRCULARS

For further information, request Circulars 15, "Renewal of Copyright," 15a, "Duration of Copyright," 15t, "Extension of Copyright Terms," and 6, "Obtaining Copies of Copyright Office Records and Deposits," from:
Publications Section, LM-455
Copyright Office
Library of Congress
Washington, D.C. 20559
    OR
You may call 202-287-9100 at any time, day or night, to leave a request for forms or circulars as a recorded message on the Forms HOTLINE. Requests made on the HOTLINE number are filled and mailed promptly.

IMPACT OF COPYRIGHT ACT ON COPYRIGHT INVESTIGATIONS

On October 19, 1976, the President signed into law a complete revision of the copyright law of the United States (Title 17 of the United States Code). Most provisions of the new copyright statute came into force on **January 1, 1978,** superseding the previous copyright act of 1909, and made significant changes in the copyright law. If you need more information about the provisions of the 1976 Act, or if you want a copy of the revised statute, write or call the Copyright Office and request Circular 92.

For copyright investigations, the following are some of the main points to consider about the impact of the Copyright Act of 1976:

A Changed System of Copyright Formalities

Some of the most sweeping changes under the 1976 Act involve copyright formalities; that is, the procedural requirements for securing and maintaining full copyright protection.

The old system of formalities involved copyright notice, deposit and registration, recordation of transfers and licenses of copyright ownership, and United States manufacture, among other things. In general, while retaining formalities the present law reduces the chances of mistakes, softens the consequences of errors and omissions, and allows for the correction of errors.

Automatic Copyright

Under the present copyright law, copyright exists in original works of authorship created and fixed in any tangible medium of expression, now known or later developed, from which they can be perceived, reproduced, or otherwise communicated, either directly, or indirectly with the aid of a machine or device. In other words, copyright is an incident of creative authorship not dependent on statutory formalities. Thus, registration with the Copyright Office generally is not required, but there are certain advantages that arise from a timely registration. For further information on the advantages of registration, write or call the Copyright Office and request Circular 1, "Copyright Basics."

Copyright Notice

Both the 1909 and 1976 copyright acts require a notice of copyright on published works. For most works, a copyright notice consists of the symbol ©, the word "Copyright," or the abbreviation "Copr.," together with the name of the owner of copyright and the year of first publication; for example: "© Marion Crane 1987" or "Copyright 1987 by Milton Arbogast." For sound recordings published on or after February 15, 1972, a copyright notice might read "℗ 1987 XYZ Records, Inc." (See page 8 for more about sound recordings.) The present law prescribes that all visually perceptible published copies of a work, or published phonorecords of a sound recording, shall bear a proper copyright notice. This requirement applies equally whether the work is published in the United States or elsewhere by authority of the copyright owner. Compliance with the statutory notice requirements is the responsibility of the copyright owner. Unauthorized publication without the copyright notice, or with a defective notice, does not affect the validity of the copyright in the work. Advance permission from, or registration with, the Copyright Office is not required before placing a copyright notice on copies of a work, or on phonorecords of a sound recording. Moreover, for works first published on or after January 1, 1978, omission of the required notice, or

6

use of a defective notice, does not result in forfeiture or outright loss of copyright protection. Certain omissions of, or defects in the notice of copyright, however, may lead to loss of copyright protection if certain steps are not taken to correct or cure the omissions or defects. The Copyright Office has issued a final regulation (37 CFR 201.20) which suggests various acceptable positions for the notice of copyright. For further information, write to the Copyright Office and request Circular 3.

Works Already in the Public Domain

The 1976 Act does not restore protection to works that fell into the public domain before January 1, 1978. If copyright in a particular work has been lost, the work is permanently in the public domain in this country, and the 1976 Act will not revive protection. Under the copyright law in effect prior to January 1, 1978, copyright could be lost in several situations: the most common were publication without the required copyright notice, expiration of the first 28-year copyright term without renewal, or final expiration of the second copyright term.

Scope of Exclusive Rights Under Copyright

The present law has changed and enlarged in some cases, the scope of the copyright owner's rights as against users of a work. The new rights apply to all uses of a work subject to protection by copyright after January 1, 1978, regardless of when the work was created.

DURATION OF COPYRIGHT PROTECTION

Works Originally Copyrighted On or After January 1, 1978

A work that is created and fixed in tangible form for the first time on or after January 1, 1978, is automatically protected from the moment of its creation, and is ordinarily given a term enduring for the author's life, plus an additional 50 years after the author's death. In the case of "a joint work prepared by two or more authors who did not work for hire," the term lasts for 50 years after the last surviving author's death. For works made for hire, and for anonymous and pseudonymous works (unless the author's identity is revealed in Copyright Office records), the duration of copyright will be 75 years from publication or 100 years from creation, whichever is less.

Works created before the 1976 law came into effect, but neither published nor registered for copyright before January 1, 1978, have been automatically brought under the statute and are now given Federal copyright protection. The duration of copyright in these works will generally be computed in the same way as for new works: the life-plus-50 or 75/100-year terms will apply. However, all works in this category are guaranteed at least 25 years of statutory protection.

Works Copyrighted Before January 1, 1978

Under the law in effect before 1978, copyright was secured either on the date a work was published with notice of copyright, or on the date of registration if the work was registered in unpublished form. In either case, copyright endured for a first term of 28 years from the date on which it was secured. During the last (28th) year of the first term, the copyright was eligible for renewal. The new copyright law has extended the renewal term from 28 to 47 years for copyrights in existence on January 1, 1978. However, the copyright still must be renewed in the 28th calendar year to receive the 47-year period of added protection. For more detailed information on the copyright term, write or call the Copyright Office and request Circulars 15a and 15t.

WORKS FIRST PUBLISHED BEFORE 1978: THE COPYRIGHT NOTICE

General Information About the Copyright Notice

In investigating the copyright status of works first published before January 1, 1978, the most important thing to look for is the notice of copyright. As a general rule under the previous law, copyright protection was lost permanently if the notice was omitted from the first authorized published edition of a work, or if it appeared in the wrong form or position. The form and position of the copyright notice for various types of works were specified in the copyright statute. Some courts were liberal in overlooking relatively minor departures from the statutory requirements, but a basic failure to comply with the notice provisions forfeited copyright protection and put the work into the public domain in this country.

7

Absence of Copyright Notice

For works first published before 1978, the complete absence of a copyright notice from a published copy generally indicates that the work is not protected by copyright. However, there are a number of exceptions and qualifications to this general rule. The following are some of them:

Unpublished Works. No notice of copyright was required on the copies of any unpublished work. The concept of "publication" is very technical, and it was possible for a number of copies lacking a copyright notice to be reproduced and distributed without affecting copyright protection.

Foreign Editions. Under certain circumstances, the law exempted copies of a copyrighted work from the notice requirements if they were first published outside the United States. Some copies of these foreign editions could find their way into the United States without impairing the copyright.

Accidental Omission. The 1909 statute preserved copyright protection if the notice was omitted by accident or mistake from a "particular copy or copies."

Unauthorized Publication. A valid copyright was not secured if someone deleted the notice and/or published the work without authorization from the copyright owner.

Sound Recordings. Reproductions of sound recordings usually contain two different types of creative works: the underlying musical, dramatic, or literary work that is being performed or read, and the fixation of the actual sounds embodying the performance or reading. For protection of the underlying musical or literary work embodied in a recording, it is not necessary that a copyright notice covering this material appear on the phonograph records or tapes in which the recording is reproduced. As noted above, a special notice is required for protection of the recording of a series of musical, spoken, or other sounds which were fixed on or after February 15, 1972. Sound recordings fixed before February 15, 1972, are not eligible for Federal copyright protection. Neither the Sound Recording Act of 1971 nor the present copyright law can be applied or be construed to provide any retroactive protection for sound recordings fixed before that date. Such works, however, may be protected by various state laws or doctrines of common law.

The Date in the Copyright Notice

If you find a copyright notice, the date it contains may be important in determining the copyright status of the work. In general, the notice on works published before 1978 must include the year in which copyright was secured by publication (or, if the work was first registered for copyright in unpublished form, the year in which registration was made). There are two main exceptions to this rule.

- For pictorial, graphic, or sculptural works (Classes F through K under the 1909 law) the law permitted omission of the year date in the notice.

- For "new versions" of previously published or copyrighted works, the notice was not usually required to include more than the year of first publication of the new version itself. This is explained further under "Derivative Works" below.

The year in the notice usually (though not always) indicated when the copyright began. It is therefore significant in determining whether a copyright is still in effect; or, if the copyright has not yet run its course, the year date will help in deciding when the copyright is scheduled to expire. For further information about the duration of copyright, request Circular 15a.

In evaluating the meaning of the date in a notice, you should keep the following points in mind:

WORKS PUBLISHED AND COPYRIGHTED BEFORE JANUARY 1, 1978: A work published before January 1, 1978, and copyrighted within the past 75 years may still be protected by copyright in the United States if a valid renewal registration was made during the 28th year of the first term of the copyright. If renewed, and if still valid under the other provisions of the law, the copyright will expire 75 years from the end of the year in which it was first secured.

Therefore, with one exception, the United States copyright in any work published or copyrighted more than 75 years ago (75 years from January 1st in the present year) has expired by operation of law, and the work has permanently fallen into the public domain in the United States. For example, on January 1, 1986, copyright in works first published or copyrighted before January 1, 1911, will have expired; on January 1, 1987, copyright in works first published or copyrighted before January 1, 1912, will have expired.

WORKS FIRST PUBLISHED OR COPYRIGHTED BETWEEN JANUARY 1, 1910, AND DECEMBER 31, 1949,

8

BUT NOT RENEWED: If a work was first published or copyrighted between January 1, 1910, and December 31, 1949, it is important to determine whether the copyright was renewed during the last (28th) year of the first term of the copyright. This can be done by searching the Copyright Office records or catalogs, as explained above. If no renewal registration was made, copyright protection expired permanently on the 28th anniversary of the date it was first secured.

WORKS FIRST PUBLISHED OR COPYRIGHTED BETWEEN JANUARY 1, 1910 AND DECEMBER 31, 1949, AND REGISTERED FOR RENEWAL: When a valid renewal registration was made and copyright in the work was in its second term on December 31, 1977, the renewal copyright term was extended under the present act to 47 years. In these cases, copyright will last for a total of 75 years from the end of the year in which copyright was originally secured. Example: Copyright in a work first published in 1917, and renewed in 1945, will expire on December 31, 1992.

WORKS FIRST PUBLISHED OR COPYRIGHTED BETWEEN JANUARY 1, 1950, AND DECEMBER 31, 1977: If a work was in its first 28-year term of copyright protection on January 1, 1978; it must be renewed in a timely fashion to secure the maximum term of copyright protection provided by the present copyright law. If renewal registration is made during the 28th calendar year of its first term, copyright will endure for 75 years from the end of the year copyright was originally secured. If not renewed, the copyright expires at the end of its 28th calendar year.

UNPUBLISHED, UNREGISTERED WORKS: Before 1978, if a work had neither been "published" in the legal sense nor registered in the Copyright Office, it was subject to perpetual protection under the common law. On January 1, 1978, all works of this kind, subject to protection by copyright, were automatically brought under the new Federal copyright statute. The duration of these new Federal copyrights will vary, but none of them will expire before December 31, 2002.

Derivative Works

In examining a copy (or a record or tape) for copyright information, it is important to determine whether that particular version of the work is an original edition of the work or a "new version." New versions include musical arrangements, adaptations, revised or newly edited editions, translations, dramatizations, abridgments, compilations, and works republished with new matter added. The law provides that derivative works are independently copyrightable and that the copyright in such a work does not affect or extend the protection, if any, in the underlying work. Under the 1909 law, courts have also held that the notice of copyright on a derivative work ordinarily need not include the dates or other information pertaining to the earlier works incorporated in it. This principle is specifically preserved in the present copyright law.

Thus, if the copy (or the record or tape) constitutes a derivative version of the work, these points should be kept in mind:

- The date in the copyright notice is not necessarily an indication of when copyright in all of the material in the work will expire. Some of the material may already be in the public domain, and some parts of the work may expire sooner than others.

- Even if some of the material in the derivative work is in the public domain and free for use, this does not mean that the "new" material added to it can be used without permission from the owner of copyright in the derivative work. It may be necessary to compare editions to determine what is free to use and what is not.

- Ownership of rights in the material included in a derivative work and in the preexisting work upon which it may be based may differ, and permission obtained from the owners of certain parts of the work may not authorize the use of other parts.

The Name in the Copyright Notice

Under the copyright statute in effect before 1978, the notice was required to include "the name of the copyright proprietor." The present act requires that the notice include "the name of the owner of copyright in the work, or an abbreviation by which the name can be recognized, or a generally known alternative designation of the owner." The name in the notice (sometimes in combination with other statements on the copy, record, tape, container, or label) often gives persons wishing to use the work the information needed to identify the owner from whom licenses or permission can be sought. In other cases, the name provides a starting point for a search in the Copyright Office records or catalogs, as explained at the beginning in this circular.

9

In the case of works published before 1978, copyright registration is made in the name of the individual person or the entity identified as the copyright owner in the notice. For works published after 1978, registration is made in the name of the person or entity owning all the rights on the date the registration is made. This may or may not be the name appearing in the notice. In addition to its records of copyright registration, the Copyright Office maintains extensive records of assignments, exclusive licenses, and other documents dealing with copyright ownership.

Ad Interim

Ad interim copyright was a special short-term copyright that applied to certain books and periodicals in the English language, first manufactured and published outside the United States. It was a partial exception to the manufacturing requirements of the previous United States copyright law. Its purpose was to secure temporary United States protection for a work, pending the manufacture of an edition in the United States. The ad interim requirements changed several times over the years, and were subject to a number of exceptions and qualifications.

The manufacturing provisions of the copyright act expired on July 1, 1986, and are no longer a part of the copyright law. The transitional and supplementary provisions of the act provide that for any work in which ad interim copyright was subsisting or capable of being secured on December 31, 1977, copyright protection would be extended for a term compatible with other works in which copyright was subsisting on the effective date of the new act. Consequently, if the work was first published on or after July 1, 1977, and was eligible for ad interim copyright protection, the provisions of the present copyright act will be applicable to the protection of these works. Anyone investigating the copyright status of an English-language book or periodical first published outside the United States before July 1, 1977, should check carefully to determine:

● Whether the manufacturing requirements were applicable to the work; and

● If so, whether the ad interim requirements were met.

10

search request form

Copyright Office
Library of Congress
Washington, D.C. 20559

Reference & Bibliography
Section
(202) 287-6850
8:30-5:00 Monday-Friday

Type of work:

☐ Book   ☐ Music   ☐ Motion Picture   ☐ Drama   ☐ Sound Recording
☐ Photograph/Artwork   ☐ Map   ☐ Periodical   ☐ Contribution

Search information you require:

☐ Registration   ☐ Renewal   ☐ Assignment   ☐ Address

Specifics of work to be searched:

TITLE: _____

AUTHOR: _____

COPYRIGHT CLAIMANT (if known): _____
(name in ©️ notice)

APPROXIMATE YEAR DATE OF PUBLICATION/CREATION: _____

REGISTRATION NUMBER (if known): _____

OTHER IDENTIFYING INFORMATION: _____

If you need more space please attach additional pages.

Estimates are based on the Copyright Office fee of $10.00 an hour or fraction of an hour consumed. The more information you furnish as a basis for the search the better service we can provide.

Names, titles, and short phrases are not copyrightable.

Please read Circular 22 for more information on copyright searches.

YOUR NAME: _____

ADDRESS: _____

DAYTIME TELEPHONE NO. ( ) _____

Convey results of estimate search by telephone
☐ yes   ☐ no

C-768

PIGEON, PARTRIDGE AND DOVE, ATTORNEYS
1184 Thomas Jefferson Highway
Westchester, Indiana 12856

April 6, 1987

Will St. Charles, Marketing Director
Fast Foods, Inc.
297 Wilson Pike Circle, Suite 203
Bloomington, Indiana 12860

Dear Mr. St. Charles:

I am writing to give you my evaluation of the results of the trademark search I commissioned for you for YESTERYEARS for restaurant services. Based on the data produced by that search, I believe that you must find another name for your new hamburger restaurant.

To understand fully the reasons behind my evaluation, you must know something about the principles of trademark infringement. Trademark rights in the United States are acquired by use of the mark. The first person to use a trademark gains by that use superior rights in that mark as used for the particular goods or services it names. A new name for a similar product or service infringes the established mark if the new mark is so similar to the established mark in the way it looks, the way it sounds when spoken, and in its meaning as to be likely to confuse consumers. This standard for infringement is called "confusing similarity." Very similar marks do not have to name identical products or services to be held "confusingly similar." In your case, your proposed use of YESTERYEARS for hamburger restaurant services would infringe any very similar, older, trademark which named any sort of restaurant, since consumers could easily believe that the restaurants were owned or franchised by the same organization.

Because federal trademark registration enhances the rights that accrue to trademark owners by use of their marks, trademarks which are registered federally are the most important class of marks to avoid infringing. However, the rights of state trademark registrants and those of owners of established but unregistered marks are just as valid and must also be taken into account when assessing the availability for use of a proposed mark, although the owners of those marks may not have used their marks widely enough to gain extensive rights in their marks.

There are several federal registrations listed in the search report for YESTERYEARS for marks which include a form of YESTERYEAR as an element. However, none of these prior registrations would present a problem to your proposed use of YESTERYEARS because, as you will note when you examine the search report, the marks all name products (costume jewelry, picture frames, etc.) which are very different from restaurant services.

However, there is a federal registration for YESTERDAY'S for restaurant services, as well as one for YESTERDOG, also for restaurant services. Both these registrations are currently valid and in force, according to the information in the search report. In my opinion, your proposed use of YESTERYEARS would infringe the rights of the YESTERDAY'S trademark owners because your proposed mark used for restaurant services could be confused with that registered mark. Further, there is a notation in the YESTERDAY'S entry in the search report that the owners of YESTERDAY'S filed an opposition against the federal registration of YESTERDOG for restaurant services. This opposition proceeding was dropped, but the fact that it was filed indicates the vigilance with which the owners of YESTERDAY'S oppose what they consider infringements.

Mr. Will St. Charles
April 6, 1987
Page 2

The state registrations section of the search report lists one YESTERYEARS registration, for restaurant services, in Massachusetts. There are also two Tennessee registrations for YESTERDAY'S for restaurant services, as well as Kansas and California registrations for YESTERDAY'S for restaurant services. All of the marks which are the subjects of these state registrations would be infringed by your proposed use of YESTERYEARS.

In the trade names section of the report, which reflects phone directory listings and other occurrences of business names similar to the mark being searched, there are listings for fourteen restaurants, the names for which start with the word YESTERYEARS. There are even more listings (several pages) for restaurants which use the word YESTERDAYS in their names. Any of the restaurants named YESTERYEARS or using YESTERYEARS as a part of their name could pose a threat to your use of the name.

I am sorry the news is bad. Apparently, others have discovered before you that YESTERYEARS is a good name. Finding out the bad news now is much preferable to finding it out by means of a "cease and desist" letter.

When you decide what new name you would like to use in place of YESTERYEARS, call me. We can order expedited service on the new search report in order to have it delivered very quickly.

I am enclosing a copy of the YESTERYEARS search report. My check marks indicate marks which required our attention and evaluation.

Please call me if you have questions.

PIGEON, PARTRIDGE AND DOVE, ATTORNEYS

Lulu Partridge

LULU PARTRIDGE

LP/tb

```
SEARCH: 2512251                    T&T TRADEMARK SEARCH SUMMARY                      PAGE:   1

Number of Copies:      01
Our File:              2512251
Your File:
Client Name:           ZUMWALT ALMON & HAYES
                       LEE WILSON
Date Received:         MARCH 17, 1987
Received by:           PHONE
Mark Searched:         YESTERYEARS
Goods/Services:         RESTAURANT SERVICES
Type of Search:        FULL SEARCH
                       2735
PTO Analyst:           A. SILVA
Comments:              THERE ARE OTHER "YEAR" FORMATIVES FOR FOOD PRODUCTS.
Filed Through:         02/17/87
O. G. Through:         03/24/87

        REG#    SERIES CODE/#  TRADEMARK

   1.  R0396909  1 437931    YESTER-YEAR PRODUCTS
   2.  R1022165  3 020156    YESTERYEAR
   3.  R1188666  3 284218    YESTERYEAR LOG HOME
   4.  R0866200  2 270793    MODELS OF YESTERYEAR
   5.  R1285364  3 385418    THE COLLECTOR'S CHOICE YESTERYEAR TODAY & THEREAFTER
   6.  R0955105  2 415117    YESTERYEAR
   7.  R1231939  3 312667    CAPRI KITCHENS INC TOMORROW'S IDEAS YESTERYEAR'S CRAFTSMANSHIP C
   8.  R0000000  3 592139    YESTERYEAR, LTD.
   9.  R1150258  3 183473    VIDEO YESTERYEAR
  10.  R0993948  2 445135    RADIO YESTERYEAR
  11.  R0924393  2 371327    YESTERYEAR
  12.  R0000000  3 106068    ARTISANS & CRAFTSMEN PRESENTS YESTERYEAR
  13.  R0930728  2 362360    RADIOS OF YESTERYEAR
  14.  R1170604  3 221634    RIDE BACK INTO YESTERYEAR
  15.  R0000000  3 480768    A GRAND HOTEL. YESTERDAY, TODAY, AND TOMORROW.
  16.  R0000000  3 635565    HOPPER'S DRIVE-INN "AT HOPPER'S YESTERDAY IS BETTER THAN EVER!"
  17.  R1050377  3 072187    YESTERDAY'S ✔
  18.  R1204923  3 145849    YESTERDOG ✔
  19.  R0503813  1 512128    YESTER-LAID
  20.  R1000005  2 438772    YESTERDAY'S LAY DELIVERED TODAY
  21.  R0000000  3 549285    YESTA
  22.  R1167851  3 244007    WE'VE MADE GOOD FOOD A FAMILY TRADITION...FOR OVER 40 YEARS.
  23.  R1277339  3 391485    BUNNY OF THE YEAR
  24.  R1344901  3 473673    ALL YEAR
  25.  R1005425  3 018247    FIRST YEAR
  26.  R0673281  2 049284    GOOD YEAR
  27.  R1136346  3 202772    TENDER-YEAR
  28.  R1162999  3 206179    "SALAD OF THE YEAR"
```

HOPPER'S DRIVE-INN "AT HOPPER'S YESTERDAY IS BETTER THAN EVER!"

STATUS: PENDING
STATUS DATE: DECEMBER 15. 1986.
U.S. CLASS: 100   INT. CLASS: 42
SERVICES: DRIVE-IN RESTAURANT SERVICES
SER. NUMBER: 635.565   FILED: DECEMBER 15. 1986.
IN COMM: NOVEMBER 25. 1986.
FIRST USED: NOVEMBER 25. 1986.
APPLICANT: HOPPER'S DRIVE-IN. INC. (LA. CORPORATION):
    BATON ROUGE. LA.

✔ YESTERDAY'S

STATUS: REGISTERED   STATUS DATE: OCTOBER 12. 1976.
U.S. CLASS: 100   INT. CLASS: 42
SERVICES: RESTAURANT SERVICES
SER. NUMBER: 72.187   FILED: DECEMBER 18. 1975.
IN COMM: OCTOBER 28. 1975.
FIRST USED: OCTOBER 28. 1975.
PUBLISHED FOR OPPOSITION: JULY 20. 1976.
REG. NUMBER: 1.050.377   REGISTERED: OCTOBER 12. 1976.
REGISTRANT: GREVGOLD ENTERPRISES, INC., FORT
    LAUDERDALE. FLA.
ADDITIONAL INFORMATION: PLAINTIFF IN OPPOSITION
    ACTION NO. 61980 AGAINST (REG. NUMBER 1204923)

YESTERDOG

✔ YESTERDOG

STATUS: REGISTERED   STATUS DATE: AUGUST 10. 1982.
U.S. CLASS: 100   INT. CLASS: 42
SERVICES: RESTAURANT SERVICES
SER. NUMBER: 145.849   FILED: OCTOBER 25. 1977.
IN COMM: JUNE 30. 1976.
FIRST USED: JUNE 30. 1976.
PUBLISHED FOR OPPOSITION: AUGUST 29. 1978.
REG. NUMBER: 1.204.923   REGISTERED: AUGUST 10. 1982.
REGISTRANT: WILLIAM LEWIS. D.B.A. YESTERDOG. GRAND
    RAPIDS. MICH.
OPPOSITION NUMBER: 61980 FILED DEC. 11.1978
    OPPOSER: GREVGOLD ENTERPRISES. INC.
    MARK: YESTERDAY'S
    RN: 1050377
    OUTCOME: DISMISSED WITH PREJUDICE APR. 29.1982

PIGEON, PARTRIDGE AND DOVE, ATTORNEYS
1184 Thomas Jefferson Highway
Westchester, Indiana 12856

May 12, 1987

Will St. Charles, Marketing Director
Fast Foods, Inc.
297 Wilson Pike Circle, Suite 203
Bloomington, Indiana 12860

Dear Mr. St. Charles:

I am writing to give you my evaluation of the results of the trademark search I commissioned for you for your second proposed mark for restaurant services, THE SOUTHERN BURGER COMPANY. Based on the data produced by that search, I believe that you will encounter no opposition to your proposed use of THE SOUTHERN BURGER COMPANY and may safely adopt the mark.

Trademark infringement is caused by "confusing similarity" between two marks and is judged by the "sight, sound and meaning" test. That is, do the two marks look so alike and sound so alike and have such similar meanings that they are likely to be confused by consumers if they name similar products or services? Applying this standard, I believe that none of the marks reported in the latest search report will be infringed by your use of THE SOUTHERN BURGER COMPANY for hamburger restaurant services.

Although the words "Southern," "South" and "burger" are formative verbal elements in many of the marks reported, the degree of similarity in the entire name in each case is not such that there is confusing similarity. There are no federally registered marks that concern me, for that reason.

The state registration for BURGER COMPANY, on page 2 of the state listings section of the report, is, I believe, of little concern. This is probably only a local restaurant; the owners would have a very hard time claiming infringement, since their BURGER COMPANY is a generic or descriptive mark which is not accorded a wide degree of protection. The same goes for SOUTHERN BIG BURGER on page 1 of the trade names listing section of the report.

I have enclosed a copy of the search report for your examination. Please call me if you have questions.

I must remind you that, although this is the most reliable information available to us, it may not be absolutely complete. It is always possible that there is some valid but unregistered trademark which would be infringed by your proposed mark which did not show up in this search report because it is unregistered. That does not happen often but it is a possibility.

I have enjoyed working with you and hope that you will call me again, for more name clearances and for federal trademark registrations.

Best regards.

PIGEON, PARTRIDGE AND DOVE, ATTORNEYS

Lulu Partridge

LULU PARTRIDGE

LP/tb

```
SEARCH: 1564931                    T&T TRADEMARK SEARCH SUMMARY                    PAGE:    1

Number of Copies:      01
Our File:              1564931
Your File:
Client Name:           ZUMWALT ALMON & HAYES
                       LEE WILSON
Date Received:         APRIL 21, 1987
Received by:           PHONE
Mark Searched:         THE SOUTHERN BURGER COMPANY
Goods/Services:        RESTAURANT SERVICES
Type of Search:        FULL SEARCH
                       2735
PTO Analyst:           M. QUIN
Filed Through:         03/20/87
O. G. Through:         04/28/87


      REG#    SERIES CODE/#  TRADEMARK

  1.  R1299141  3 445486     SOUTH STREET SAUSAGE
  2.  R0000000  3 479701     SOUTH PHILLY STEAKS & FRIES
  3.  R0000000  3 628246     SOUTH PHILLY STEAKS & FRIES
  4.  R1195742  3 251489     THE BIRGER COMPANY
  5.  R0961578  2 412731     BERGER DU NORD
  6.  R1108813  3 134470     WESTBERG
  7.  R0000000  3 636886     WESTERN BACON CHEESBURGER
  8.  R0000000  3 457446     WESTERN BACON CHEESEBURGER
  9.  R0000000  3 617549     LOUISIANA GROCERY & FEED COMPANY
 10.  R0951518  2 408035     MONTANA MINING COMPANY
 11.  R1001861  2 455296     THE MISSISSIPPI RIVER COMPANY
 12.  R1094808  3 130997     THE GREAT LAKES STEAK CO.
 13.  R0000000  3 635172     CALIFORNIA CASTLE BURGER
 14.  R1274617  3 243878     THE CHICAGO DOUGH COMPANY
 15.  R0943498  2 336620     SOUTH-OF-THE-BORDER-FOOD-NORTH-OF-THE-BORDER-STYLE
 16.  R1051023  2 434015     SOUTHERN SUN
 17.  R1203138  3 050509     SOUTH OF THE BORDER
 18.  R1190331  3 206847     SOUTH-OF-THE-BORDER-FOOD NORTH-OF-THE-BORDER-STYLE
 19.  R1224619  3 263033     SOUTHERN HOSPITALITY CORPORATION
 20.  R1183327  3 284356     SOUTH FORK
 21.  R1301041  3 453072     SOUTHERN SPORTSMAN
 22.  R1381755  3 485872     SOUTH SHORE HARBOUR
 23.  R1363838  3 527728     SOUTHWEST CHILI
 24.  R1382649  3 485873     SOUTH SHORE HARBOUR
 25.  R1369553  3 527867     SOUTHERN SKILLET
 26.  R1362575  3 476421     THE SOUTHERN COOKER HOME STYLE RESTAURANT & BAR
 27.  R0663884  2 029348     SOUTHERN BELLE
 28.  R0676424  2 055839     SOUTHERN GEM
 29.  R1294693  3 408142     SOUTHERN CHEF
 30.  R1134242  3 179349     THE TASTE THAT MADE THE SOUTH LOVE CHICKEN
 31.  R1237818  3 357172     "PUT SOME SOUTH IN YOUR MOUTH"
 32.  R1006533  3 021811     BRITLING B & W BLUE BOAR SERVING RIVER CITIES OF THE SOUTH
 33.  R0991004  2 463926     COLEMANS BAR-B-Q SOUTH'S FINEST
 34.  R0917391  2 337022     DIXIE KITCHEN SOUTHERN FRIED CHICKEN
 35.  R0000000  3 429633     DIMITRI'S OF SOUTHFIELD
 36.  R1321426  3 479230     FANDANGLES SOUTHWESTERN CHAR GRILL
 37.  R1432565  3 613615     THE FLAVOR OF THE DEEPER SOUTH
 38.  R1271169  3 401646     JOSE D MCMILLAN'S SOUTHWEST AMERICAN CANTINA
 39.  R0901311  2 328416     BURGER KING
 40.  R1074687  3 116697     BRESTBURGER
 41.  R1148467  3 230105     MR. BURGER
 42.  R1162108  3 186527     THE ALL AMERICAN BURGER
 43.  R1353461  3 461821     BAGELBURGER
 44.  R0754745  2 099490     BABY BURGER
 45.  R0557104  1 519480     MEXIBURGERS
 46.  R0918210  2 346026     BUN N' BURGER
 47.  R1231457  3 291455     CIRCUS BURGERS
 48.  R0979612  2 447406     DIXIE BURGER
 49.  R1401673  3 555227     FRANK R. BURGER'S
 50.  R1286599  3 421953     GET THAT URGE BURGER
 51.  R0996582  2 445062     HARRISBURGER
 52.  R1023506  2 452850     IN-N-OUT BURGERS
 53.  R0947715  2 374501     THE ALL AMERICAN BURGER
```

```
SEARCH: 1564931                    T&T TRADEMARK SEARCH SUMMARY                    PAGE:   2

 54.  R0000000  3 074986   NORTHWESTERN WILD RICE COMPANY
 55.  R1291368  3 389943   NORTH AMERICAN LOBSTER COMPANY
 56.  R1406214  3 510036   "THE CHILI" COMPANY
 57.  R0000000  3 579397   A ASPEN SKIING COMPANY
 58.  R0984772  2 412799   A CONSOLIDATED FOODS COMPANY RESPONSIVE TO CONSUMER NEEDS C
 59.  R1137070  3 194053   BABY DOE MINING COMPANY
 60.  R0000000  3 565496   BISHOP'S CATTLE COMPANY
 61.  R1404446  3 558751   BOSTON SEAFOOD COMPANY
 62.  R1283795  3 411635   BREAD & COMPANY
 63.  R1249391  3 339652   CALHOUN ST. OYSTER COMPANY
 64.  R1400791  3 487807   CALIFORNIA YOGURT COMPANY
 65.  R1358291  3 502946   CANOOKY COOKIE COMPANY
 66.  R1407145  3 541979   CHICAGO SANDWICH COMPANY
 67.  R1394430  3 483343   CLASSIC CARRIAGE & CAR COMPANY
 68.  R0000000  3 330625   COGBURN'S STAPLES & CHILI COMPANY
 69.  R1145349  3 203820   EMILE'S GERMAN FOOD COMPANY INC.
 70.  R1279316  3 413424   GREAT AMERICAN PIZZA COMPANY
 71.  R1074298  3 116966   MONTEREY WHALING COMPANY
 72.  R0245567  1 264614   SOUTHERN
 73.  R0741380  2 128860   SOUTHERN
 74.  R0852882  2 287995   SOUTHERN
 75.  R1321001  3 467019   SOUTHERN
 76.  R0438082  1 522783   BURGER
 77.  R0888786  2 301797   BURGER
 78.  R1006094  2 431247   BURGE'S
 79.  R0976072  2 426429   BURGIE!
```

RELEASE FOR USE OF PHOTOGRAPHS

In return for good and valuable consideration, receipt of which I acknowledge, I hereby grant to
_____ (the "Agency"), its clients and any other persons or
entities with whom it may contract for the use of such photographs, the unlimited right and
permission to use the photographs described below (the "Photographs"):

Subject(s) of Photographs: _____

_____

Date(s) Photographs Taken:_____

_____

Location(s) of Photographs: _____

_____

I further grant to the Agency the right to crop, edit, and otherwise alter the Photographs and to
combine them with other photographs or graphic elements, and I waive my right to inspect the
Photographs or any version of them or any finished advertisement or printed or other materials into
which they may be incorporated. I further understand that by signing this release I waive any
claim I might otherwise have for invasion of privacy due to the publication of the Photographs and
I hereby consent to their publication in any form in any medium or periodical or other publication,
alone or in conjunction with any printed matter which may be published with them. I warrant that I
have reached the age of majority and have every right to grant the permissions herein granted.
Further, I represent that I have read this document before signing it and understand its provisions.

_____   _____
Signature   Date of Signature

_____
Print or Type Name

Resources

Copyright	<u>**United States Copyright Office**</u>

Copyright Office
Library of Congress
Washington, D.C. 20559

Public Information: 202-479-0700 (to talk to a Copyright Information Specialist, who can answer your questions about copyright registration procedures and other matters connected with functions of the Copyright Office and can recommend and send to you appropriate free Copyright Office publications to educate you further, from 8:30 until 5, Monday through Friday)

Reference and Bibliography Section: 202-707-6850 (for information on searching the status of a copyright, from 8:30 until 5, Monday through Friday)

Forms and Circulars Hotline: 202-707-9100 (for ordering free Copyright Office publications and copyright registration forms, 24 hours a day)

Copyright Registration Forms

The Copyright Office will send you a supply of blank copyright registration forms free of charge if you call the 24-hour Forms and Circulars Hotline and leave your name on the Hotline answering machine along with information on what forms you need. It is important to use the right type of copyright registration form. The types of registration forms and the sorts of works they register are:

Form TX is used for non-dramatic literary works, including all types of published and unpublished works written in words or other verbal or numerical symbols, except for dramatic works and certain kinds of audiovisual works. You will need this form—whether your work is fiction or non-fiction, poetry or prose—to register a work that is a textbook, reference work, directory, catalog, advertising copy, computer program, data base, or other non-dramatic literary work.

Form SE is used for serials, that is, all works issued or intended to be issued in successive parts bearing numerical or chronological designations and intended to be continued indefinitely (periodicals, newspapers, magazines, newsletters, annuals, journals, etc.).

Form PA is used for works of the performing arts, including published and unpublished works prepared for the purpose of being performed directly before an audience or indirectly by means of any device or process. Some examples of works in this category are musical works (including any accompanying words), dramatic works (including any accompanying music), pantomimes and choreographic works, motion pictures, and other audiovisual works.

Form VA is used for published and unpublished pictorial, graphic, and sculptural works, including two-dimensional and three-dimensional works of fine, graphic, and applied art, photographs, prints, and art reproductions, maps, globes, charts, technical drawings, diagrams, models, pictorial or graphic labels and advertisements, as well as "works of artistic craftsmanship." Use Form VA for labels and advertisements if the copyrightable material in them is mainly pictorial or graphic; use Form TX if it consists mainly of text.

Form SR is used for sound recordings, that is, works that result from the fixation of a series of musical, spoken, or other sounds. Form SR should be used to register the claim to copyright in the sound recording itself. Form SR may also be used to register both the sound recording and the musical, dramatic, or literary work fixed in the phonograph record (or tape, disk, or cassette), as long as the same person or organization owns the copyright in both the sound recording and in the work which was recorded.

Form RE is used for any renewal application, regardless of the class in which the original registration was made. A renewal application can be made only for works that were already in their first twenty-eight-year term of copyright protection on January 1, 1978 (that is, works originally copyrighted between January 1, 1950 and December 31, 1977). Renewals can be made only during the last calendar year of the first twenty-eight-year copyright term.

Form CA is a supplemental registration form used to correct an error or amplify the information in the initial registration application form after it has been filed with the Copyright Office or a registration has been issued by the Copyright Office.

Form GR/CP is a form used as an addition to a basic application on Form TX, Form PA, or Form VA if you are making a single registration for a group of contributions to periodicals. The copyright statute provides that a single registration for a group of works can be made if all of the following conditions are met: all of the works are by the same author, who is an individual, all of the works were first published as contributions to periodicals (including newspapers) within a twelve-month period, each of the contributions as first published bore a separate copyright notice and the name of the owner of copyright in the work was the same in each notice, one copy of the entire periodical issue or newspaper section in which each contribution was first published must be deposited with the application, and the application must identify each contribution separately, including the periodical containing it and the date of its first publication.

Most works will fall naturally into one of the five main categories of copyrightable material. If your work contains copyrightable material falling into two or more classes, choose the one class that is most appropriate for the work as a whole. If your work, however, is an audiovisual work consisting of components which could fall into several classes, choose form PA. If your claim to copyright includes a claim in the sound recording, use Form SR.

Use only the official Copyright Office application forms to apply for registration. The Copyright Office at one time refused to consider applications made on forms which were photocopied from the printed Copyright Office forms. In recent years, however, the Copyright Office has actually encouraged the use of such photocopied application forms. You may submit photocopied application forms so long as they are clear, legible, copied onto a good grade of white paper and printed head-to-head, that is, copied so that when you turn the sheet over, the top of the second page is directly behind the top of page one. Because certificates of copyright registration are reproduced directly from the application forms filled out and submitted by applicants, the Copyright Office will reject any photocopied form which does not meet these requirements.

Copyright Office Publications

The Copyright Office also publishes a variety of excellent short pamphlets and circulars written in simple language on an assortment of copyright-related topics. A list of the most helpful of these publications, along with their corresponding publication numbers, follows. (An asterisk (*) denotes an especially informative publication.)

You may order single copies of these publications by calling the Forms and Circulars Hotline number given above or by writing the publications department of the Copyright Office: Information and Publications Section, LM-455, Copyright Office, Library of Congress, Washington, D.C. 20559.

Publication Title	Publication Number
* Copyright Basics	1
Limitations on the Information Furnished by the Copyright Office	1b
* Copyright Notice	3
Copyright Fees	4
* Mandatory Deposit of Copies or Phonorecords for the Library of Congress	7d
* Works-Made-For-Hire Under the 1976 Copyright Act	9
Recordation of Transfers and Other Documents	12
Renewal of Copyright	15
* Duration of Copyright	15a

Trademark directories list marks which are already registered in the United States Patent and Trademark Office. Various publishers have compiled such directories; most are aimed primarily at lawyers. However, a trademark directory may be very useful during the process of choosing or designing a new trademark, since it can tell you what *not* to name a product and how your new logo design should *not* look. Several trademark directories are listed below.

The Trademark Register of the United States
$288.00 from The Trademark Register, National Press Building 1297, Washington, D.C. 20045 (800-888-8062)

This is a big, fat book filled with tiny type which lists, by category of goods or services named, every trademark currently registered in the United States Patent and Trademark Office. It is designed for use by lawyers and marketing departments of large corporations, but could be helpful to other users as well. It looks forbidding and the correct interpretation of the information it contains is crucial to its effective use, but anyone can learn to find her or his way around in it with a little practice. As a way of eliminating further consideration of and work on proposed trademarks that are, in fact, not available for use, this comprehensive directory, correctly used, has no peer. It is, however, really of use with regard to word marks only. However, the same publisher also publishes *The Trademark Design Register of the United States.* That directory is far more useful to graphic designers, since it depicts registered design trademarks. It is available from the publisher at $267.00.

The Compu-Mark Directory of U.S. Trademarks
$435 from Compu-Mark U.S. 7201 Wisconsin Avenue,
Suite 400, Bethesda, MD 20814 (800-421-7881 or, within
Maryland, 301-907-9600)

This trademark directory consists of seven paper-bound volumes which give all the information available in *The Trademark Register of the United States*, plus several other categories of information regarding registered trademarks and those which are the subjects of pending applications for registration. Certain supplementary publications, such as quarterly update supplements, are available at extra charge. The extra information available in this directory is probably much more useful to trademark attorneys than to the average advertising creative person. The same goes for the additional information available through the supplementary publications, which, in any event, are expensive. This directory does not show registered design trademarks and the publisher does not publish a design mark directory.

A "trademark collection" is not an exhaustive compilation of all trademarks registered in the United States, as are the directories listed above. However, a collection may be of use in the trademark selection process. The following two collections of design trademarks are good ones.

American Trademark Designs
by Barbara Baer Capitman
$6.95 from Dover Publications, Inc.,
31 East Second Street, Mineola, NY 11501

This paperbound book is a handy tool for preliminarily searching the availability of design trademarks. It makes no pretense to being a complete listing of American design trademarks, but includes, rather, 732 of the most famous (and therefore most dangerous to infringe) marks. For the price, it is a good reference book for the shelf of every graphic designer.

Trademark Designs of the World
by Yusaku Kamekura
$5.95 from Dover Publications, Inc.,
at the address shown above

This paperbound book is a compilation of design trademarks from all over the world. Its 699 trademarks are not all well-known in the United States, but some are known internationally and should be avoided by U.S. companies. Less useful than the collection mentioned above, perhaps, but still an inexpensive reference to many foreign design marks.

The United States Trademark Association

The United States Trademark Association
6 East 45th Street
New York, NY 10017

212-986-5880

Founded in 1878, the United States Trademark Association promotes the interests of trademark owners, encourages the proper treatment of trademarks, advises lawmakers on trademark legislation, and serves as a clearinghouse for information and publications useful to its members. Association members are corporations which own trademarks, trademark lawyers, and advertising agencies, graphic designers, and public relations firms, among others. Membership information is available by calling the Association. However, the Association is also useful to non-members. Some of the resources available from the U.S.T.A. are listed below. Anyone whose work involves the creation of new trademarks or the advertising of established marks should consider obtaining some of the publications listed and/or using some of the Association's services.

U.S.T.A. Publications

Trademark Management

$16.50 from Clark Boardman Company, Ltd.,
435 Hudson Street, New York, N.Y. 10014
(1-800-221-9428 or, within New York State,
call collect, 212-645-0215)

This small paperback is written for real people instead of lawyers and gives real information and advice on the proper use and management of trademarks. It is the most useful publication of its kind and no copywriter or art director should be without one.

Also available from the U.S.T.A. are several excellent short publications on various subjects connected with trademarks. At this writing, the list of available publications was being revised; call or write the U.S.T.A. for information concerning the titles and prices of those of interest to advertising creative people.

U.S.T.A. Services

Library: The Association maintains a library that offers researchers access to information on trademark law and proper trademark management. Of most interest to advertising creative professionals is the U.S.T.A.'s extensive collection of manuals on proper usage of and graphic standards for trademarks.

Trademark Inquiry Program: Through this program, the U.S.T.A. answers questions from the media on the proper use of trademarks. This is a handy number to have if you are mentioning someone else's trademark in any publication.

Both of these services are free, even to people and companies who are not U.S.T.A. members. The U.S.T.A. library may be used only by prior arrangement, however, and materials are not lent. Anyone may ask trademark usage questions by calling the U.S.T.A. at the number shown above.

The U.S. Patent and Trademark Office

Patent and Trademark Office
Washington, D.C. 20231

General trademark information: 703-557-INFO
Status information for particular trademark applications:
703-557-5249

Trademark Office Publications

The Trademark Office does not publish the number of informative pamphlets that are offered by the Copyright Office, but it will send you, at no charge, a booklet called "Basic Facts About Trademarks" if you call the Trademark Office general information number, shown above or write the Trademark Office at the above address. This booklet contains a great deal of useful information about the benefits and mechanics of trademark registration as well as detailed information on certain materials that are required to be filed with any registration application.

In spite of the availability of this clearly written booklet and of the fact that no attorney is required to help you or a client make application for federal trademark registration, it is far more usual for a trademark application to be prepared and filed by an attorney on behalf of the applicant than for an applicant to file without an attorney's help. Because the rules and requirements that govern the sufficiency of the application and the registrability of the trademark are complicated and sometimes almost incomprehensibly niggling, even to attorneys, it is much wiser to use this booklet as an informational document only and to hire a trademark lawyer to prepare any registration application. Really.

Trademark registration is hard to get and takes a long time under the best of circumstances; filing the original application may only be the beginning of a long, drawn-out correspondence with the Trademark Office before a registration is granted. Not having the help of a competent lawyer only delays things and can easily result in the rejection of the application on grounds that have little to do with the inherent registrability of the mark.

False Advertising	**National Advertising Division of the Council of Better Business Bureaus, Inc.**

845 Third Avenue
New York, NY 10022

212-754-1320

The National Advertising Division of the Council of Better Business Bureaus (the NAD) promotes truth in advertising. Among its other activities and services, it offers several publications to assist advertisers in creating ads that won't cause them problems.

NAD Publications

There are two useful free publications available from the NAD. The Children's Advertising Review Unit of the NAD publishes a set of guidelines for creating advertising aimed at children; ask the NAD to send you a copy of the CARU "Self-Regulatory Guidelines for Children's Advertising." Also available free of charge is the "Better Business Bureau Code of Advertising," which deals primarily with retail advertising.

Council of Better Business Bureaus, Inc.

1515 Wilson Boulevard
Arlington, Virginia 22209

703-276-0100

Council of Better Business Bureaus Publications

A highly-regarded and widely-used publication of the Council of Better Business Bureaus, Inc., is *Do's and Don'ts in Advertising Copy. Do's and Don'ts* is looseleaf-format publication, which is updated monthly. It is a compilation of rules, regulations, and standards governing advertising (including visual elements of ads) and is designed for use by advertisers and the people who create advertising for them.

Do's and Don'ts is probably the best source available for detailed information about false advertising law. At $275 per year ($160 for annual renewals), *Do's and Don'ts* is expensive. However, if you consider that some lawyers charge $275 per hour, it seems like a bargain.

Direct Mail Board of Review

23 S. Fourth Street
Lebanon, PA 17042

717-274-6599

DMBR Publications

The Direct Mail Board of Review is a new self-regulatory association of mail order advertisers. Staffed by volunteers, it offers a kit to people interested in its goals of promoting responsible advertising and conduct by mail-order merchants. The kit, which contains, among other things, the DMBR's "Code of Business Ethics"and its '"Standard of Advertising, "can be obtained without charge from the association.

Federal Trade Commission

Sixth Street and Pennsylvania Avenue, N.W.
Washington, D.C. 20580

Main Number: 202-326-2000
Public Reference Section: 202-326-2222

FTC Publications

The FTC does not publish as many helpful publications to guide the public as the Copyright Office. One reason is that false advertising law is too complicated to lend itself to summary in short publications. Another is that the FTC is an enforcing agency; its "publications" are the decisions handed down by courts in cases brought by the FTC.

However, the FTC does offer a free "Advertising Practices Rules" packet, which consists of several small booklets that set out the FTC's regulations with regard to advertising. This packet is available for the asking from the Public Reference Section of the FTC, at the address and number given above.

Office of Consumer Affairs
U.S. Department of Commerce

Office of Consumer Affairs
U.S. Department of Commerce
Washington, D.C. 20230

202-377-5001

Commerce Department Publications

The Commerce Department's Office of Consumer Affairs publishes a very helpful booklet called "Advertising, Packaging, and Labeling." This booklet is full of information on complying with FTC (and other government agencies') regulations regarding advertising and includes information on the laws and regulations governing packaging and the labeling of products. An invaluable primer for the advertiser, it is just as useful to anyone who creates advertising, and is available free by calling or writing the Office of Consumer Affairs at the number or address shown above.

The Office of Consumer Affairs also publishes four other informative booklets on related topics, also available free of charge. They are "Product Warranties and Servicing," "Managing Consumer Complaints," "Credit and Financial Issues," and "Consumer Product Safety." Order them for your reference bookshelf when you ask for "Advertising, Packaging and Labeling."

Index

Afterword

Your comments and questions are invited. Address either or both to the author: Lee Wilson, Attorney-at-Law, P.O. Box 24594, Nashville, Tennessee 37202, 615-256-7200 or, by telecopier, 615-256-7016. Pertinent comments and good questions will be employed to make subsequent editions of this book more responsive to readers' needs and concerns.

You are also invited to subscribe to the quarterly newsletter published by the author on legal topics which are of interest to advertising creative people. To subscribe, photocopy the coupon printed below, fill it in, and mail it and your check for $25, made payable to July Publications, to the address shown on the coupon.

YES, I'd like to subscribe to **Ad Infinitum**, the quarterly advertising law newsletter published for graphic designers and advertising creative professionals. I understand that I may request a refund at any time for all unmailed issues of the newsletter.

Name_____

Company_____

Mailing Address_____

_____

_____

Send me **Ad Infinitum** for: one year ($25) ____, or two years ($50)____. My check for $____, payable to July Publications, is enclosed.

Mail to:
July Publications
P.O. Box 24594
Nashville, Tennessee 37202